BIG BAD ASS

· BOOK OF ·

DREAMS

D0061530

BIG BAD ASS
· BOOK OF ·
DREAMS

Klaus Vollmar

and

James Napoli

STERLING INNOVATION
An imprint of Sterling Publishing Co., Inc.

New York / London
www.sterlingpublishing.com

Library of Congress Cataloging-in-Publication Data

Vollmar, Klausbernd.
  Big bad ass book of dreams / Klaus Vollmar and James Napoli.
      p. cm.
  ISBN 978-1-4027-4784-7 (pbk.)
  1. Dream interpretation--Dictionaries. 2. Dream
interpretation--Humor. I. Napoli, James. II. Title.
  BF1091.V64 2010
  154.6'303--dc22

                          2010002694

10 9 8 7 6 5 4 3 2 1

Published by Sterling Publishing Co., Inc.
387 Park Avenue South, New York, NY 10016
© 2010 by Sterling Publishing Co., Inc.
Distributed in Canada by Sterling Publishing

This book contains material from *Dream Symbols* © 1997 Sterling
Publishing Co., Inc. Originally published in Germany under the title
Handbuch der Traum-Symbols © 1992 by Konigsfurt Verlag

c/o Canadian Manda Group, 165 Dufferin Street
Toronto, Ontario, Canada M6K 3H6
Distributed in the United Kingdom by GMC Distribution Services
Castle Place, 166 High Street, Lewes, East Sussex, England BN7 1XU
Distributed in Australia by Capricorn Link (Australia) Pty. Ltd.
P.O. Box 704, Windsor, NSW 2756, Australia

Interior design by Alicia Freile, Tango Media
Interior art © shutterstock.com

Sterling ISBN 978-1-4027-4784-7

For information about custom editions, special sales, premium and
corporate purchases, please contact Sterling Special Sales
Department at 800-805-5489 or specialsales@sterlingpublishing.com.

Contents

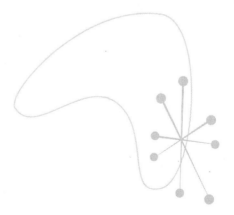

Introduction

"In a very curious way a dream teaches us how easily our soul is capable of penetrating every object while—at the same time—becoming that object."

—NOVALIS

YOU'RE WELCOME FOR THE TIP

Surely Freud would agree that it all comes back to penetration.

The book presented here is a unique, modern dictionary for contemporary people who want to gain a more detailed insight into the images of their dreams. We start with the assumption that each dream image always has more than one meaning. In this way, a dream symbol is different from, for instance, a mathematical symbol. Each dream symbol and image is not only dependent upon the content of the whole dream, but also on the personality of the dreamer. And then we turn the tables a bit on Freud and Jung and question the personality of those who first came up with these symbols! This is dream analysis—bad ass style!

Tips on How to Use This Encyclopedia

"I always have been—and am to this day—a dreamer. But who cares, as long as dreaming is a tool for searching?"

—GEORGE SAND

I f you are unable to determine the meaning of one or more of the images in your dreams (including your daydreams), look under the key word and let yourself be inspired by the meaning that is expressed there. The interpretations and explanations are formulated to guide you to new ideas, insights, and emotions.

In addition, reading this dream-symbol encyclopedia can be useful even for interpreting those dreams that pose no particular difficulty. Looking up symbols—even if they seem to be "obvious"—might help to deepen your understanding of and insight into your dreams. It may make you aware of other ways of interpreting certain images, which in turn will help you to look at your dreams more creatively and openly.

It may also be useful to browse through the book without a specific dream in mind, because it will not only stimulate your dream activities, but also help you to deal with your dreams more imaginatively.

An additional advantage of reading about the many different symbols is that you will become more familiar with the history of dream interpretation. Many of those involved in dream research have understood the same images to mean totally different things. When we realize this, we not only learn something about the times and cultures during which these interpretations were formulated, but we also gain a greater understanding of the complexity of our dreams. Seldom does a dream image have only one meaning. Rather, it points in many different directions at once, and at least a few of them have been recognized throughout history.

It is important for you who use this encyclopedia to find your own relevant and complex meanings among all the possible interpretations. The interpretations presented in this book are meant to introduce new—and up until now unknown—possibilities, assisting in the exploration of your dreams.

—Klaus Vollmar

Or you could browse through the book when other people insist on describing their dreams to you and find ways to mock them. That'll teach them!

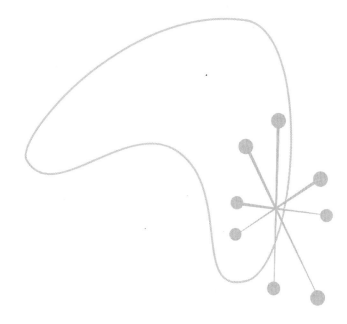

Dream
Symbols

ABBEY: Even though the abbey or cloister has no real meaning in today's world, in a dream it points to the fact that the person is looking for something. The Latin word monasterium points to "monaster"—your own star, your own self (that Jung compares to God). Peace, spiritualization, meditation, and quietness lead you to self, but so does discipline. You have discovered your path and must follow it.

DON'T BE A JERK

What are you complaining about? There are people who wait their whole freaking lives for an abbey dream, and here you're having one! That means you've discovered your path in life, bozo. Jeez, you're tough to please.

ABDUCTION: Repressed urges, similar to Bomb, Attack, Surf, Explosion and Electricity, Defloration, Flames, Violence, Greed, Harem, Skin Rash, Wire (High-Voltage), and Hooker/ Prostitute. Longing to be rescued from a situation, but the strength to do something is missing.

YOU'RE WELCOME FOR THE TIP

If you can interpret bombs, flames, violence, greed, high voltage wire, and skin rashes as a sign that one's circumstances will improve noticeably, then you will probably make a terrific congressman. Come to think of it, the whole harem/hooker/prostitute thing could come in handy there as well.

ABORTING: See Toilet.

ABORTION/MISCARRIAGE: Emotions are facing reality. Also, you want to discard inner conflicts, as in Sewage/Waste. Fear of accidental pregnancy. Physical changes. Separation from a loved one or a favorite. Unhealthy (neurotic) behavior.

ABUNDANCE: It symbolizes excess—be content with less. But it may also suggest being in the flow, where everything needed is forthcoming.

ABYSS: Precipice. This dream usually appears when we are in crisis, or when a crisis has almost been overcome, making room for its deeper meaning. Difficulties in life, critical situations, require decisions. You are looking for help. A challenge to look deeper inside, accepting your own deeper soul.

QUICK FIX

Look deeper inside and accept your own deeper soul. Yeah, like that's going to happen.

ACORN: Precaution; well-known phallic symbol.

SNAP OF THE FINGER

Your mind's way of reminding you to use protection, and wear an acorn next time.

ACTOR: See Theater. You are pretending to be something that you are not. You want to be the center of attention and admiration. Also, you are trying to discover your own potentialities.

ADAM: Returning to the origin of masculinity, this is often the symbol for Father. As the first Man, you also want to be the "top man." Be more vigorous in shaping your life. This symbol rarely occurs today, as is the case with most religious symbols.

LISTEN UP, THIS IS IMPORTANT

The real reason this symbol rarely occurs today is that men are all whipped.

ADDRESS: Whether it is your own or somebody else's is important. Your own address may point to the fact that you are too self-absorbed; some other person's address, that you should become more aware of others. A "good" address means social advancement, a "bad" address social demotion.

ADMINISTRATOR/PUBLIC SERVANT: Often appears in a dream when you are suffering from lack of self-worth. Also addressed here is the dreamer's "responsibility to govern," which means facing the problems and developing the capabilities to manage his own issues. In that sense, it addresses self-determination. Such concerns are surely influenced by the dreamer's attitude toward power and acceptance. Freud is said to have dreamed as a young man that he was a public servant, which might help explain his ambitions.

ADMIRAL: See Captain, a symbol of manliness, like Abbot, Athlete, and King. A person of authority. Authority over Water. Water relates to the emotions, compulsive tendencies, or, less often, being particularly sensitive. A leader and example, but the Admiral also represents masculinity that has rejected aggressiveness. The dreamer is very self-confident, able to steer the ship of life (although sometimes aggressively). There is a sexual connotation here, since a ship is generally thought of as female. One wants to rule and own women. After all, the Admiral is a seafarer, and a symbol of unrestricted sexuality.

ADOPTION: Taking on something foreign—giving aid. Longing for the "child within." Here you should always ask what is missing that would make you happy. What would you like to take on?

ADULTERY: See Stranger, Intercourse, Sexuality. Also Friend, Foreign Language.

ADVENTURE: Being unsure about one's surroundings or fearful of a risky relationship while—at the same time—yearning for it. Life is becoming boring; you are looking for adventure and daring in a world that is perceived as being empty. Opposite of the working routine.

An adventure dream may also refer to a chance to become more intimate with oneself. Be glad about the dream; you are gaining self-knowledge and getting closer to your goal!

Determine what kind of adventure it is and what your feelings are. And do remember that adventure may sometimes take place in the internal rather than in the external world.

YOU'RE WELCOME FOR THE TIP

Finally going to the bathroom again after three days of constipation does not qualify as an internal adventure.

ADVERTISEMENT: A long-overdue situation needs to be resolved; otherwise, it will become public. Or it is absolutely necessary to make it public. Let the world know about your wishes and longings.

Too much self-congratulation and advertising of oneself, but also creativity and inspiration.

ADVICE: Searching for direction and support from the outside. Friendship and help.

AFRICA: The dark continent, our own shadow, our own hidden side, and our own urges/drives. (See Primeval Forest/Jungle.) It is the continent of hunger and of chaotic political situations, chaos, heat, thirst. That which is black, dark, and from which all female creativity originates.

BARE FACTS

Not to be confused with the song "Africa" by Toto. If that ends up in your dream, then you're just lame.

AGENT/SPY: Points to too much fantasizing. Wanderlust, being shallow. Make inquiries before coming to a decision; search for the truth first. This is a frequent dream symbol when life is boring and has no excitement. But this symbol may also be a general sign of searching. Ask yourself what it is that you are looking for (and what it is that you want to find).

Also addressed here may be a life lived intensely and dangerously. It is the image of the male hero that appears when the dreamer is showing little masculinity, and in rare instances, also, when such masculinity is present in a woman or man.

On the other hand, this dream image also appears when the dreamer has an unconscious suspicion that, in most cases, is unfounded. It is helpful in such cases to adopt a positive attitude to life (positive thinking).

AIR: Symbol of essence and awareness. Insight, ideas, imagination, and creative thinking, as well as a rich intellectual life. Effortlessness, but also a warning not to be a "happy-go-lucky" sort of person. Air is also a symbol of opportunities in the future. Thick, muggy, smoky, and bad air have negative meanings; fresh, morning, or spring air mean youth and well-being.

AIRPLANE: See Flying. Airplanes and flying are considered symbols of far-reaching thoughts, ideas, and new insights.

According to Freud, the plane is a phallic symbol. It is able to overcome gravity.

ALCHEMIST: Pharmacist, chemist. Spiritualization. Inner strength is solidifying; character ennoblement. Also: Adventure. Warning: Look out for too much romanticizing.

ALCOHOL: "Muddying the water," lack of clarity, unscrupulousness, intoxication, emotionalizing, melodrama. It may be a concrete warning of too much alcohol consumption. The symbol may also be a challenge from the unconscious, demanding more clarity and deliberation. Is life lived in a fog? Are important problems being repressed? In another sense, this symbol may be pointing to positive social skills and communication, as well as the healing aspect of euphoria.

Astrology: Symbol of Neptune.

QUICK FIX

You may be in denial about your addiction to analyzing
dreams about alcohol. Analyzing Alcohol Dreams
Anonymous can help. The first step is admitting you
are powerless against trying to figure out your alcohol
dreams. Sometimes a fifth of bourbon is just a fifth
of bourbon.

ALLIGATOR: Fear of being swallowed up by tasks and work. Pay attention to your animalistic aggressions.

ALMOND: An erotic symbol. Bitter almonds mean disappointment; sweet almonds mean good luck.

ALPHABET: Wholeness and complete spiritual richness is realized. Order. Highly oriented toward the abstract, as also when dreaming about numbers.

ALTAR: Well-known holy place; a place of power, spirituality, personal growth, and development. Ideals that are held dear are addressed and should be either elevated or sacrificed. The altar is the place of transformation and ascent.

AMAZEMENT: Good things are going to happen to those who did not expect anything.

AMBER: Petrification, narrowness (restricted lifestyle), as in: Siege, Elevator, Village, Cage, Trap. A warning about arrogance. Also jealousy, like all types of jewelry (gems).

AMPUTATION: Losing something of oneself. Always restricted and needs are ignored (see Abortion, Funeral, Divorce, and Death). Expression of fear of loss and an invitation to discard nonessentials. Important: Which limb is being amputated?

YOU'RE WELCOME FOR THE TIP

As just noted, this image can occur as a result of divorce. In such a divorce dream, the amputated limb is usually hemorrhaging huge amounts of cash.

ANCHOR: A symbol of security, as in Family, Home, and Notice-of-Intention-to-Marry. The desire to be grounded in spite of all the emotions. Self-confidence, but also standstill.

ANESTHESIA: Calming, unconsciousness. But often also anguish, and a defense against anything lively and spiritual.

ANGEL: See Flying. Messenger from God. In a broader sense, angels are messengers from the higher self who is guiding the dreamer. Or a woman or man we love is being placed on a pedestal.

According to Jung, animus figures often represent still unfinished, not yet understood, but surprisingly new intellectual gifts, power of reasoning, or character ideals.

During the night of November 10, 1619, René Descartes had three consecutive dreams during which the angel of truth appeared to him. On the basis of this revelation, the 23-year-old Descartes developed his philosophy. Lightning.

Opposite: clear counterimage of Devil.

ANIMAL: The animal, compulsive nature of human beings. Instincts, according to Freud and most other dream interpreters, removed from awareness (animus); or awareness removed from instinct (anima) in human beings. The image of the suppressed or of the shadow, suggesting a chance for integration.

The type of animal in the dream is important. Jung suggested that we find out more about the innate character of the animal we have dreamed about. According to Freud, small animals always symbolize children and siblings, while wild animals are a symbol for sexually excited or exciting people, evil urges, or passions.

ANTLERS: Aggressive, physical male drive, as in Rifle, and all other weapons. Unfaithfulness. Antlers mounted on the wall are reminiscent of sexuality (fertility) in the past.

ANVIL: Resistance. Toughness, becoming passive endurance. May also point to a sadomasochism that is not expressed. Also: a romantic look back at the period when craftsmen flourished.

SECRETS TO MAKE YOU LOOK GOOD

If you want to get some action this weekend, you might consider nixing your romantic look back at the period when craftsmen flourished.

APE: Developmental difficulties. Points at the same time to increased rigidity. You need to allow yourself to be more playful and happy. Leave room for the animal side of you (the ape is considered one of the most sexual animals). The ape is the shadow of the ego, the soul of instinct, the most ancient and most human creature.

It is a symbol of imitation, which points to self-ridicule as well as a lack of autonomy. Pay special attention to the type of ape that appears in the dream.

QUICK FIX

Don't worry. All this stuff about apes in dreams will never be taught in the public schools if we have anything to say about it.

APPLAUSE: Approval. Vanity based on fear of rejection or success. Often a sign of avoiding criticism.

One is surrounded by envy and jealousy. A warning not to be so vain. Also an expression of the need for recognition. You should compliment yourself and others. In any case, you want others to pay attention to you. What are you doing to make it happen?

APPLE: Health and natural- ness; also renewal of life and the symbol of immortality (the golden apple). Seduction and sexual symbol for breast. (The ideal in the Middle Ages was to have breasts like little apples.) Something that turns into something good (and deservedly so—for instance, William Tell's apple) or, less frequently, something that turns into something bad (see the Apple of Paris).

According to Freud, the apple, like almost every other Fruit, is the symbol for breasts, particularly when there is more than one apple. In psychoanalysis, apples are generally considered a typical sexual symbol. According to C. G. Jung, they are a symbol of life, an ancient fertility symbol, as are the pomegranate, fig, and quince.

STRETCHING THE TRUTH

However, also in the Middle Ages, having breasts like little quinces was a total drag.

APPLICATION: Desire or Fear of making one's needs known and/or to plan for them. Manipulation by others, or wanting to manipulate others. Relationship proposal: Yearning for a long-term relationship.

Looking for something that is not easily obtained. What are you applying for? Are you confronted with new tasks that require talents you don't know you have?

APRICOTS: Female sexual symbol, well-being. One of the most common erotic symbols for skin, often used as a metaphor in contemporary pornography.

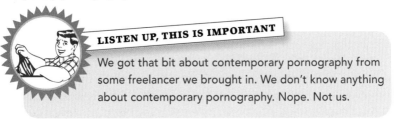

LISTEN UP, THIS IS IMPORTANT

We got that bit about contemporary pornography from some freelancer we brought in. We don't know anything about contemporary pornography. Nope. Not us.

AQUARIUM: Artificial living space. Unnatural, deep (repressed) desires for a more natural lifestyle.

ARABIAN: Longing to be "wild." May also appear as a symbol for the masculine world and misogyny. Fanaticism and danger of war, but also romanticism (Lawrence of Arabia). This symbol also, and always, addresses the dreamer's own urges (in the case of women, the masculine side).

ARCHER/ARCH OF A BRIDGE: Tension, overcoming contradictions.

ARENA: A room where the ego is placed in the center, as in Amphitheater. Struggle, the determination to achieve, and striving for success. If you are in the center of the arena, it is necessary to be active, self-promoting, and bold. If you see somebody else in the center, you are too passive.

ARISTOCRAT: Inferiority complex. You feel inferior in your social environment. Symbol of self-worth, wanting to advance but being aware of your shortcomings. Sign of romanticizing social status by holding onto ideals uncritically, even those that should have been discarded long ago. What do you really want out of life?

ARM: The basis for action, reaching for or getting something. Wanting to accomplish something ("the arm of the state," for instance). Also see Beggar.

ARMAMENT: Separation and disarmament, distancing, which may be positive or negative. Protection from emotional pain. See Knight.

ARMCHAIR: Resting, being peaceful, as in Evening, Worship, and Prayer, but less religious in meaning. It may, however, also be a sign of laziness or boredom, and point to the fact that you act like a ruler.

ARREST: You feel your life is exciting, seen and lived like a detective story, but you are feeling guilty. Certain habits need to be changed immediately if you want to avoid complications. You have caught the "culprit" that was residing inside you, which means that you have come face to face with yourself, your motives, and intentions, and have understood the consequences.

YOU'RE WELCOME FOR THE TIP

Or, you should just be locked up like the degenerate you are.

ARRIVAL: Beginning. Obvious meaning: one part of life is completed; something new is about to take place. A goal is reached. See Adventure.

ARROW: Focus and concentration on a goal. This image is a "point of reference," and suggests the way you have—or should have—developed. In addition, the arrow is a male sexual symbol and a symbol of aggression.

ARTERIES: See Blood, Red. Life is in motion, as is your circulatory system.

ARTIST: A well-known symbol for a life lived freely and creatively.

ASCENSION: The obvious meaning is success through effort. Where do I want to go? Is the goal worth the effort? See Stairs, Ladder.

ASHES: Something has come to an end, has been completely dissolved. Ashes often signify weakness, the loss of vitality, and act as a reminder to enjoy life and have fun. Symbol of the Phoenix, the Bird that, after total self-condemnation, sets himself on Fire, only to be born again by rising from the ashes. In that sense, the ashes are a sign of rebirth, transformation, and, in the last analysis, of Birth and Death.

One feels burned out, with no interests (depression, as in Abyss and Murder). Insults, disappointments, illness, and the death of a loved one can create such dreams. Guilt, blame, and atonement for transgressions (Ash Wednesday, the mark on the forehead). Glowing ashes point to self-reflection and purification.

According to C. G. Jung, ashes were seen in the olden days as protection from demons, particularly against the angel of death. In addition, ashes are the product of cremation. The physical shell must be completely destroyed before the soul can become free.

QUICK FIX

Do you dream about ashes? Do you occasionally feel burned out? Are you depressed, lacking in interests? Ask your doctor about Corsysil. Clinical trials report an 80 percent recovery rate. Side effects may include nausea, dizziness, rectal itch, bleeding from the eyes, and dry mouth.

ASPARAGUS: Not only Freud considered this a phallic symbol.

DON'T BE A JERK

Look, pal, if we stopped to comment on every phallic symbol in the book, you wouldn't be able to lift the thing.

ASS: See Buttocks.

SNAP OF THE FINGER

"Buttocks" begins with a B. That's coming right up; it's the next letter in the alphabet. Come on, don't skip ahead now. Show a little self-control.

ASSASSINATION: Hopeless situation; it is essential that something be done. Fear of political instability, Ruler. Greater attention needs to be paid to everyday occurrences.

ASSAULTS/ATTACKS OF ILLNESS: Breaking out of what is considered the norm. Repressed drives. See Termination, Surf, Fire, Electricity, Abduction, Defloration, Flames, Violence, Greed, Harem, Skin Rash, Wire (high-voltage), and Prostitute. In the form of ecstasy, it has a sexual meaning. If your dreams are about severe seizures (particularly when specific organs are involved), consider seeing a psychologist.

ASTROLOGY: Cosmic connectedness, ancient and profound wisdom, or superstition, relinquishing responsibility for oneself. Search for one's own star.

SECRET TIP

See also **Whatever You Need To Believe.**

ASTRONAUT: Expanding consciousness; seeing and being given much news. Exploring the hereafter and other realms.

ASYLUM/EXILE: Having committed a crime against society; bad conscience, often due to tax evasion.

ATHLETE: Symbol of sexual masculinity, the Hero. Masculine power, as in Bear. Frequently appears as a dream symbol when one is feeling weak.

Advice that one ought to get involved in fitness. Often, also, the dream symbol for simplemindedness.

STRETCHING THE TRUTH

In more contemporary cases, the athlete is also the dream symbol for the elusive trillion dollar endorsement deal.

ATLAS: Orientation in the world. He who carries the weight of the world on his shoulders: troubles and burdens. Longing to travel to foreign lands and have new experiences.

ATOM BOMB: See Bomb, Explosion. Worry about humankind or at least about the immediate surroundings. Fear of death and war as in Shot. Recommends taking greater responsibility for the larger questions of life and asserting greater influence upon things affecting society and the community.

BARE FACTS

If you should awaken feeling refreshed and ready to face the day after a dream about an atom bomb killing everybody in the entire world, you seriously need to take some downtime.

ATTACK: Similar to Being Run Over, only more aggressive, and accompanied by the fear of losing property.

ATTIC: The place where forgotten goals and expectations are hidden. According to Jung, the place of the first sexual experience, as in the fairy tale "Sleeping Beauty," where the princess is pricked by a spindle in a room under the roof of the high tower. Here in the attic are the intellectual taboos, the sexual ones, and the taboos of independent conscience. In the attic are the thoughts that we don't dare explore and the attitudes we don't dare express.

Poverty, perspective, advancement.

ATTORNEY/LAWYER: A need for fair and proper self-treatment and self-analysis. The search for what is "proper." You are making demands. A symbol of fair treatment for the self.

Call for help, or business problems. Points to career difficulties.

Question of fairness, or the opposite of it, is being addressed. Points to powerlessness, or unused persuasive skills.

COMMUNICATION

So in dreams, the lawyer represents seeking fair treatment and taking care of yourself. This is a rare, positive image of the lawyer in our society. We must not forget, however, that most lawyer dreams are billed hourly.

AUDIENCE: This may symbolize the way you portray yourself. In the extreme, it represents exhibitionism. Often what is hiding behind this dream is the desire for fame. On the other hand, it is the image of a search for your own world and a real Self. It also points to a manipulated secondhand experience that is, like television, often a substitute for reality.

SNAP OF THE FINGER

Remember, having a manipulated secondhand experience is a perfectly normal part of our sexual development.

AUGUST: Vacation time, harvest time, relaxation. Also heat, laziness, and eroticism.

AUNT: As with every female symbol in the dream of a man, it is a symbol of the man's feminine side. In the case of a woman, the image of the aunt in a dream often refers to her own shadow; only in exceptional cases would it represent an ideal. The feminine to which one feels attracted. The aunt, as is the case with the Uncle, often symbolizes "wholesome common sense."

LISTEN UP, THIS IS IMPORTANT

See also **Aunt Bee, Mayberry, Nonthreatening, Plump, Asexual, Don't Even Want to Think About Her Having Sex, Least of All With Barney Fife,** etc.

AUTHOR: Independence. A person who is creating his/her own life. The smart man or smart woman is not necessarily the wise man or wise woman! Here is the need to be productive and produce something of intellectual value. Everybody has something worthwhile to say. Communicate it and express yourself. Maybe you have to speak up more often, and more clearly? Do you want to give somebody a piece of your mind, openly and honestly?

YOU'RE WELCOME FOR THE TIP

Did I mention authors are also known for their prodigious lovemaking ability? . . . What did I say? Come back, you haven't finished your drink.

AUTUMN: Time for harvesting and utilizing, a time of becoming aware about life, reaching new goals. Allow yourself peace and quiet, reflect on your circumstances. Harvest, maturity, success, and prosperity.

AWAKENING: You are becoming more aware of yourself or certain characteristics, or you fear waking up to something dreadful (a bad surprise). Reflects a positive development in awareness, new perspectives, desire for something new, a new beginning, as in Opening, Baby, Birth.

AXIS: Movement of life, the wheel of life (or Wheel of Fortune). You are concentrating on your center—"navel gazing."

DON'T BE A JERK

When dreaming about the Wheel of Fortune, don't buy a vowel. It's a completely useless strategy.

BABY: See Child. A dream known to be a portent of good news, success, and advancement. A wish is fulfilled, a childhood wish. Or, it may suggest that the dreamer is childish and immature, wanting to be taken care of. Often this image corresponds to a feeling of helplessness. This is also the symbol for a loved one ("my baby," "sugar baby," etc.).

If the baby is perceived as a threat, the dreamer might be afraid of an accidental pregnancy, as in Abortion. Also, it may suggest fear of letting go of one's children.

In another context, longing for rebirth and a new beginning. Always ask yourself what you would do differently if you could start over again.

BACKPACK: See also Luggage. The burden that you are carrying around with you, or relaxation and moving about in nature.

SECRETS TO MAKE YOU LOOK GOOD

The backpack also has strong associations with the time you bummed around Europe after college. Women, see also **One Night Stands With Guys Named Claude.** Men, see also **One Night Stands With Women Named Ulrike.**

BACKYARD: Hidden place, secrets. Poverty and the unconscious.

BACON: Conscious or unconscious wishes to get something or someone. Also "Bring home the bacon."

BAD LUCK: Points to trouble. On the other hand, it might be a sign that you can make good connections and have someone you can rely on. Always remember that what appears to be bad luck in the beginning often turns out later to be good luck.

BADGE/INSIGNIA/DECORATION: A symbol of belonging, of which you have dreamed repeatedly, from which you feel rejected. How was the sense of belonging demonstrated? Was the badge given/awarded for something?

BADGER: A lot of work is ahead of you. Occasionally, but rarely, a sexual dream symbol.

BAG: The symbol of the unknown and the surprises that life has in store. Because it is similar to a *surprise package*, the bag is often a symbol for secrets ("letting the cat out of the bag"). On the other hand, it might also point to obstacles and burdens. It is the image of the burdens that you are carrying. It is important to pay attention to what is inside the bag.

BAKER: See Baking, Cooking. The domestic male, the practical and creative male.

BAKING: Like Cooking, this image is connected with transformation. See also Alchemist. Urge for domesticity. Being contented and convivial, as in Communion. Often refers to creativity.

What are you baking, and what is the recipe?

BALCONY: Command, focus, and planning. Symbol of female breasts.

BALDNESS: Intellectualization (the crown chakra). Also brutality, or effects of radiation. Intellectual failure. According to second-century dream interpreter Artemidorus, loss of relatives or objects.

BALL (DANCING): Dissatisfaction with the social situation (similar to Aristocrat), or enjoying social recognition. A ball also is considered the place where one is introduced to social/cultivated passion.

BALL/GLOBE: Completeness, wholeness. The dynamics of the psyche that bring contradictions into harmony. The symbol of the all-encompassing "completeness of the cosmic soul." You are on the path of individuation and able to view it from many perspectives. The glass ball (hollow inside) is like the soap bubble. Since the Middle Ages it has been a symbol of impermanence. A solid globe made of glass or a crystal ball is a symbol for all-knowing, or the pretense of being all-knowing.

YOU'RE WELCOME FOR THE TIP

You may be surprised to see that there are three different kinds of balls in dreams, and none of them directly reference the testicles. Man, Freud was asleep at the switch on that one.

BALLOON: Flying, weightlessness. Being or have been depressed. But this is a warning that you are losing ground. It is also a symbol for arrogance and social advance, similar to Aristocrat, Auction. Less often a symbol of ideas. Is the balloon flying or bursting?

According to Freud, a phallic symbol (particularly in the case of a zeppelin).

BANANA: Fruit. Generally, a well-known phallic symbol. As monkey food, a symbol for delighting in silliness and boisterous nonsense.

STRETCHING THE TRUTH

Or, as Carl Jung once put it, "Is that a symbol for delighting in silliness and boisterous nonsense in your pocket, or are you just glad to see me?"

BANDAGE: Support, help, and security, as in Apothecary, Medication. Fight (protective bandaging), shackled and handicapped.

BAND-AID: Part of the body is injured and needs to be protected (with a Band-Aid), held together, or "hidden."

BANK (SAVINGS BANK): Fear of losing money, a warning against being wasteful, but also power, recognition, and energy. See Money, Wealth.

BANKRUPTCY: Fear of loss, making excuses, freeing yourself of debt. Often a feeling of being at the end of your rope, not knowing what to do next, usually due to exhaustion and denial, instead of facing the situation. Desire to come clean and start all over again. What would you like to do differently?

A warning dream. Important to be more careful how you use your energies. A need to tell the truth to others and to self.

SNAP OF THE FINGER

Some bankruptcy dreams may include the appearance of a man with bad hair telling you how to consolidate your debt into one easy monthly payment. Do not listen to this man. And for God's sake don't call the 800 number.

BAR: An erotic or forbidden place; relaxation, similar to Armchair, Bench (sometimes with erotic meaning).

BAR (CHOCOLATE): See Sweets.

BARBED WIRE: Boundaries or injuries. See Sting.

BARBER/HAIRDRESSER: The way you care for your hair shows your attitude toward your own sexuality. Vanity, as in the case of all jewelry.

BAREFOOT: See Foot. Being grounded. Asceticism, health, frequent vacations.

BARENESS: Naked, Stripping. A frequent dream symbol when you want to hide something. Or search for the "naked truth."

BARKING: Warning that danger is lurking. Aggression.

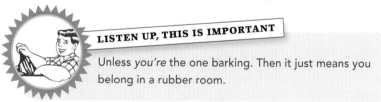

BARN: Making use of your own abilities. Success and well-being, but also a place of adolescent sexuality.

According to Jung, the barn is a place where demons and ghosts reside, but also a place of protection against rain and cold.

BARRICADE: In dreams about obstacles. A barricade signifies a logical boundary or self-limitation.

BARRIER: Restriction, limitation, or establishing boundaries. A frequently occurring dream symbol when feeling confined and unable to move forward. Also see Amputation, Cage. Balking at something, holding back. Sign of social force. Taboo.

Difficulty in making social or business contacts. To have hit a brick wall. Usually points to a challenge.

BASEMENT: House. A scary place where, according to Jung, we lose our soul or rediscover it. It is the unconscious, the dark, the impenetrable, that which we repress.

The foundation of your life. A longing for greater security.

You are coming into contact with your unconscious.

YOU'RE WELCOME FOR THE TIP

You could also come into contact with a sump pump down there, especially during the rainy season.

BAT: The symbol for Vampire, sucking, being sucked dry. Dull, compulsive, dangerous emotions. On the other hand, this dream symbol expresses great sensibility, having radar-like skills and useful instincts.

BATH: Suggests cleansing (possibly a ritual cleansing, from sin). This type of washing usually refers to "cleansing of the soul." It often also refers to relaxation and recuperation. At the same time, the image of a bath is always connected with the "fountain of youth." The symbol is similar to Shower, Sauna, Soap. Cold water means trouble; and so does hot water—"getting into hot water." Water that is too hot means unconsciousness.

BATHROOM/BATHHOUSE: A place for cleansing, as in Bath. An erotic place where clothes are taken off (see Physician). Often refers to the psychoanalyst's office, particularly during sessions. A place of emotion.

BATON: See Rod.

DON'T BE A JERK

We're not even going there.

BATTLE: Erotic symbol, overstimulation, and overwork.

BEACH: The border between consciousness and the unconscious; or a desire for vacation and relaxation.

BEAKER: See Mug, Cup, Goblet.

BEARD: Symbol of the ruler, of male strength and vitality, of aid from a wise man; wisdom increasing with age. Nurturing your masculine side. Indicates male superiority and authority (the beard of the prophet). A beard being cut off almost always means loss of vitality and fear of impotence. However, there is also another side to the image of a beard being cut off—exposing the face, approaching the world with openness. In this context, shaving off a beard in today's setting might also mean an increase in potency.

Astrology: Symbol of Saturn.

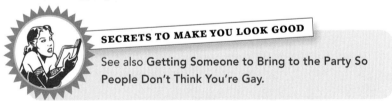
BEAUTY: In fairy tales, as in dreams, the image of beauty is another expression of truth and honesty. At the same time, it symbolizes vanity,

good luck, and great success. In the Oriental tradition, it is the most sought-after dream for luck.

BED: Longing for domestic bliss and quiet, also erotic encounters. Often points to sexual problems; if that is the case, the type of bed points to the sexuality of the dreamer. In the *I Ching*, the bed always stands for intimacy.

According to Jung, the bed is always a place of security and caring, also the symbol of Sleep and the unconscious. The place where people are born and die; the symbol of the circle of life.

YOU'RE WELCOME FOR THE TIP

Don't let this idea about the type of bed a guy has representing his sexuality get around. Guys already spend enough time picking out cars as extensions of their penis. Let's not open up the playing field.

BEDROOM: A place of relationships, their problems, and their beautiful moments.

SECRETS TO MAKE YOU LOOK GOOD

And yes, in case she asks, being awakened in the middle of the night with the question, "Honey, do you feel like talking?" *is* one of the beautiful moments.

BEE: An industrious person. As with all insects, positive social behavior and the desire for personal development. A bee also points to honey, as sweet, nutritious food (and the slang expression for a girlfriend or boyfriend). Do you need to do something nice for yourself? Being threatened by a bee means tension in your life (you are asked to conform to society); also, it often refers to problems with teamwork.

Astrology: The sign of Virgo.

BEE STING: Sexual intercourse. In ancient Greece and Rome, when a girl dreamed of a bee sting she was said to be in love.

BEER: Alcohol. Happiness, social life, and either fogginess or inspiration.

Astrology: Symbol of Neptune.

SECRET TIP

See also **Simpson, Homer.**

BEGGAR: Symbolizes the fight for existence, inferiority complex, fear of poverty. Somebody is giving you a gift. Do you need to learn to ask for something or demand it?

BEING CHAUFFEURED: Great wealth. Archetype for clergyman.

BEING HOARSE: Something is taking your breath away.

BEING RUN OVER: This may point to an inferiority complex or a feeling of being overwhelmed.

According to Freud, this image, particularly in men's dreams, appears when sexual intercourse is problematic and one's id can't be actively lived out.

BELL: Steadfastness, trustworthiness, joy, and harmony. The bell is inseparably tied to time. This dream poses a question about what hour has just been tolled.

Hearing a bell ringing means that something new is happening. The sound of the bell is often thought to be the sound of a "heavenly message." "Wanting to hang something on the great bell" means that you either have arrogantly exaggerated about something because of your craving for admiration, or need to make something known that you would rather hide.

Since the beginning of the fifteenth century, bells have been a symbol for the Fool and, at the same time, for Vanity.

A bell can also symbolize the school bell—which means this might be a good time to talk about that dream where you're running down the hallway in just your underwear. In case you were wondering, it means you're a loser.

BELLY: Determine if real intestinal problems exist. The belly represents the kitchen of the body, the place of transformation Alchemist, but also the place of desire and physical urges. It can also stand for wealth that belongs to the dreamer.

Often points to a connection between the will and the emotions, between conscious and unconscious needs. A flat belly often points to unfulfilled sexuality; a fat belly to too much sex (or substitution for sex) and excess. The medieval Swiss philosopher Paracelsus said that everybody has an alchemist in his belly.

BENCH (PARK BENCH): Resting, tranquility, as in Armchair, Worship. A long bench points to procrastination.

BERET: See Hat. Finding your spiritual identity. Protect yourself from intellectual influences and mental manipulation.

BERRIES: You are having fun and pleasure. Having a desire for berries is often an expression of sexual desires. But it may also be a warning that you are becoming careless. (This interpretation was found in ancient Persia.) A yearning for health and nature, as in Farmer, Farm, Ear (of corn), Sowing.

BICYCLE: Getting ahead under your own power. Individualism and independence—you are pursuing your own path. The type of bicycle points to the personality of the dreamer: if a kid's bike—childlike or childish; a sports bike—fast, vigorous; an old bike—you feel old. Trouble-free riding: you are pursuing your own path and have no problem with it.

BARE FACTS

There's also the iconic image of the old lady on the bicycle in *The Wizard of Oz*. The one who turns into the Wicked Witch and wants to kill Toto. And she has those flying monkeys—those horrible flying monkeys that freak us out to this day! No, no! Not the flying monkeys! Get away, get away! Agghhh!

BILLIARDS: Finding success around several "corners." Fun and relaxation. See Ball. The ability to set something in motion. Fertility.

BINOCULARS: Don't get into a panic about every little thing; don't magnify everything you see out of proportion. Or bring something closer toward you, including something you want to remember. This might also refer to searching for access to your subconscious. To see more clearly what is invisible.

BIRCH: Young, slender girl. The birch combines black and white in its bark, implying contradictions.

During the Middle Ages, a magic protection against witches and evil spirits.

BIRD: Spiritual content. An attempt to get a better perspective. This symbol also has an erotic meaning. In addition, it may imply that you want to be different, as in the myth of Icarus.

BIRD WOMAN: A creature of myth, symbolic of excitement and temptation, the anima in her heavenly and at the same time animal role, threatening and destroying. Also a symbol of the wise woman (for instance, night owl) and a symbol of death.

BIRTH: First, this image expresses actual birth, maybe your own, that of your children, or others'. Wishes, fears, pain, and the joy of becoming "a human being" may be expressed here, as well as the dreamer's interaction with his or her children. In addition, the beginning of a generally promising, creative time. Creating something new. Complete state of happiness and clarity. On the other hand, often a longing for rebirth, in the sense of personal changes. This image also appears frequently just before or just after having started a new project. Occasionally, it also may express a resistance to letting go of the old, to maturity and completion. With this symbol the question is: What do you want to do with your life and where do your desires lead you? See Child.

YOU'RE WELCOME FOR THE TIP

See also **Baby**, and that whole bit about the pointlessness of existence. Always worth revisiting!

BIRTHDAY: A common symbol for luck in any form. The birthday is a magical time when wishes are fulfilled, but where somebody could also cast a spell over you ("Sleeping Beauty"). Important are the gifts, the kind of celebration, and how old you became. Gifts usually represent characteristics of the dreamer or the person the dreamer is meeting and are an indication of how rich your life is on account of them. In addition, a birthday is a celebration of your personal existence, and your individual characteristics are the gifts. They are worthy of being honored. Pay attention to the overall flavor of the birthday party. How did you feel?

STRETCHING THE TRUTH

One noted researcher reports that only in our dreams do all of the schmucks at the party sing "Happy Birthday" in the same key.

BISHOP: Symbol of masculinity, as in: Author, Pope, Father, Wise Man.

BITE: Aggression ("sharp tongue"), chopping up. Often points to the animal side in humans. Vicious personality, social inhibition, in many ways relating to the acceptance/rejection of one's own "animalistic" side. Also, on another plane, reference to eating habits and the ability to chew. See Eating, Teeth. Who is biting whom? Being bitten by an animal: contact with one's own drive. See Animal, Vampire.

SECRET TIP

Also applicable to common slang. "This bites," as in one of our researchers clearly grasping at straws to come up with something to say about a dream.

BLACK: A symbol of emotional stagnation or a depiction of the unconscious or the unknown. Grief and death, but also magical power and fertility. In earlier books about dreams, black animals are always seen in an unfavorable light, while white animals are always considered positive images.

BLACKBERRY: Connected with nature. All Berries have a sexual connotation (clitoris).

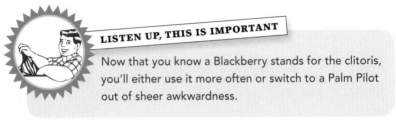

LISTEN UP, THIS IS IMPORTANT

Now that you know a Blackberry stands for the clitoris, you'll either use it more often or switch to a Palm Pilot out of sheer awkwardness.

BLACKBIRD: See Bird. Subtle sign of hope. If the bird is singing, happiness and the need to be more casual. Points to the carefree life of birds: they neither sow nor reap.

BLACKBOARD: Memories of something repressed. Points to fears and difficulties during your time in school. At issue here is knowledge and being tested. See Table.

BLEEDING: Life, passion, courage, or disappointment, as in Blood. Also giving in and going with the flow, as for all Water symbols. Dreaming about menstruation. Injury or shock. The secret of life. Is the bleeding accompanied by pain?

BLENDING: Illusions, usually of grandeur. Too much sun, too little shade, overexposure; a challenge to illuminate your own dark side.

BLINDNESS: Danger! You are not seeing something or you're avoiding taking responsibility for something or reflecting on something. You are unaware. Appearance gives no clues. Are you looking for new insights?

BLOOD: Red. "Blood is a very special liquid" (Goethe: *Faust, Part I*)—it is that which is alive, the driving substance expressing fire and passion (something that Freud and Jung agreed on). Life, love, and passion, but also injury and disappointment. Blood also—and often—points to Mother, and can symbolize soul and will. When the "voice of the blood" is speaking, a very special sensibility or domination of one's urges is being addressed.

Exchanging blood (or drinking blood) represents a joining of life forces (brotherhood). The blood of Christ is symbolically served at communion; it has a universal healing power.

Loss of blood usually means loss in love; blood transfusion corresponds to the strengthening of vitality. See Menstruation, Bleeding.

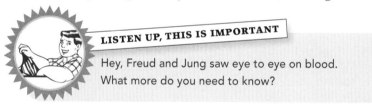

LISTEN UP, THIS IS IMPORTANT

Hey, Freud and Jung saw eye to eye on blood. What more do you need to know?

BLOSSOMS/BLOOMING: As in Spring, joy, abundance, physical aspects of the emotional life, sexuality (particularly female sexuality).

According to Freud, a reference to female sexuality. White flowers mean sexual innocence; red flowers mean sexual maturity.

BOAR: Animalistic male instincts, as in Buck and Bull.

BOARD: That which is flat, smooth, and connects. The function of the board is important.

BOAT: See Ship.

BODY: To see one's own body in a dream implies a tendency toward narcissism, being in love with oneself. Or you have lost contact with your body, and the forgotten body is making itself known in your dream.

BOMB: See Atom Bomb. Aggression and destruction, fear of war, as in Bayonet, Siege. Frequently indicates that you are being too domineering and aggressive, or need to be more so. According to psychoanalysis, a bomb explosion symbolizes orgasm. A picture of an exploding bomb also points to an act of freeing oneself and of unloading. Addressed here is removing and shattering boundaries.

BONES: Referring to life experiences, the spiritual and emotional backbone of life, but also "ossification."

BOOK: Being well-read and wise is an obvious interpretation. Also, a suggestion that one ought to turn more often to the "real world." In the "Book of Life," one's own inner wisdom is written, which means that we find here the script for our life. The content of the book is important as well as its title and the color of the cover. Compare also Author.

BOOTS: Being grounded, mobile, and getting ahead. A symbol of something new. A sexual symbol.

BOOTY/LOOT: Getting something through one's own efforts and trouble. A state of "have-mode," according to Erich Fromm, as in Auction, Stock Market, Attaché Case.

BORDELLO: See Hooker. New experiences. One is doing something for money that would be better left undone. Expression of calculated sexuality. Desire for or fear of licentious sexuality. Usually symbolizes wanting to break conventional boundaries and a search for new ways of expressing lust.

BARE FACTS

Also a search for new, creative ways to part with your money.

BORDER: A frequent dream symbol for those who are being restricted and are feeling a lack of possibilities. You need to overcome the obstacles in your path and, at the same time, be reminded that it is limitation that brings forth the mastery. See Hedge.

BOREDOM: See Snake, Time, Haste.

BOTTLE: See Container. Male and female sexual symbol, but according to Freud, always female. What kind of ghost or spirit is bottled up inside? See Glass, Vase.

BOWLING: On one hand, you may want to take it easy, look for relaxation and fun; on the other hand, bowling expresses power and agility. Last, but not least, this symbol could point to hidden aggression, if a powerful throw "bowls over" the pins.

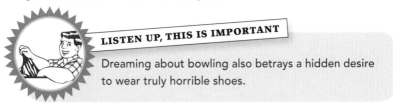

LISTEN UP, THIS IS IMPORTANT

Dreaming about bowling also betrays a hidden desire to wear truly horrible shoes.

BOX: See Container. Love affairs and relationships, but also your own burden. What is inside the box? Also, female genitalia.

According to Freud, a symbol of the female body, as with all musical instruments or a Church.

SECRET TIP

Wow! A church is a symbol of the female body? Man, you can get away with some screwed-up stuff in your dreams, can't you?

BOXING MATCH: Ability to assert yourself. Aggression. A frequent symbol for work/profession or marital situations, it can also point to a positive fight.

BRAIDING: See Thread. The act of connecting the threads of life, meaning different situations and personal characteristics.

BRAKES: Obstructions; lack of mobility, inhibition. Often, this dream symbol is an incentive, but also a compulsion to be more accurate, more moderate. It is important to establish what is putting on the brakes and what is being held back. On rare occasions, it is a sign of security.

BRANCH: Twig, Tree. Looking for help, support (Don't saw off the limb you sit on). Symbol of the back, or at least the shoulders. Connected or being close to nature.

Does the tree have leaves or are they already on the ground? If it is a broken or sawed-off branch, you have too much on your plate.

BRASS: See Metal. Usually points to a desire for success and prosperity.

BRAWL: Repressed aggression, and a desire for physical closeness.

BREAD/ROLLS: Life-sustaining food, strengthening, nurturing substance. Economic security, as in Bureaucrat, but not as materially oriented as Shares, Auction, Attaché Case. Because of its shape, often the symbol for female genitalia. In addition, this symbol also relates to everyday life ("Give us this day our daily bread"). Pay attention: Are they big or small rolls? According to Jung, the womb. A frequent symbol when sexual urges remain at the preintercourse stage (oral sex). Freud calls this a regression into the oral phase.

STRETCHING THE TRUTH

An informal poll of dream-symbol experts found that once they knew the truth about bread, over 60 percent of them were grossed out. The other 40 percent just used extra butter.

BREAKDOWN: An obstacle dream, gloating. Bad luck, Embarrassment.

BREAKFAST: New beginning, good beginning.

BREAST: Longing for connectedness, tenderness, rest. Those you take to your bosom become related. According to ancient Germanic law, families gave their members names of body parts in order to indicate how closely they were related. Somebody with the name "bosom" was a close blood relative.

BARE FACTS

Somebody with the name "bosom" was also teased mercilessly in eighth grade.

BREATH: Life energies (Prana). An exchange with the environment.

BREATHLESSNESS: Exhaustion, having a lot of staying power, patience.

BRIAR: Problems and difficulties, as in Bush, often between partners.

BRICKLAYER: Building something, a challenge to be more productive.

BRIDE/BRIDEGROOM: See Marriage. A specific event concerning your own development. A desire for a partner, for bonding, or looking for balance between internal and external contradictions. Are you seeing your dream partner? Such a dream partner often depicts your ideal soulmate. Rarely, it signifies a warning of unwanted pregnancy. See Baby. An unhappy or ugly bride or bridegroom often points to conflicts with your partner.

Alchemy understood these symbols as a connection between opposites. According to Jung, the images connect the masculine and feminine parts of the soul and are a symbol of light and fertility.

STRETCHING THE TRUTH

Two of Freud's early patients, newlyweds, described their recurring dream of being the miniature bride and groom on top of the wedding cake. Made of marzipan, they were then eaten by both the best man and the maid of honor. Freud was inconclusive in his analysis of this dream, but he did point at them and laugh.

BRIDGE: A frequent symbol in dreams and mythology, the bridge spans a gulf. It is often a place of danger and of falling; you are crossing a boundary. In the Catholic faith, the patron saint of bridges is Saint Napomuk. Uniting, reestablishing relationships; contradictions are bridged. If the dreamer has self-confidence, the fear of the abyss may be going away, but although the bridge becomes wider and is safe, it is still a place of danger. The condition of the bridge is important. How are you feeling on the bridge? When you have crossed the bridge, you have done a lot of inner work. Changes have taken place (you have reached the other shore).

In the Koran, the bridge over hell is as thin as a thread and can be crossed only by the righteous. In Celtic lore, there exists a bridge of horror that is also as narrow as a thread. The bridge always spans an abyss in which spirits, the devil, or God resides. Often in the dream one must bring a sacrifice in order to cross the bridge. For that reason, we often see chapels on the bridge where a sacrifice has to be offered. Jung related the symbol of the bridge to the unconscious. He saw the unconscious as different islands in the sea. For him, a bridge connected these islands and is therefore a symbol of working toward a strong consciousness.

SECRETS TO MAKE YOU LOOK GOOD

So, this Saint Napomuk is the patron saint of bridges. Great, now we know who to cuss out when there's a backup at the tolls.

BROOCH: As with all other jewelry, it refers to vanity or cultivation. You want recognition, to amount to something, or to receive a gift.

BROOK/STREAM: See River, Water. Flowing emotions, allowing oneself to let go and give in, as in Cliff. Should you go with the flow, or are you just drifting about? Similar symbols are Flying, Sled, Parachute. Longing for quiet and nature. Also, keep in mind that the movements here refer mainly to the emotions.

BROOM: Cleansing, as in Bath, Trash Can. Popular symbol for a witch. Pointing to a problem that needs to be resolved. Phallic symbol, magic wand.

BROTHER: In the case of a man, the second ego. You are dependent only on yourself; you walk unaided; or your masculine side needs to be strengthened. In the case of a woman: strengthen your masculine side.

SECRET TIP

A "brother" in a dream can also convey a repressed desire to be the protagonist in a 1970s blacksploitation film. (See **Shaft.**)

BROWN: Nature, nature connected, vitality, groundedness. Also vacation and sunshine. Clay, mud, feces. It also might point to subjugation.

BUCK/RAM: A dream symbol for earthbound vitality, lechery. The buck and the rooster have been allegorical since the Middle Ages for male—but also witchlike—horniness and carnal lust, the animalistic, and the wild; but this also stands for stupidity. The task is to make the buck into a gardener, which means growth and development, and gives him human qualities.

YOU'RE WELCOME FOR THE TIP

A buck is also a symbol from the male ritual of hunting. If a hunter shoots a buck in his dream, he is actually castrating himself. There, think about that the next time you put on an orange vest, drink a can of beer from a tube in your hat, and go slaughtering Bambi.

BUCKLE: Holding something together. Something is connected, understood.

BUD: Refers to energy that should be used for your development. The same as in Tuber, Flower, Fruit.

BUFFALO: A well-known symbol for male sexual urges as in Bull, Buck.

BUG: How you view the bug depends on your personal relation to it. As a germ or virus, it does not seem to offer any great threat. As a slang expression—"to bugger someone"—it has a sexual connotation.

In Egypt, the scarab (black dung beetle) symbolizes rebirth; later it became a symbol of luck. In our culture today, the june bug is generally a symbol of luck.

SNAP OF THE FINGER

Impress your friends! The next time you see a bug, point out how it can often symbolize buggering someone. They'll be sure to thank you for it!

BUILDING: See House. According to Freud, Jung, and some current dream analysts, a building always represents the dreamer. The condition of the building is important, as is the atmosphere in and around the building, and where it is located.

BUILDING SOMETHING: A building, like a House, almost always symbolizes the human body and personal identity. Pay attention to the type of building you see in the dream. The process of building usually points to independence—rebuilding oneself during hard times.

BULL (WILD): The bull/steer and Tiger are always personifications of drives and urges. Running after a bull in a dream means you are in conflict with your drives. You must always confront the bull or the tiger in your dream, because both have something important to say. The bull is a symbol of masculine (originally feminine) strengths, fertility, and potency. Also indicates that animalistic urges have been mastered. See Buffalo, Buck.

BULLDOZER: Energy for pushing something out of the way; or are you feeling pushed away?

BARE FACTS

Or are you awake, and are they just demolishing your house? See also **Deadbeat Dad.**

BURGLAR: The need to get something on the sly. Greed (you are "breaking into" yourself). You can't trust people around you. Somebody is violating the dreamer's boundaries—emotionally or physically (another person is breaking in). Something new is coming, and there is fear of loss (as in Thrush) through changes. What has the burglar taken from you?

BURIAL: See Funeral.

BURNING: A frequent warning dream when risks are too great. See Flames, Fire, Light.

BUS: Moving forward quickly on the road of life, but in contrast to Car, it is oriented toward the community. You want to force your way to your goal alone—something that is not always a good idea. Less force and more patience would be better. It is reminiscent of the collective, the power of many. Going on a trip, changing location. What is the condition of the bus? How is the trip proceeding? See Driving.

BUSINESS: Usually is connected with present business. You are either too busy or not active enough. As in Factory, the image of "business" is also a symbol for monetary transactions, which, in turn, depend on the interaction of the dreamer's individual characteristics. What kind of business is it? What does the business sell, and what is your role in the transaction?

BUSINESSMAN: This dream image refers to the masculine side of men and women. Either it is the result of feeling self-confident or it indicates the need to be more self-confident. The businessman stands for the exchange between people. He is the one who guides the flow of goods and, in that capacity, is the negotiator between nature and people. The property of the businessman points to the talents of the dreamer, as do the goods he sells. The way in which he is moving the goods may be an indication of how the dreamer uses his energies.

YOU'RE WELCOME FOR THE TIP

Note: The image of a naked businessman can indicate a weakness in PowerPoint.

BUSY DREAMS: Usually, these are signs of a great deal of activity during the day (less often, a suggestion to be more active). In contrast, being an observer in the dream means to be less passive. These dreams may also point to too much stress, indicating that your life has become too frantic. Try to determine whether you see yourself as being very active in the dream or if you seem to be disappearing from view.

BUTTERFLY: One's own transformation (from Caterpillar to butterfly); also the image of inspired lightness and the soul of the child. The image of the butterfly is that of "spiritus," the connection between mind and soul. In this sense, it is a symbol for enthusiasm and salvation/happiness.

BUTTOCKS: Those who don't "cover their ass" show how vulnerable they are. Or they don't have to hide their disadvantage, such as "The Fool" in early Tarot decks.

According to Freud, an infantile sexual symbol.

CACTUS: Defense, brusqueness, distance, hate-love and, in general, contradictory emotions. This image often comes up in dreams when you are in a situation in which you fear you have been injured. It points to the need for new boundaries and distance. This need for boundaries is often an expression of your sensitivity. Are you often acting irritably toward the world around you? Or, are you feeling overwhelmed by the intensity of your emotions? Take your emotions seriously and look for an appropriate way to express them.

BARE FACTS

Or, you could just be dealing with a lot of pricks.

CAFE: Obvious symbol for a place of rest, relaxation, and enjoyment. Meeting place, intellectual stimulation. What did you choose to eat?

CAGE: A symbol for narrowness and being deprived of freedom, as in Elevator, Village. Restrictions, however, are felt more strongly, similar to Sewer, Amber, Trap. On the other hand, this dream symbol can have positive meanings, particularly when the cage is seen from the outside. Then it usually is a symbol of protection and taming (of wild urges). In addition, the cage can also seem like fencing, because fences create protection, giving you the peace you are seeking.

CAKE: Reward. Food is often a sign of love that you either receive or give. Emotional and intellectual needs.

CALENDAR: Impermanence; fear of age and death; make use of your life (Carpe diem!—seize the day). On the other hand, this dream image may also appear because you fear being mortal; you are afraid of things that could have long-standing consequences; you feel overwhelmed and overburdened by responsibilities. In the end, this dream is asking you to have a productive life and to enjoy it.

YOU'RE WELCOME FOR THE TIP

Also, remember to pay attention to the type of calendar in your dream. For men, for instance, a swimsuit calendar points to you being a sexist pig who has some screwed-up ideal of the perfect woman; for women, a teddy bear calendar might indicate your secret desire to repel all potential male companionship. And, as we know, teddy bear calendars are a gateway drug to having teddy bears in the back window of your car, which pretty much puts the nail in the coffin.

CALF: Youthful inexperience. Childlike, naive.

CALLING CARD: Advancement. Symbol of a desired identity.

CAMEL: Adventure, deprivation, travel. Symbol for patience and quiet, but also for stupidity. The ability to "overcome dry periods." In addition, this is a symbol of the search for what is essential.

COMMUNICATION

Closely related to the cameltoe dream, which indicates that you've had that pair of pants too long. (Women only.)

CAMERA: Methodical, technical perspective. Suggests you look at something more impersonally and objectively—look through the objective! You should document something very carefully. The film in the camera refers to the initial screen, the creative power of the soul, where external impressions leave their imprint.

CAMPING: See also Tent. Longing for relaxation and vacation. Sense of community, longing for a simpler life.

YOU'RE WELCOME FOR THE TIP

Camping dreams can also indicate a sick longing for chiggers, having to relieve yourself in the woods, and hearing weird noises outside your tent all night. Honestly, we'll take the hotel room.

CAN: See Container, Tin. Female sexuality. What is in the can, and what can you do with it? According to Freud, cans, containers, and boxes all symbolize the female womb.

CANARY: Happy, comfortable home, as in Singing. Being locked up, as in Cage.

As with all Birds, what is also addressed here are freedom and intellect. A bird flying high in the sky symbolizes sexual ecstasy that, in the case of the canary, is (only now, or already) present in the beginning stages.

LISTEN UP, THIS IS IMPORTANT

Not to bring the room down or anything, but these little guys are also sent to die in coal mines.

CANDLE: A symbol of life, particularly a burning candle. May also point to specific festivities. See Light.

Already, in antiquity, the candle was a male sexual symbol. Also, according to Freud, a phallic symbol. A broken candle symbolizes impotence.

CANNIBAL: A grabby kind of person by whom you feel overwhelmed. The desire to establish an intimate relationship with somebody. You feel you are eaten up by something, usually a relationship.

CANNON: Weapon. A symbol for immense, massive energy. This dream image may also refer to your personal drive and power, force, and ability for achievement. You carry out your actions either too strongly or not strongly enough.

CAP: Hat. Consciousness and thinking. Are you living too much in your head? It also addresses the fact that you keep something hidden or that something seems to be hidden. The verb "to cap" also points to completion, the end of a situation. In fables and fairy tales, the cap often plays a significant role as a magical covering for the head, allowing the person to become invisible. It also points to the fact that you may be too visible. Or that you might pay more attention to yourself and be more outgoing. See Shadow.

CAP (WOMAN'S): This symbol often appears when the dreamer is longing to get married. It indicates the transformation from girl to woman. It points to the head and seat of consciousness. See Helmet.

CAPE/CLOAK: Searching for warmth or a place to hide.

CAPITAL CITY: This symbol always takes on the meaning of Ruler and Government.

CAPTAIN: A guide that is determining the proper (emotional) course. A person of respect. Symbol for father, or for yourself. Also prosperity, dignity, and worldly experience, in the sense that you know the strength of your own soul.

CARAVAN: Symbol of an adventurous trip. You are in search of a pilgrimage. Burdens are being shared.

CARDS: Cards can appear in dreams in many different forms—such as postcards, maps, entrance cards or tickets, playing cards, and business cards.

In the case of playing cards, it implies that you do not take life seriously enough and are taking too many risks. It also may be a suggestion to look at life more as if it were a game and to be less serious. It is important whether you have good or bad cards in your hand. If you dream about a particular card, find out the meaning by checking out books about reading cards.

With postcards and maps, refer to the place or area pictured on them. If you can't make any connection with the picture, postcards and maps may be an expression of a desire for travel and vacation.

Tickets and business cards point to areas that are normally unavailable to you. In the case of tickets, the specific area depicted is most important: what you are admitted to is an indication of the direction you should take in your life. In the case of business cards and credit cards, it is the person who carries them who is important. A business card shows that you are, or want to be, successful.

LISTEN UP, THIS IS IMPORTANT

Don't forget the many interpretations of the rank of hands in poker. Flush: Your life is going down the toilet. Two Pair: You have grown an extra set of testicles (men only). Full House: Despite your best efforts, somehow there's another damn kid on the way. Royal Flush: Your life is going down the toilet, but this time it's while you are still on the throne.

CAREER: Career dreams often indicate the importance of work in daily life. Such dreams imply either that we take our careers too seriously, or that we should pay more attention to them. In any case, career dreams appear only when tension exists in this area. Less often, the career itself can be seen as a general symbol of wanting to get ahead.

CARNATION: An attempt to voice a desire that can only be expressed through flowers.

CARPENTER: Architect, builder of the roof—in other words, consciousness, intellect, and the mind. One who builds knowledge and awareness.

See also **Karen & Richard, 1970s Soft Rock.**

CARRIAGE: See Wagon. A symbol of personality and status. What kind of carriage is it?

CARTOON, ANIMATED: You are trying to get through life by hook and by crook. You have the ability to find the comic in every situation.

CASH REGISTER: See Money. The image of a cash register often means limited access to the world around you, which is blamed on money. You would rather have more than be more, indicating greed.

On the other hand, the cash register is a place where money is kept in an orderly fashion, protected, and saved. In this case, Money is a symbol for your abilities and talents.

CASTRATION: Loss of masculinity and vitality. As a dream image, it is almost always a sign of repressed physical urges. This symbol refers mostly to inferiority complexes and feelings of guilt. In rare cases, castration points to a deep-seated denial of masculine sexuality. At the time of Sigmund Freud and Carl Jung, castration dreams were relatively frequent. Now, they happen relatively seldom, since our attitudes to sexuality have changed. A woman is not likely to see herself as a castrated man; today, aggressive masculinity is accepted by men and women as an important aspect of themselves, which does not need to be punished with castration. Castration dreams today are mostly seen as referring to work and vitality. Also, castration dreams dreamt by women and men are often a reference to their relationship. If a relationship is problematic and a partner feels restricted, fantasies and images about castration are normal. Castration dreams, in rare cases, might have a positive side: one is liberating oneself from burdensome tasks. See also Donkey, Genital Organ, Sexuality.

COMMUNICATION

See? When a relationship is problematic, castration fantasies are normal. We just saved you a bundle on couples counseling. Tell me this entry alone wasn't worth the price of the book. Yes, we know we used the word "entry." Get your mind out of the gutter—or, as we call it, Freud's office.

CAT: The emotional side of the dreamer, as well as the unconscious willpower of the dreamer. On one hand, it is a symbol of deception and cunning. It always refers to a woman, since the cat is connected to the archetypal female. On the other hand, the cat is a symbol for independence, lust, and self-will, again exclusively referring to women. It is a symbol of female sexual organs (pussy) and sexual aggression. But it is also a sign of physical agility, orgasm, and freedom. If a man or a woman is having a cat dream, it always addresses the feminine side (anima).

LISTEN UP, THIS IS IMPORTANT

Cats also represent something that takes great pleasure in ignoring you and doesn't give a crap whether or not you exist, as long as you feed it and give it a place to live. See also **Musician.**

CATERPILLAR: See also Worm. Caterpillars only eat what is not complete. They are greedy and fat. On the other hand, a butterfly was once a caterpillar. Therefore, the caterpillar stands at the beginning of transformation. This symbol almost always points to the process of transformation.

CATHEDRAL (DOME, AS IN "HOUSE OF GOD"): Holy place, self-contemplation, quietness in times of unrest, as in Chapel and Church, only stronger because of its size and more intense. Nostalgic, remembering old times. Structuring one's own life, great works, correlating many different strengths, fulfilling one's calling.

Security and a place of quiet. It often suggests the need to take time out for contemplation.

CAVE: See Barn. Womb of the mother, uterus, and security, as in Family and Dam.

According to Freud, a symbol for vagina; protection and femininity. The original dwellings in which human beings lived, with their animal drives. According to Jung, a reminder that human beings developed from animals.

CEILING: Limited in your thinking and ideas. In the dream, either the ceiling is falling on top of you, creating a feeling of being confined or crushed, or the ceiling is immensely high and you are trying to stretch in order to reach it. In one case, more intellectual effort is called for; in the other, you are overextending yourself intellectually.

CELLO: Harmony, as in Choir. Depth, being grounded, and movement into the unconscious. Are you playing or are you listening?

According to psychoanalysis, the female body.

CEMETERY: Funeral, Death. Longing for rest and relaxation in times of overwork and stress. A classic place for ghosts.

CENTER/MIDDLE: You are looking for your own center, the quiet pole in your life. Ideal and balanced.

CHAIN: Close ties, in a positive sense. Chains have been a symbol for shackles and bondage as far back as the second century.

CHAIR: Need for rest.

CHALK: Points to school and learning; also debts being written on a chalkboard.

CHAMOIS/ANTELOPE: Skillful, with modest requirements, and shy.
  Astrology: Corresponds to the sign of Sagittarius.

CHAMPAGNE: See Sparkling Wine. Advancement, happiness; be good to yourself, treat yourself well. Longing for luxury, as in Oysters. At the same time, it is a warning not to be too extravagant. Taking a bath in champagne is considered a symbol for titillating sexuality and decadent luxury.

COMMUNICATION

Recent studies have shown that taking a bath in champagne is a bit more than a freaking symbol for titillating sexuality and decadent luxury. It pretty much *is* titillating sexuality and decadent luxury. Oh, and as for "Champagne: See *Sparkling Wine*"? There's no comparison, you philistine!

CHANCE: If something happens by chance in a dream, it is usually a message that you can attain something without expending great effort, or that a situation will resolve itself without extra effort.

CHAPEL: A place of quiet and contemplation. Particularly in times of stress it points to reflection. A romantic place.

According to Freud, a symbol for women, as in Church.

CHARITY: Improved financial situation for the giver, worsening financial situation for the receiver (see Beggar). On rare occasions, this can also mean the reverse. It points to hard times to come, or fear of poverty (see also Asylum, Rags, and Counterfeit Money). A warning about being petty and stingy, and about self-deception.

CHARM/MASCOT: Make sure you pay attention to what is pictured or written on the charm.

CHEESE: Property and prosperity. Or, something is not quite right or something is going to waste. See also Milk.

CHESS: A symbol for the fight of the white (affirming) against the black (rejecting) energy in all of us. The outcome of this battle is determined by our awareness. See also Game, Fight.

CHESTNUT: Autumn, play, food, fertility.

CHIEF/BOSS: Symbol of male authority, as in Father. You are really your own boss. Or the "chief" is a symbol of your own, higher authority or the ability to self-govern. Positive interpretation: positive masculinity, "ruler" over your own affairs. Seeing yourself as a chief is usually a wish-fulfillment dream or a compensatory dream: you feel inferior and inadequate, or you are not making good use of your powers. According to Jung, it is usually the voice of the domineering, masculine side of us.

CHILD: Either a positive symbol that refers to new possibilities, or a hint that we are resisting maturity and completion. The child represents the essential in us that we want to see mature. We are supposed to tell the truth ("children and fools speak the truth") and be less complicated ("if you become like children . . .").

If women dream about a child, it is usually because they are longing to have one, or are looking for something new, meaning a change in lifestyle is about to occur.

Also a symbol of the prime of life and continuity. A sick child points to emotional difficulties. Pay attention to what attitude the child has in the dream. These attitudes want to be supported and made conscious.

According to Freud, the child may represent a regression or one's own genitals ("my little one," my penis). It is still true today that regressive tendencies are involved when an adult dreams about a child.

However, we ought not to dismiss Freud's belief that "reclaiming one's own childlike simplicity" can also be a positive process that allows us in later years to become lively and even revive a sense of eroticism. The symbol of the child appearing in a dream is always connected with vitality, the joy of life, and sexuality.

CHIMNEY: See Smoke. Cleansing, but also pollution. A phallic symbol. See also Tree, Stairs.

CHOCOLATE: Often appears when the dreamer is really hungry. Symbol for temptation.

CHOIR: Fusion, happiness, harmony (heavenly choir), and a sense of art. How can you become part of a group and remain in it? Are you part of the choir or are you a listener?

CHURCH: Similar to Chapel, Cathedral. A debate about the meaning of life. Contemplation is asked of you. According to Freud, a symbol for woman.

CHUTE/SLIDE: Sliding down, meaning closing in on the unconscious. Devotion, enjoyment of life, but also insecurity. See Slipping, Falling.

CIGAR: See Cigarette. Phallic symbol that also represents the father.

CIGARETTE: Once the image of intellectual activity, cigarettes now indicate dependency and addiction. Symbol of taking a break. According to Freud, a phallic symbol.

CIRCUS: The uncommon but controlled manner of using emotions, drives, and the body. Traditionally, the image of the circus is the exact opposite of what is taking place in everyday life, as in Gypsy and Actor.

CITY: See Palace, Fort. On one hand, and as far back as the Middle Ages, the city has been a well-known symbol for Mother, since cities provide protection and resources and are usually surrounded by a wall (uterus). On the other hand, it may also stand for Father and "father state." It is a symbol of progress on the road to self-development, as well as a symbol of the emotional environment of the dreamer. A large city represents a source of contact, a hectic lifestyle, and stress.

According to Freud, a symbol of woman.

YOU'RE WELCOME FOR THE TIP

So the next time you say New York is a great walking city, just remember you're strolling around inside a uterus. The same goes for you, Paris!

CLAW: The fear of the animalistic. Also, "claw" implies grabbing. It can represent the dreamer's own wild and greedy grabbing for a world that he is either "dreaming" about or actually living. Is the animal threatening you with its claw?

However, the claw could just as easily be a "healthy" sign if you are very timid. It might, however, suggest that you need to control your greed instead of living it out.

CLIFF: See Abyss. Fear of Falling. Falling down the precipice means either fear of difficulties and adversity or a challenge to let go (see Shot, Brook, Elevator, Trapdoor). Moving up a cliff indicates that adversity can positively affect the outcome; the situation is improving.

You want to get some perspective on your life. It may also mean that you have difficulty advancing socially, as in Climbing, Obstacle, Exam/Test, Summit.

CLIMBING: You have high ambitions, but the path is often dangerous and difficult, in contrast to *walking* uphill, where you also want to advance, but the path usually is not difficult or dangerous. See Career, Ladder, Stairs.

CLOCK: See Mandala and Time. According to Freud, the clock is a symbol of menstruation, because it measures cyclical periods. The ticking of the clock, also according to Freud, corresponds to the pulse of the clitoris during sexual excitation. Is it possible to transfer this meaning to the rhythmical impulses of a Quartz watch?

CLOSET: Possessions. Hiding something. According to Freud, a symbol of the woman's body.

CLOTH: Protection and covering/disguise/masking. Pay attention to the color and its symbolism.

CLOTHING: See Dress/Clothing.

CLOUDS: Illness, sorrow, and grief. They represent the mood of the dreamer. Gentle white clouds in the sky during good weather symbolize happiness and reverie. "Dark clouds on the horizon" point to difficulties ahead. The blending of yin and yang is interpreted by the Chinese to mean sexual union. When rain is falling from the clouds, it means that lovemaking has reached its highest point of exaltation.

SECRETS TO MAKE YOU LOOK GOOD

Or, to put it another way, when rain is falling from the clouds, the authors of dream books have reached their highest point of euphemism.

CLOVER: The four-leaf clover is a well-known symbol of good luck. The three-leaf clover points to the normal and the everyday. According to Freud, the three leaves symbolize masculinity.

CLOWN: Do not take life so seriously: lighten up, play. Fear that you are making a fool of yourself due to an inferiority complex, or you are demanding too much of yourself and others. The actions and the mood of the clown are important.

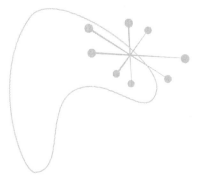

CLUB: The primitive weapon of the Giant. Its phallic shape points to undifferentiated drives. You are being hit over the head with something, in the sense of being overwhelmed.

COAL: Energy that rises from the unconscious. As fuel, it points to passion. A well-known symbol for Money.

According to Freud, the symbol of libido. According to Jung and the alchemists, a symbol for transformation since, in the process of burning, coal is transformed into warmth and ashes.

COAT: Protection, defense, and isolation. The type of coat indicates the type of protection.

According to Freud, the coat also stands for a condom, and is a symbol for the genitals.

COAT OF ARMS: Advancement, ambition, vanity, and the need for power.

COCOA: Sweets. People are laughing at you, or you are laughing at somebody.

COFFEE: Social gathering, mental stimulation, enjoyment of life. May also point to addiction. Coffee also indicates a need to be more mentally alert and have better concentration.

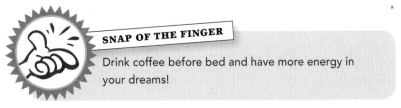

SNAP OF THE FINGER

Drink coffee before bed and have more energy in your dreams!

COFFIN: See Funeral, Grave. Also dowry, inheritance, and a task that needs to be tackled.

COIN: Money. You either need or have money. Coins are always connected with your energies and talents. Fear of impending poverty, as in Savings, Food.

COLD: As in Ice, Snow, projecting isolation. It is a symbol of an aloof personality and emotional neutrality. Or it could be a hint to exercise more detachment.

COLLAR: Order, good grooming, advancement.

COLOR: Psychological experience. See specific colors—Red, Yellow. Colors are very important if they are a function of a symbol. According to some modern dream research, people who dream in color are particularly temperamental.

COMB: Vanity. Searching more diligently (combing through). See Hair.

COMMUNION (CHURCH SERVICE): Longing for religious rituals, or having an aversion to them. Betrayal by or acceptance into a social group. The $64 million question: "How do you feel about religion?"

In addition, important here is the duality of bread and wine: the material versus the spiritual world.

SNAP OF THE FINGER

Drink enough wine with your bread and you won't give a rat's ass about duality or betrayal or any of that happy horse puckey.

COMPANION: See Brother, Friend.

COMPASS: Focused thinking and acting. Which course do you want to choose for your life? It often poses the question of reorientation. But with the compass, you are sure to find your way. In other words, you can trust your own power and your own fate.

COMPASS (INSTRUMENT FOR MAKING CIRCLES): You are running around in circles; but also a sign of completion, as in Mandala.

COMPULSION: A very important dream symbol that often allows us to see clearly our internal or external compulsions. Should you be more assertive and show more strength? Or should you try not to force things and situations?

COMPUTER: A symbol of mental discipline and the ability to coordinate. Help at work, impersonal perfection, indifferent precision; what is missing is the soul and the emotions. Warning: too career oriented.

SECRET TIP

See also **Carpal Tunnel Syndrome, Huge Time Suck, Spam from Natural Male Enhancement Firms, Staring at the Screen and Saying "What?" While Waiting for Something to Happen,** etc.

CONCERT/ORCHESTRA: A desire for harmony, because in a concert many voices create a harmonic whole. In that same sense, out of many experiences, one may create a life of harmony. When dreaming about an orchestra, it usually indicates a longing for a richer, more meaningful life. Are you part of the orchestra, or are you conducting it?

CONDUCTOR (OF AN ORCHESTRA): Figure of authority, similar to Chief and Admiral, only here it is in a harmonious atmosphere. You want to be the guide to ensure that everything is harmonious.

CONDUCTOR (OF A TRAIN): Control. Are you going in the right direction?

SECRET TIP

Occasionally, the train conductor and the orchestra conductor will be combined in a dream. This is usually an indicator of a deep need to be validated (the train ticket) at the same time as hoping to get in a French horn–player's pants.

CONFECTION/CONFECTIONER: Sweets. Fun and winning.

CONFESSION: Benefiting from communication and honesty. Needing to free yourself from guilt and/or from morals that are too rigid. This symbol is similar to Punishment.

CONSTIPATION: Difficult emotional work ahead. The process is faltering.

SNAP OF THE FINGER

If you are plagued by persistent constipation dreams, send yourself off to sleep by repeating the ancient Hindu mantra "Om Metamucil padme."

CONSTRUCTION SITE: Building. Planning one's life, creating one's livelihood, and spurring personal growth.

CONTAINER: Bottle, Box, Vase. These containers symbolize the body of the woman and female sexuality, at least in men's dreams. The male body and male sexuality is seldom, if ever, represented by a vase. If a container symbolizes male sexuality, it appears in the shape of a barrel or bottle. For men and women alike, though, a vase may represent the innermost part of the person in the sense of the unconscious. But here the image usually appears in the form of a box (Pandora's Box) or a treasure chest.

What is inside the container is important (the spirit in the Bottle—the genie). Ever since Sigmund Freud, containers have been seen as referring to sexuality; if the container is empty, impotence. Pouring liquid from a container or removing a cork from a bottle is, according to classical psychoanalysis, usually a symbol for intercourse.

SECRETS TO MAKE YOU LOOK GOOD

You may find yourself in a dream in which many people are gathered around containers called Tupperware. Do not be concerned. Nothing sexual can ever happen around this substance or the people who sell it.

CONVERSATION: Quiet conversation indicates the pleasure of making contact. Openness, in the form of arguments, usually reflects inner conflict.

CONVERSION/CHANGE: A scene of conversion or change usually points more to mobility and to the hope that a situation can be changed.

COOK (FEMALE): The other "mother" who is not trying to educate and punish, but the woman who cares for you, spoils you, and does not discipline you. In addition, this dream symbol shows the inner power of the woman and her ability for transformation. See Cooking, Kettle.

COOKIES: Indulging in sweets. In general, the time for sweets is in childhood, but you are still enjoying sweets. Are you longing for your childhood?

Do you wish to have the protection and care you had when you were a child? Is "sweetness" missing in your life? Maybe you should make more room in your life for security and childlike enjoyment. According to Freud, cookies with a smooth surface represent nakedness.

YOU'RE WELCOME FOR THE TIP

Indeed, the slang term "cookie" can also refer to someone you find sexually attractive. However, given a choice between such a person and an actual cookie, take the cookie. Yes. Mmm . . . cookies.

COOKING: Change and emotional development, exactly as in Kitchen. May also point to seething/boiling with anger. On the other hand, cooking may mean bringing something to conclusion and maturity. What is being cooked? What are you supposed to prepare? Do you want it well done?

COOKING LESSON: Desire to improve your domestic skills, usually meant as a contrasting symbol to Cooking, Roast.

COMMUNICATION

Note: The desire to improve your domestic skills went out in 1952.

COPPER: Symbolizes success, sensitivity, and appreciation of life.
Astrology: Symbol of Venus.

CORAL: Symbol for the beauty of life. And, since the coral is a water creature, emotions are also addressed here. Are you using your emotions as the key to a happy life?

CORD/ROPE: You would like to lasso somebody.

CORK: Taking out a cork means intercourse or ejaculation. The cork-screw is usually a phallic symbol.

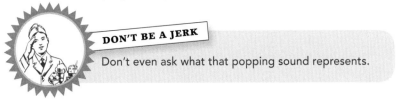

DON'T BE A JERK

Don't even ask what that popping sound represents.

CORNER OF A HOUSE: A complete persona or a "person with corners and edges."

CORNERS AND ANGLES: Take a chance on being more open and direct in your communications. It is also possible that somebody is hiding something from you. Or are you hiding something?

CORN-ON-THE-COB: A phallic symbol.

BARE FACTS

Although, you must admit, one of the tastier phallic symbols around.

COSMETIC: Points to improving your image—also to vanity. In a dream, it may often be a hint that you are caring too much or too little for your soul.

COUCH: Quiet, rest, as in Armchair. Couch almost always has a sexual connotation. What is the color of the couch; who is on it with you?

COUGHING: A negative answer in a very important matter; fear of the future and dissatisfaction. Coughing is almost always connected to an unconscious need for distance and rejection. See Cold, Lung.

COUNTERFEIT MONEY: Dishonesty and pretense. Your values are too materialistic. Fear of poverty, similar to Charity, Asylum, and Beggar, however not as intense. Here, it is rather a case of not quite trusting your assets.

COUNTRY FAIR: Vanity and bustling activity, joy, and Feast.

BARE FACTS

See also **More Grams of Saturated Fat Than You Can Shake a Stick At.**

COURT: Bad conscience. You are sitting in judgment of yourself. Don't be so hard on yourself. Search for justice. Are you always trying to "get it right"? Is it important for you to have certainty and a clear direction for your life?

COUSIN: That which is familiar, usually your own characteristics.

COVER (AS IN BEDCOVER): Protection and warmth, hiding, being secretive. To be under the same cover with someone else indicates intimate connection and trust.

COW: See also Milk. A symbol for mother. It appears only very rarely in men's dreams, and only when there is a strong connection to the mother. It has also been a prophetic symbol—of a lean or productive year. Remember Pharaoh's dream about the seven lean and the seven abundant years, as interpreted by Joseph? In India the cow is seen as the earth itself, and in Egypt the cow represents heaven (Hathor).

LISTEN UP, THIS IS IMPORTANT

Some of you may not remember Pharaoh's dream about the seven lean and the seven abundant years. Some of you have lives.

COWBOY: Adventure, individualism. Exaggerated craving for admiration. Longing for directness and being closer to self. See Rifle.

CRADLE: Baby. If this image is not a desire for a child, it usually symbolizes new ideas. See Scale.

CRAFTSMAN: Vigor, practical intelligence, and being constructive.

CRANE (MACHINERY): To remember something, to find something, to lift and remove something old.

CREAM (FOOD): See Milk. Heavy food. Taking pleasure in sweets.

CREAM (LOTION): Points to the "character mask" in everyday life. You want to be more beautiful. However, cream also indicates "balsam for the soul." In a deeper sense, the beauty of the soul is addressed here, and a beautiful soul is, in at least one sense, a true soul.

LISTEN UP, THIS IS IMPORTANT

As with the two kinds of conductors, so too can cream dreams be combined, as in your finding yourself putting lotion on a cake or using frosting as a sunblock. This usually indicates a desire to indulge in smearing food on yourself or, conversely, to preserve a cake (a celebration) a little longer. Either way, you're out of your tiny little mind.

CRIMINAL: See Burglar. Loss; moral conflicts, often of the sexual variety.

CRIPPLE: Emotional or mental handicap. In this dream symbol an important part of the shadow is expressed: your own weakness and neediness, for example. This dream symbol often appears when you are feeling overly important and are tending toward arrogance. Often a challenge to become more responsible, compassionate, and helpful. In addition, the image of the cripple is also related to Beggar, which may point either to becoming more humble or to greed and a hunger for possessions. See Illness, Crutch.

CROCUS: New life is emerging.

CROSS: Symbol for direction and order. It appears in classic dreams, where it is the cross of the victor, the cross of God's praise and honor, and also a sign of victory. According to Jung, it appears in a dream about agony (cross to bear).

According to Artemidorus, the second-century dream interpreter, it is a favorable sign for those who are going on a sea voyage, because ships were made of wood, and the masts took on the configuration of a cross. For nonseafaring people, however, it is a sign of bad luck.

CROSSING: Here it is always a matter of weighing alternative solutions. What do the different paths look like, and where do they lead?

CROW: Symbolizes misfortune or death because of its black color. See Darkness. It may also be a symbol of an aggressive woman. It was an early Christian symbol of faithfulness. See Bird.

CROWDS: A sign that you need more freedom and space, as in Prison and Cage. You feel crowded (this could be an actual sensation). Are you able in your everyday life to articulate your point of view and assert yourself? Do you need more space?

SNAP OF THE FINGER

Recurring dreams of wanting to rip the heads off of people in crowds could indicate unresolved anger issues. Please send someone else to the bank and post office for you for the next six months.

CROWN: Hat. Symbolizes power, fame, and influence. Points to a high level of awareness that is related in yoga to the crown chakra (*Sahasrara*). See King/Queen.

Since the Middle Ages, a crown made of straw has symbolized impermanence, which is still part of today's interpretation. The crown of straw also points to the Harvest—experiences from the past are now useful.

CRUTCH: Fear of life, inhibitions, and inferiority complexes, or being freed from them. See Invalid, Bridge.

CRYING: Release from pain, letting go. See Water, Tears.
Crying, according to Freud, meant ejaculation.

SECRET TIP

This is one case in which Freud was wrong. Everyone knows that men are much better at learning how to ejaculate than they are at learning how to cry.

CRYSTAL: Harmony and clarity. See also Glass, Mandala, Star.

CUBE: Being on the path of individuation. As far back as ancient Greece, geometry was considered the path to self-realization. According to Plato, the cube stands for Earth.

CUCUMBER: Phallic symbol. Recuperation and health.

YOU'RE WELCOME FOR THE TIP

May also turn up in dreams about rock musicians trying to impress the ladies.

CUP: See Thirst. Refers to female virtues and emotions, and the needs of the soul. According to psychoanalysis, a symbol of female sexuality.

See also Mug, Beaker, Goblet.

CURL/HAIR: Temptation and youth.

CURSE: Great caution is called for. You are getting caught up in guilt.

CURTAIN: Wanting to hide something; confusion—"can't see through it." On the other hand, it might be necessary for you to "draw the curtain" closed for protection.

CUSHION: A need for quiet.

According to Freud, a symbol of the female.

SNAP OF THE FINGER

See also **Cushion, Whoopie.** According to Jung, a symbol of something that makes hysterical fake fart sounds.

CYPRESS: See Tree. Memories of vacations. Longing for Warmth. Slender and graceful.

DAM (DIKE): Built-up, repressed aggression, similar to Steam. Controlled feelings and suppressed desires. Also protection and security, as in Anchor, Arch, and Buoy.

COMMUNICATION

Repeated and intense dreams about dams may indicate a repressed sexual attraction to public figures with dams named after them. Yes, you may have the hots for America's thirty-first president, Mr. Herbert Hoover!

DAM (RAILROAD EMBANKMENT): This symbol always points to a road that is certain and predetermined. Also, the dam could possibly have sexual-erotic meaning as a first sexual experience. The dam is also a term used for the perineum, the area between rectum and genitalia.

DANCE/DANCER/DANCING: A frequent dream of women, expressing joy and sorrow about one's body. The rhythm of life, specifically the female's. To this day, many native peoples depict important life events in dance, and it often happens that a new situation is introduced during a dream in the form of a dance. Similar to Swimming.

Dancing with a partner refers to the roles people play in a relationship. Who was leading?

Desire for a partner; dynamic expressions within a relationship (playfulness).

According to Freud, all rhythmic body movements are a symbol for intercourse. According to Jung, a female dancer expresses the principal archetype of the female. See Ball (Dancing).

DARKNESS: Well-known symbol for our shadow, which depicts something invisible. Fear of people, emotions, thoughts, actions, and situations we don't understand, since they are in the dark. Ambiguous premonition, not knowing, secrets. Walking into your own darkness, where more awareness is called for. The task almost always is to become more aware (Light), to shed light on something intellectually, or to deal more consciously with the unknown. Your own shadow is now visible, which brings great progress and freedom. There are also "light shadows"— Angel and Fairy—but they are seldom addressed in dreams.

Also, do not lose sight of your path in the dark.

DASHING UP: A symbol for ascending.

DATE (FRUIT): A symbol of female gender. According to Oriental interpretations, a fruit pointing to a passionate love affair in the making.

DAUGHTER: The creative feminine that has many possibilities open to her for development. See also Moon. This image also represents the dreamer's need for new and unique powers.

DAWN: A new beginning; energy and youth. Postponing something until tomorrow. Either you are waiting to see or you are simply too lazy to do what you feel you need to do, but this can sometimes be quite proper and healing.

DAY: Confidence; infinite possibilities (the whole day lies ahead). Increasing awareness.

DEAD PERSON: In the past, dreams about dead people were rather frequent; today, they are relatively rare. The land of the dead is that of the unconscious where the Shadow resides. A dead person, according to Jung, is first and foremost a representative of unconscious incidents. See also Death.

DEAD-END STREET: You don't know how to proceed, you have no solutions. This can be a positive image if you see yourself turn back. Learn from old mistakes. Often the image appears in fearful situations where you are being pursued. This fear can be overcome if you understand that you need to turn around (or back out) in order to free yourself. If such a fear-based dream image appears, experiment with different behaviors. Changing your behavior almost always leads out of the dead-end situation. The experience of a dead-end street is, from a developmental point of view, absolutely essential.

COMMUNICATION

Dead-end dreams are extremely common among people who work in retail. (See **Food Court.**)

DEAF: Not wanting to hear something, being uncomfortable. Also, either too much or too little compliance. Not being fully aware of one's environment or surroundings. In rare cases, the experience of real physical symptoms during sleep.

DEATH/KILLING: If it is the dreamer dying, it never has any connection to a real, impending physical death. Rather, it is a reference to the need to change one's path in life and allow old attitudes to die. Death usually means that radical change is necessary.

Basically, there are eight different levels of this symbol:

1. An indication that a necessary end has come to a certain phase. It is a transition to something new.

2. The desire to shed something (attitudes, behavior, situation, etc.).

3. A suggestion to come to terms with death and the fear of death,

meaning a search for fulfillment and productivity.

4. A limit has been reached and there is an inability to know how to go beyond that limit.

5. A suggestion to take better care of one's health.

6. Something is dying inside.

7. A close connection with somebody deceased.

8. A desire for peace, solitude, and harmony ("the death of fear").

According to Jung, dreaming about death means letting go of something that has died; it is a symbol of transformation and a new beginning.

QUICK FIX

Having repeated experiences of dying in your own dreams is an unnerving experience, but, as we pointed out above, it is actually symbolic of so many things, none of which actually involves your physical death. So try, just this once, not sleeping in adult diapers.

DEBRIS/RUBBLE: Internal debris, a challenge to start "cleaning up" and recognizing the gifts and the chances that are hidden behind existing problems.

DEBTS: An obvious reference to material that burdens you and to real debts and mortgages. Your life is out of balance, meaning that you are confronted with guilt feelings in order to allow you to resolve them. Also, unconscious punishment for actual financial burdens.

DECEASED: See Death.

DECEPTION: A symbol of the unconscious. It is a suggestion to become more alert and more clear; or have you been engaged in (self-) deception lately? If that is the case, this symbol shows that you are already more conscious, more alert, and more clear.

Points to sexual inhibition, angst. Who has betrayed whom?

DECK: Ship, Travel, relaxation. Are you on the upper or lower deck? This would tell you whether you are centered more in the head or the belly.

COMMUNICATION

You could also be out on the deck of a ship, flush with the bloom of young love, letting the wind whip through your hair just a couple of days before you hit an iceberg and one of you plunges to your death in the icy deep. Sorry, *Titanic* was on cable again last night.

DEER: A symbol for a woman or girl.

Astrology: According to teacher Johannes Fiebig, a traditional symbol for the zodiacal sign of Cancer.

DEFENSE: See Fight, War, Armament, Jewelry, Attorney.

DEFLORATION: To be deflowered. See also Flower.

You are either losing your innocence, or opening yourself up to the pleasures and joys of life. Something is being pointed out here that cannot be undone. In addition, this dream symbol points to very profound experiences.

BARE FACTS

See also **Back Seat of Car.**

DEFORMED, BEING: Emotional wounds that may lead to insecurity and fear. You are unable to evolve fully and have lost your balance. You are longing for your own needs to be fully revealed, which would again make you beautiful. See Invalid, Cripple. This dream symbol may indicate fear of failure. It may also indicate that a possible failure (being deformed) can be prevented.

DELAY: Fear of missing something.

DELIVERANCE: Always a longing for freedom.

BARE FACTS

Especially freedom from inbred mountain men who want you to squeal like a pig.

DEMONSTRATION: Were you participating or watching? What were your feelings during the dream? Who demonstrated for what? And the most important questions that you have to ask yourself are: What would I be demanding or wishing for? What purpose motivates me?

DENTIST: A stressful situation. Is there a reason for you to dream about aching teeth? Fear of illness and pain.
Astrology: A symbol of Saturn.

DESERT/WASTELAND: Emotional isolation and loneliness. The place where fear and temptation and ghosts reside. See T. S. Eliot's *The Waste Land*. Withdrawal and asceticism. Symbol of the peak experiences that will lead toward self-realization. But the dreamer has to get all the insights and power from himself; there are no teachers. An illustration of the new and unknown.

DETECTIVE: The thrills and dangers of everyday life. This dream symbol often points to your search for your personal, as yet unknown, abilities and possibilities, but also to danger.

DETOUR: Pursue goals more directly, or a detour is necessary. The detour may represent the quickest road to your goal. (The Chinese say, "If you want to make haste, make a detour.")

DEVIL: Usually this symbol indicates that the shadow needs to be better integrated with the Self, or a reference to a one-sided intellectual attitude like Mephistopheles's in Faust. A black devil represents darkness and death; a red devil is the messenger of light and passion who is keeping close company with the wild. A green devil represents nature, which usually appears in the form of a snake, cat, or goat (all are symbols for the Devil). The Devil symbolizes the animal nature of human beings and their connection to the earth.

Like Ahriman (an ancient Persian version), the Devil is the antagonist of light, descended from the heavens in the form of a snake. In Hebrew he is Satan, the picture of evil lust; in the New Testament, he is the antagonist of the Church, embodying the absence of God among peoples. According to Irenaeus, a third-century Greek theologian, the Devil is really an angel who has fallen because of his arrogance. As Lucifer (who brings light), the Devil is considered a creature of light. In Dante's *Divine Comedy*, Lucifer has three heads, lives in the darkest parts of the earth, and is the enemy of the Holy Trinity. In the eyes of Christianity, almost all gods of native tribes were considered devils. In that sense, the Devil also symbolizes everything that is natural, original, and has the spark of light.

YOU'RE WELCOME FOR THE TIP

If you dream that you have literally shaken hands with the devil, then you have probably just signed your first mortgage—or paid for digital cable.

DIALECT: If it is the dreamer's own dialect, this image points to identity or psychological rigidity. If it is a foreign dialect, it points to a side of the dreamer that is unknown to him. Connections the dreamer can make to the dialect are important.

DINOSAUR: Frequently the grandparent or parents, ancestors, etc. Memories from childhood situations, because, from the perspective of small children, their parents seem very large.

The image points to inherited or early childhood experiences. In the end it is also a fascination with all that is huge and monumental; either you desire to be in command, or you're in love with your own status.

BARE FACTS

A dinosaur also symbolizes something that vanished without our being able to tell exactly why. This could indicate some stress around that jackball who never did call you back after the first date.

DIPLOMA: You would like to excel intellectually or be recognized publicly. Or are you craving too much recognition?

DIPLOMAT: Be diplomatic, more careful with the words you use, and with your actions. Often a need for awareness of the world and the self.

DIRECTOR: Who in your life is the director? Do you feel that your life is determined by outside circumstances? In the last analysis, such a dream image points to inner strengths and weaknesses of the ego, which usually directs the course of life. See Government.

DIRT: Feelings of being unclean, which are a burden to the dreamer. Frequently, sexual feelings, which parents have told their children are "dirty." What is often addressed is the task of cleansing oneself or cleaning up a situation.

DISCOVERY: Something new or something forgotten is awaiting you. What has been discovered? These are always personal, often unknown, qualities.

DISCUSSION: Frequently appears during work on unsolved intellectual problems (during the day); it is an unconscious problem-solving strategy, or perhaps a hint that a particular problem can only be solved collectively.

DISH/JUG/CHALICE: As in the symbol of the grail, emotional capacity and the soul itself. What is inside the dish is important. See also Cup, Container.

DISHES/CHINA: Domesticity. Broken china is commonly considered bad luck (in contrast to broken Glass).

DISMEMBERING/BREAKING UP: Do you have the feeling that you are falling apart? Dismembering often comes up in a dream when there is a fear of the breakup of a love relationship. In mythology, it frequently represents alienation and estrangement, and the dismembered person is then sometimes put together again by the gods. See also Mosaic, Puzzle.

DISOBEDIENCE: Symbol of liberation, but also of irresponsibility.

DISORDER: Chaos from which anything may evolve. A challenge to put more order into your life.

DIVING: Either exploring the depths of the soul or trying to deny something. Diving is an image of flight. It also means regression into a prebirth condition and a preparation for rebirth (a new beginning). Diving dreams always deal with an Adventure where the dreamer is surrounding himself with Water (emotions). Such experiences may be ecstatic or full of fear. In most cases, however, they are an image of liberation. After all, moving in water is easier than on land. See Submarine.

Yes, we can easily see how a diving image represents a return to the calming waters of your time in the womb. However, why you are spearing fish in there is anyone's guess.

DIVINING/DOWSING ROD: Being grounded, emotional sensibility.

DIVISION: Separation, estrangement, and loss. Depending on the context, this image may also refer to social skills.

Division often points to the individuality of the dreamer, because individuality is indivisible.

DIVORCE/SEPARATION: Either a desire for or a fear of separation. This symbol also may indicate separating things out—differentiating— which points to your ability to make judgments.

DOCK: Groundedness, security, as in Anchor and Buoy. Being at home, coming home, as in Parents' House, Family.

DOCTOR: See Physician. Helper, healer, wise man, adviser, and leader. Symbol of the healing power residing within, which you can trust. On the other hand, "Doctor" as a title points to the appearance that we would like to present to the outside world. If that is the case, this is a message to seek your true self.

DOG: The animalistic. A symbol of instincts to be used and guided by conscience. The dog may also appear as a guard to protect property and defend against attack. He may symbolize a true friend. The dog is the closest creature that humans come to call "friend." It may also represent part of the dreamer—for instance, the shadow.

The dog as a pet almost always points to our instinct or loss of instinct, particularly when it is a trained dog, which in this case does not imply cultivation, but rather the destruction of instincts. The dog is also a creature that needs to inspect its environment, that looks for and finds information. In the Tarot, the two images of "the Fool" and "the Dog" always appear together. A vicious dog means envy and unscrupulousness. According to Jung, the dog is the undertaker who buries the Corpse. The dog with its instincts is seen as aiding the process of dying and resurrection (like Anubis in ancient Egyptian mythology). According to Greek mythology, the dog from hell, Cerberus, stands on the border between life and death.

Also may point to fear of rejection—e.g., "dog" as an unattractive female.

DOLPHIN: The smart, wise mammal; highly developed, intellectual emotions.

DONKEY/ASS: The obvious meaning is stupidity, but also stubbornness, sexual energy, and vitality. (In the language of the sixteenth century, "driving an ass" meant to arouse the penis.) Today this symbol is seen differently, since the proverbial stubbornness of the ass can be interpreted as strength. He follows his own intuition and possesses a sense of what is his. And in the pursuit of his urges, the ass can also be very smart.

According to the second-century dream interpreter Artemidorus, if you see an ass that is carrying a load, a burden has been removed from you.

The most widely read book of the Middle Ages, *Physiologus*, relates the ass to the custom of castration.

Folklore: Luck in love.

DOOR: A new beginning. See also Gate. In ancient Egyptian dream interpretation, if the door is open, it is a sign that a favorite visitor is coming.

According to Freud, symbol of the female sexual organ. According to Jung, symbol of a transition from one phase to another.

DOORMAT: You are feeling inferior or stepped on. Everything dirty seems to be unloaded on you.

DOVE: The animal without trickery. As with all Birds, a symbol of sexuality as well as intellectual euphoria and ecstasy. A symbol of peace and creative thoughts. Doves can also be experienced as spirits or demons that one is unable to shed. In that sense, the dove is also a symbol of fear and disgust.

In the Christian Church, the white dove is the symbol for the Holy Ghost and is usually female. According to early Christian understanding, the dove is also the opposite of the Snake. According to Jewish tradition, the dove is the messenger of God. Today the "Christian-influenced" image of the dove of peace is a particularly favorite notion, as described in the best-selling book *Jonathan Livingston Seagull.*

YOU'RE WELCOME FOR THE TIP

Jonathan Livingston Seagull = Tuesdays with Morrie, except with a seagull.

DOWNHILL: Letting go; fear of "going down" (to the depths of emotions, or a reference to sexuality, etc.) as in Falling.

DRAGON: Fear of a woman, usually the partner or mother. Great wealth and luck. The dragon might be threatening and combative (Blake related it to mental battles). Often, as in depictions of St. Michael or St. George slaying the Dragon, a symbol of desire that needs to be resisted in favor of intellectual development. Points to one's own "poisonous" and destructive side. Are you hoarding too much? What do you want to own?

According to dream interpreter Artemidorus, wealth and treasure. The dragon is also a Chinese symbol for luck.

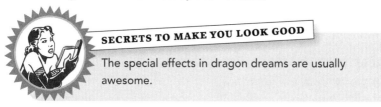

SECRETS TO MAKE YOU LOOK GOOD

The special effects in dragon dreams are usually awesome.

DRAWER: See also Closet. An image of secrets and possessions.

SECRET TIP

Also, a drawer full of underwear with dirty magazines underneath points to adolescence.

DRAWING: This symbol suggests that you look at something very carefully and realistically. Also, there is a need to be more active.

DREAM: It symbolizes the unconscious; awareness is demanded.

DRESS/CLOTHING: An image of poverty. Symbolizes the role the dreamer plays in the world and how he presents himself—"clothing makes the man." The type of clothing refers to the social standing of the dreamer, either the one he occupies or the one he would like to occupy. According to Freud, it points to nakedness, which is hidden under the clothing.

DRINK: Images of a drink usually appear when the dreamer is actually thirsty. It can also relate to taking pleasure in love. What did you drink?

See also Thirst, Cup, Glass, Water, Wine, Tears.

DRIVER'S LICENSE: Symbolizes identity. You have been recognized as mature enough to become a Leader. You can move freely (symbol of freedom). Loss of driver's license, loss of identity, immaturity. Searching for the driver's license, searching for one's identity.

DRIVING: Always refers to your life's journey, to the growth you have achieved. Here, particular emphasis is placed on your mobility. What kind of Vehicle are you using? How is the trip? Are you driving yourself or are you being driven? Check more closely Driving a Car, Train, Airplane, and Bicycle.

According to Freud, a symbol for intercourse.

According to psychotherapy, the analytical process itself.

DROWNING: Sinking into the unconscious, helplessness, lack of planning in your life. Being swept away by the flow of emotions.

Fear of being swallowed up by the unconscious. As in Suffocating, where the issue is to get more air, here it is a matter of being safe in the Water, about feelings and (emotional) needs that tap more energy and inner strength.

DRUGS: Opium. Murky, foggy; a message to be more awake, more clear, and more focused.

Astrology: Symbol for Neptune.

DRUM/DRUMMING: Movement, something new, excitement. According to the latest research, if a person has frequent dreams in quick succession about drums, it might indicate that the nervous system is in a state of alarm.

Arrogance, exaggerated self-importance, enjoying contact.

DUCK: Symbol of female friendship, but also falsehood.

COMMUNICATION

Oh, those evil, duplicitous, phony ducks. One minute they're your friends, the next minute they're falsehood itself. Don't you just hate them? Freakin' ducks.

DUEL: See Duet. Problems with your environment, contradictory emotions. This dream symbol may also have sexual aspects. A frequent dream image when one is at war with oneself: I am torn!

DUET: Contradictory thoughts and feelings, as in Duel, but more harmonious. Harmony, particularly in relationships.

DUNES: Memories of travels. Something is temporary, fizzling out. See also Quicksand, Sand, Beach.

DWARF: A fairy-tale figure, a helper, and a symbol for being connected to the earth. Are you feeling small and inferior? Should you be more humble? Also a symbol of the shadow, of what is minuscule and invisible. You still feel like a child; or you know how huge the world and cosmos are and feel small again, like a child.

DYING: According to psychoanalysis, wanting to get even with somebody. See Death/Killing.

DYING FOREST: Often a suggestion that the foundation of the dreamer's life, the unconscious, is disturbed. An exploitative worldview has taken over. The dreamer needs to find and stop the ways he is exploiting himself—and others. See also Forest.

EAGLE: An ancient symbol for rulers and power, the eagle can, like the phoenix, rejuvenate himself and thereby become immortal. The eagle possesses superior viewing power, but there is also a warning connected to the symbol—bold plans and actions can turn dangerous. The eagle is an ancient symbol of freedom. As an endangered species, it symbolizes a rare but also most powerful animal. Like all Birds, it points to the connection between heaven (spirit) and earth.

A white eagle is a symbol of happiness and spirituality. With a lame wing, the eagle points to constriction and restrictions, similar to the symbols of Amputation and Cage.

Freud saw in the eagle a distinctive and powerful sexual symbol. For C. G. Jung, it was a symbol of transformation. For William Blake, it was the marriage between Heaven and Hell. The eagle is also viewed as the symbol of the (high-flying) genius.

YOU'RE WELCOME FOR THE TIP

Dreams of the bald eagle indicate a long-overdue acceptance of one's receding hairline.

EAR (OF CORN): Symbol of fertility and well-being, also a phallic symbol. Here it is usually a question of how productive you are—what has grown inside you, and what you want to harvest.

Astrology: The sign of Virgo.

EARRING: See Jewelry. Are you greatly invested in your outward appearance? Or should you listen more carefully, as in Ear?

SECRET TIP

Also relates to piercings, which indicate a desire to piss off one's parents.

EARTHQUAKE: Enormous event, severe emotional upset; often hinting at self-destructive energies. Sign of general insecurity.

According to Jung, always a blow to one's point of view or convictions. Something confronting you can be handled only if you totally abandon your old convictions. In that sense, this dream symbol is always a sign of getting another chance and making a new beginning.

SECRETS TO MAKE YOU LOOK GOOD

There is also, of course, the sexual connotation, as in "the earth moved." However, even in dreams, this phrase is usually hyperbole, used to soothe the fragile male ego.

EASEL: Creativity.

EAST: From the East come awareness and enlightenment. See also the Bible story of the three wise men from the Orient. The Sun rises in the East. A dream about the East is almost always connected with a longing for higher consciousness, greater clarity, and better self-understanding.

EATING: Grounding, taking something in, being touched by sensual pleasures. In the widest sense of the word, it always points to emotional or spiritual food. What do you have to do to nurture your soul?

LISTEN UP, THIS IS IMPORTANT

We don't want to say you have heinous eating habits, but even the fast-food joints in your dreams are offering several low-fat alternatives.

EBB TIDE: Emotional relaxation, or lack of energy, calming of one's emotional life. A poor financial situation.

EBONY: Black, Wood, Beauty. In the fairy tale "Snow White and the Seven Dwarfs," ebony plays a role.

ECHO: Usually the result of noises in the immediate environment. Otherwise, you ought to pay more attention to the impact of your own words; everything that you send out is coming back to you. Also, it is frequently a symbol of the soul, where everything resonates. You are hoping for a reaction from the world around you. It may refer to remembering something that was said a long time ago, and that now may possibly be seen in a new light.

EGG: Symbol of beginning. Many mythologies depict the earth as having developed from an egg. Symbol of rebirth—Easter eggs. Also, that which is fragile. Longing for or fear of pregnancy, as in Baby, Birth. In the Koran, virgin women are compared to well-preserved eggs.

According to Freud, female sexuality and motherhood.

Astrology: Symbol for Cancer.

STRETCHING THE TRUTH

Many test subjects report dreaming of *scrambled* eggs. You don't need a Ph.D. to know how screwed up these people are.

EIGHT: Symbol of wholeness, completeness, the eight-fold road of Buddha, an octave in music. Grounding, since the dice, as the symbol of earth, have eight corners. In rare cases, a sign of being fixed and motionless. Also: Pay attention!

Infinity—the sign of infinity is a horizontal figure eight. In rare cases, "8" is also the sign of an outcast (ostracism).

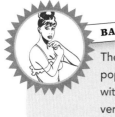

BARE FACTS

The number eight is also the centerpiece numeral in a popular game of billiards—a game played on green fur with a bunch of balls dropping into holes. We mean it's very similar to golf. Why, what were you thinking?

ELECTRICAL CORD: The energy of the dreamer is addressed here.

ELECTRICAL WIRE: See Wire. Energy transformation.

ELECTRICITY (POWER PLANT): Symbol for energy, supply, and transformation of power; or you may be under tension. If there is an accident in a power plant, and you can't handle internal tension, this indicates repressed urges—see also Termination, Attack, Fire, Surf, Defloration, Flame, Violence, Greed, Skin Rash, Wire (High-Tension), and Hooker/Prostitute.

ELEPHANT: Perception of your own power; or you are not letting anybody near you. The power of the unconscious is not available to you, and you are afraid of it. Points to thick-skinned people who are unaware of their destructive powers (the elephant in the china shop). Warning of one's own repressed sexuality. A need to be more patient (thick-skinned), or perhaps you have too much patience. Tusks and trunks are sexual symbols. The image of a sick or weak elephant points to emotional injuries. If it is a peaceful elephant, you are handling your unconscious issues comfortably.

According to early Christian belief, as described in *Physiologus*, one of the most widely read books of the Middle Ages, the elephant has no sex drive and is a powerful enemy of Snakes. Elephants' hair and bones were burned inside the house as a protection against evil spirits.

STRETCHING THE TRUTH

Research reveals that the reason the elephant has no sex drive is that it works hard all day and when it comes home, it just wants to veg out in front of the TV. So like us, our animal brethren.

ELEVATOR: See also Ladder, Stairs. Emotional changes and the degree of those changes are expressed here. Caution, remaining aware of reality. If the elevator is moving up fast: advancement, high hopes. If the elevator is moving down fast: fear of letting go. See also Abyss and Trapdoor. If the elevator gets stuck: inferiority complex or strong inhibitions.

A symbol of Kundalini, vitality in Yoga. Advancement and wish for self-affirmation; or, fear of Falling and Shooting. Being constricted as in Siege, Amber, Village, and Trap, except not so extreme. Emotional transformation; becoming more aware without effort.

EMBARRASSMENT: On one hand, admitting imperfection—not being what you would like to be. On the other hand, breaking through limiting conventions. This dream may also point to the end of long-standing behaviors and/or attitudes. See also Puddle.

Indicates the inability to communicate and express your needs clearly. Part of the Self is lost or was put aside and is not being lived.

SNAP OF THE FINGER

The word is "embarrassment" and the "see also" is "puddle." You really don't even need us anymore, do you?

EMBRACE: The desire for closeness, but fear of restriction and boundaries. Problems in bonding. Pay attention to who is being embraced.

According to Freud, desire for sexual union.

EMBROIDERY: If you are doing embroidery, it indicates that you may need to calm your nerves.

COMMUNICATION

If what you are embroidering is a straitjacket, you may need trained professionals to do the nerve calming for you.

EMERALD: One of the hardest gemstones, the emerald symbolizes character or the innermost soul.

EMERGENCY ROOM: Ambulance, fear of accident; you are looking for help.

EMIGRATION: Trying to find a new field of activity/employment, but also fear of necessary reorientation. Could also be interpreted, as in Giving Up/Getting Out and Foreign Countries/Abroad, as a warning for being unrealistic. See also Asylum/Exile.

END OF THE LINE: Either you are at the end of your rope, feeling exhausted, as in Blindness, or you have reached your goal.

ENEMY: Contradictory ideas, attitudes, and aspects within the self. Often those which you want to deny. See also Ruler.

On an objective level: people in your surroundings whom you reject. On a subjective level: one's own characteristics and mistakes.

ENGAGEMENT: See also Marriage, Wedding. Symbol of at least a temporary union. An unknown side is integrated. It is symbolically important to whom you have become engaged.

YOU'RE WELCOME FOR THE TIP

Dreams of engagement are often followed by dreams of wedding planning. Well, actually, wedding planning is a nightmare.

ENTRANCE: Openness. Sexual meaning seems apparent.

ENTRANCE (AS IN PERFORMING): Often fear of success or a more generalized fear of failure (particularly when stage fright is part of the dream). "Where do I have to appear?"

ENVELOPE: See Letter, Post Office. Are you expecting an important announcement?

STRETCHING THE TRUTH

Ninety-eight percent of dream test subjects report enormous letdown upon finally opening the envelope that contains the important announcement, only to find it is an offer for a low rate on a balance transfer.

ERASER: To undo something, to get rid of something, to repress and forget facts. Faulty and indecisive actions.

ERECTION: Erections during a dream are normal, but here we are talking about a dream of erection. Symbolically, this points either to fear of impotence or to the joy of masculine power. This symbol is about willpower and vitality within men and women. It almost always poses the question of how goal oriented and focused your actions are. For men as well as for women, this dream can be interpreted as the need for hetero-, auto-, or homosexuality.

According to Freud, women dreaming of erection indicates penis envy.

BARE FACTS

As the years go on, erection dreams gradually change, becoming dreams in which the subject is searching high and low for someone to write a Viagra prescription.

ESCAPE/FLIGHT: Repression, particularly when you are afraid of examining your own shadow (thoughts and feelings that you are unaware of), as is often the case in dreams about flying. Are you running away from part of yourself? You might have good reason for it! However, in a dream, escaping is a sign that whatever you are running from wants to be understood and accepted—otherwise, it would not appear in a dream. Whenever you are fleeing, you are also *looking* for something. Ask yourself what your goals are.

EVENING: Time for reflection, a comfortable, peaceful time. Often an expression of the need for rest when being overwhelmed. This symbol frequently appears when the person is in a stressful or out-of-balance situation. It may also appear after a stressful period. The evening as the "twilight of one's life," or taking a rest at the end of a day's work, is often a sign of life lived with purpose and accomplishments (you may rest on your laurels).

The evening is, in part, a sign that you are reaching deeper layers of the unconscious. Less frequently, the image of being at the end of the day may also be expressing a painful loss.

EVENING MEAL (DINNER): Longing for, or fear of, happy Family and a cozy Home. "Often appears" when all of this is being missed, or when it is simply too much to cope with. Enjoyment of the retirement years (Evening) indicates a zest for life and sensuality.

EXECUTION: Don't panic when you have such a dream. This is a symbolic expression and not a threat. In some cases, the image of an execution can be particularly positive, because something is finally dying that has bothered you for a long time. If you are the one who is being executed, this symbol indicates strong negative emotions, self-doubts, and guilt feelings. If somebody else is being executed, it symbolizes the Other—usually characteristics or behavior that you must urgently discard. See also Death.

Psychological and mental reorientation. Changes need to be made.

EXILE: Feelings of estrangement and abandonment. Longing to belong. Or are you seeing a part of you that you have "condemned into exile"? Repression. See also Hermit and Asylum/Exile.

EXPLOSION: Emotional outburst, intense (inner) conflict. Repressed urges, as in Electricity, Attack, Surf, Abduction, Defloration. You really should allow yourself to "explode" now and then! It is important to look at what is exploding, and what form the explosion takes.

EXPRESS: Stress, hurry, and importance.

EYE: Mirror of the soul, window of vitality and willpower. Since the eye also represents the image of the Sun, this dream symbol points to vitality and courage. Here, body, mind, and soul are synonymous with heart, consciousness, and emotion. Often a sign of inner restlessness. Fear of missing something or being left out. Being aware of something but not wanting to see it, or simply being curious. Become a better and more thorough observer. Greed ("eating" with the eyes).

The color of the eyes and its symbolism is important.

In our culture, green and blue eyes are very much eroticized. In Islamic countries, people protect themselves studiously from the "evil eye," but being stared at in a dream is considered a good sign: it means being considered an important and interesting person.

Freud and Jung both considered the eyes—because of their shape—to be a female sexual symbol (the blinding of Oedipus is a castration symbol).

Looking yourself in the eye in a dream means self-knowledge; it is a challenge to have courage and to see yourself as you really are. It is important who is looking, in what manner, and what direction. Open eyes show recognition and openness; downcast eyes mean a weakening of willpower.

COMMUNICATION

It is said that the eyes are the window to the soul. Similarly, the mouth is the window to the gastrointestinal tract, although somehow that notion never caught on.

EYEGLASSES: Help, or an obstacle to, seeing something more clearly. Refers to your own perception and the courage to hold to your own subjective convictions. Insight, vision, perspective, as in Eye, and sometimes Bird, but with assistance. Also an expression of your own emotions that are either endangered, protected, or sharpened. Sunglasses point to summer, vacation, and Blending. Also "seeing the world through rose-colored glasses." Protective glasses point to work.

SNAP OF THE FINGER

Dude, get laser surgery, and you never even have to *dream* about glasses again!

EYE SPECIALIST/OPHTHALMOLOGIST: See also Eye, Physician. One ought to take a closer look and seek help in obtaining objective insights.

QUICK FIX

Plus, it helps if you can read all the letters on the chart.

FABRIC: Everything is connected to everything else. Fabric symbolizes the "thread of life," a suggestion to "weave" together the threads of experience and your own personality to create a whole. See also Thread. The type of fabric is often a mirror of your emotions.

You either want to hide something or want to present something in a favorable light. Pay attention to the symbolic meaning of the colors.

According to Freud, a symbol of the female body.

SECRET TIP

Also, fabric store. A fabric store dream is a very clear symbol for an excursion into the depths of hell. At least for some of us.

FACE: Facial expressions stand for the emotional situation of the dreamer, for the way he respects and judges himself. They are a symbol of the dreamer's identity, willpower, and power of intuition. A disfigured face reflects rage, aggression, fear. A distorted face indicates internal turmoil. An uneasy or inscrutable face expresses the search for identity. Is the face a Mask, is it made up, or is it open and free?

FAIR/EXHIBITION: Communication, contact. See Masses.

FAIRY: Desire for advice and help from the outside, as in Parents, Physician, and Pharmacist. Tendency toward childishness. The fairy is a being of the soul.

According to Jung, it points to the feminine side (anima) in men and women. The "good fairy" is the liberated female or the fertile mother; the "bad fairy" is the female temptress who needs to be set free.

Astrology: The symbol for Cancer.

SNAP OF THE FINGER

Traditionally, fairies were said to live in another dimension, just beyond the reach of what we know as normal. For a glimpse of this world in your everyday life, check out public access television.

FALLING: A warning not to be such a realist. It might be better to just let go, as in Abyss, Cliff, Shot, Parachute, Flying, and be more open to something new. Also fear of being destroyed, as in Descent. Points to loss due to miscalculation on the part of the dreamer (see the myth of Dædalus and Icarus), or is a sign of unjustified euphoria and arrogance. This symbol often appears in dreams during times when a person has difficulty achieving orgasm and during an acute midlife crisis.

Doubt and insecurity. You need to let go, as in Brook, Leaf, and Parachute. Dreams of falling often appear if you are in the process of transition to a new stage in life. Particularly when you are trying out something new, you will first, just as in the dream, fall flat on your face. A falling dream happens again and again if you are fighting against your own limitations. It is very helpful to change falling dreams into flying dreams.

According to Freud, falling dreams are always sexual. In the case of women, the question revolves around giving in to erotic desires ("fallen" women). Freud has dealt with the symbol of falling extensively in his *Interpretation of Dreams*.

STRETCHING THE TRUTH

May also indicate falling prices! We mean it: everything must go! Every refrigerator and appliance in our showroom at drastically reduced prices! We make the deals and pass the savings onto you! (Known in psychological circles as the "Crazy Eddie" dream; indicates the dreamer's desire for low, low, rock-bottom prices on electronics.)

FAME: Dissatisfaction and longing for acceptance.

FAMILY: Fulfillment of the need for protection and security, as in Notice-of-Intention-to-Marry, Bureaucrat, Tree Trunk, Sidewalk, and Parents' House. On an objective level, one's "own" family that is often unconsciously experienced aggressively. On a subjective level: needs, emotions, and partly reflecting the characteristics of self. It can also refer to other groups (at work, friends, etc.)

According to Freud, a symbol for secrets.

BARE FACTS

See also **The Source of All Your Problems.**

FARM: The "innate" side of the dreamer (the instinctive urges). Acceptance and integration of instinctive urges, material success, grounding, and health.

FASHION: Personal style or vanity, as in Jewelry and Mask.

FASTING: Refusal to accept anything from the world around you. Vanity. You ought to take up less space. The motive for the fast is important.

FAT: Too much of a good thing. Often combined with disgust.

FATHER: Chief, Teacher, King. A person who teaches the laws of life. The archetypal father figure stands for the need for security, order, authority, and achievement (Mars), and awareness/consciousness (Sun).

Having it appear in dreams is often an expression of a bad conscience. If the dreamer has a problematic relationship with his father, the father in the dream would appear as the Pope, or as Almighty God—the Father, who guides and controls the dreamer's world.

According to Jung, the image represents the one who generates and creates, the intellectual principle, and the one who gives life.

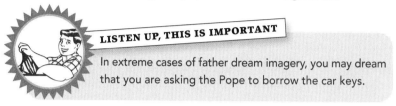

LISTEN UP, THIS IS IMPORTANT

In extreme cases of father dream imagery, you may dream that you are asking the Pope to borrow the car keys.

FAUCET: Not only in Freud's understanding: a phallic symbol.

FAX: Effective communication, working through information received. The power to communicate, not least about emotional concerns. Perfect symbol for Transference, which plays a prominent role in psychoanalytical dream interpretation.

COMMUNICATION

Also a perfect symbol for a screeching, ear-splitting tone that one hears when one's so-called friends have their fax set on autodial.

FEAR: We are confronted with many different fears in dreams, but they always refer to obstacles that are a mirror of our everyday—often unconscious—fears and insecurities. Nightmares often have physical causes: we have eaten too much, smoked too much, or drunk too much alcohol. Often it is fear of illness (hypochondria), that needs to be overcome. It is important to determine what frightened you.

Usually, this is about literal fear, or about undoing a mistake. On the other hand, such a dream might also suggest letting go of unnecessary fears. Fear can escalate into nightmares, showing the way to personal development. Fear is also connected to being too narrow, and is usually a sign that the dreamer is in search of a more broad, liberated alternative to his or her present lifestyle.

STRETCHING THE TRUTH

You have no doubt heard Franklin Roosevelt's famous phrase, "We have nothing to fear but fear itself." While a comforting thought, any moron can see that it does not apply to dreams. Being dragged through mountains of broken glass by the guy who works at the deli, who can now suddenly fly, or looking up at a fifty-foot-tall Gorgon with the head of your ex-girlfriend pretty much shoots old FDR's theory right out of the freaking water.

FEAST: Longing for social contact, as in Communion. Eating can refer to all kinds of needs that you are trying to satisfy.

FEATHER: Travel, ease of movement with which you can let yourself go gently, as in Leaf. Compare also Bed, Pencil/Fountain Pen. A white feather means innocence.

FENCE: Isolation; feeling secure, or feeling restricted. See also Wall.

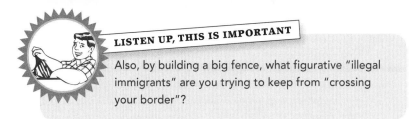
FERN: Recreation and vacation. A good time to bring into reality what you have planned.

FERRY: A sign of transition (sometimes also initiation) that plays a major role in fairy tales, mythology, and dreams. The ferry brings you to the other shore, traveling to another world. See also Bridge. A new goal for your life's journey.

FIELD (AREA): Symbol for women—your field of work/profession. (This patriarchal interpretation, which often does not correspond to the dreamer's conviction, is nevertheless appropriate because our internal attitudes do not change at the same rate as our ideology. Our conscious awareness is much more eager to change than our subconscious).

FIELD (E.G., CORNFIELD): Productive stage in life, particularly when the furrows are clearly visible. It may be the symbol of a fertile woman or mother (Gaia, the earth mother; also Demeter). Pointing toward work (one has to work the field). Hard, crusty clods indicate problems or paralysis.

For people living in a city, it is often also the symbol of rustic romanticism, similar to Farmer and Furrow, or wanting to escape from the city, becoming interested in the country for environmental reasons.

FIGHT: Symbolizes a problematic way you deal with aggression. Behind it is almost always the wish to deal with aggression more effectively and constructively. Contradictory thoughts and actions.

FILTH/DIRT: The desire for cleansing (due to a bad conscience), as in the expression "to wallow in dirt." According to Freud, sexuality. This association, however, was mostly relevant during the Victorian era, at the beginning of this century.

FINGER: Manual dexterity. According to conventional psychoanalytical theory, a phallic symbol.

FIRE: A frequently occurring dream when fearing or yearning for inner fire or passion. Warning: Be careful, because here, it is always the fire of life that is being addressed. Either it is destroying something or it is giving a signal. Accumulated urges, as in Termination, Attack, Surf, Electricity, Defloration, Flames, Greed, Harem, Skin Rash, Wire (high-voltage), and Hooker.

FIRE BRIGADE: The dreamer is fascinated with Fire, but not admitting to it. Fear of too much internal fire.

And let's not forget dreams about the firemen themselves. Right, ladies?

FIREFLY: As for Light, extending kindness and help. As in Spark, here it can also mean spark of the soul.

FIREPLACE: Confined physical urges, family, comfortable home; also, Fire.

According to Freud, a female sexual symbol.

FIREWOOD: Impetus, a short affair.

FIREWORKS: Playing with illusion. Points to how special an occasion is. Blending passion, lust, orgasm, and enthusiasm.

FISHING: Repressed aggression, or too little aggression, as in: Attack, Surf, Fire, Flames, Violence, Greed, and Wire (high-tension). Feelings of inferiority, repression, as in Termination, Attack, Harem, Skin Rash, and Prostitute. Fear of war or aggression, but also desperate search for physical or personal closeness.

FISHING ROD: Being dependent on somebody, or wanting somebody to depend on you, often with sexual undertones (the happy hooker). To reach for something way down deep (see also Water). Quiet and contemplation.

FIVE: The fundamental human being, a person in harmony—because a person, hands and legs extended, forms a pentagram. Also related to the five senses. The connection between the female and the male. Five also means "quintessence," the fundamental sense, the essential. In China, the number of the center.

FLAG: Passion, intellect (Air, Wind) and idealism; but also war. See also Standard.

FLAME: See Flames.

FLAMES: See Fire. A positive sign of your vitality if the flame is under control; otherwise, aggression and discharge of physical urges. According to ancient Egyptian dream interpretation, great monetary gain.

According to Freud: A symbol of male genitalia (since he considered the oven to represent the woman's womb).

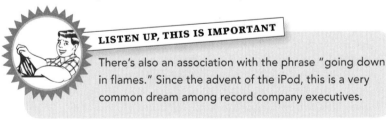

FLASHLIGHT: See also Light. One is unable to tolerate the dark side of the Self or others. At the same time, however, it is a light in the darkness, a symbol of insight and hope.

FLEA: Overexcitement, stress, as in Fly. A hint that you need to pay more attention to the small things in life.

FLEET (OF SHIPS): An emotional conflict situation, fear of emotional conflict.

FLOATING: Going forward by the most simple means on the Water of emotions. The dreamer should not just drift along. This is dangerous, because when you're floating, it is difficult to steer. On the other hand, you may trust that the water will carry you. It is very important to note how the trip is proceeding.

FLOOD: Being overwhelmed; an enemy is about to attack. Fear of drowning in emotions; being thrown back into the world of animals; being thrown back into the world of physical urges. The female archetype. The powers of the intellect and reason standing against the assault of nature on the conscious, civilized life. You need to learn how to "swim," which means being ready to swim in the water like a Fish. Both meanings are included here: to swim, and to give in and flow with the river of life, staying flexible.

A sign of being very emotional. You are overwhelmed, swept away, and, in the dream, you are afraid of this even if you would really like to give in. Incoming and outgoing tide: the rhythm of tension and relaxation in everyday life.

Feelings seem to be taking over. A feeling of being imprisoned because of physical drives and unconscious needs. Warning of psychotic behavior. If this dream image is accompanied by fear and appears often, a need for psychotherapy is indicated.

Seething emotions. A frequent dream symbol when fearful of one's own emotions.

SNAP OF THE FINGER

Fight the fear of a flood dream by sleeping in scuba gear. You will send a message to your subconscious that you are ready to meet the flood head-on, and your partner will spend a peaceful evening, lulled to sleep by the calming rhythm of your Darth Vader–like breathing device.

FLOOR: External and internal foundation, personal attitude. Always refers to being grounded, as in Foot and Basement. The floor can also be seen as a barrier between you and the ground. See also Stone/Clay (Floor).

FLOOR (IN THE SENSE OF A FOUR-STORY BUILDING): Level of awareness, level of physical presence.

FLOWER: Traditional symbol for emotions ("Say it with flowers"). Beauty and fertility. Growing and fading away, like life. Expectations of and hope for love and relationships of importance are the type and the color of the flower. Red roses point to sexual love; white roses and other flowers, to innocence; blue flowers, to the strength of the soul and emotions. Snowdrops point to overcoming the cold of winter; asters, to autumn and death. Picking flowers is considered a symbol of sexual experience.

In the Middle Ages, flowers with broken stems meant sexual intercourse. In India, in dream interpretation, the flower is the symbol of the highest pleasure. In Freud's dream interpretations, the flower is dealt with extensively and symbolizes women, tenderness, female genitals, and genitals in general, as in Blossoms (see Anaïs Nin's *The Delta of Venus*).

According to C. G. Jung, flowers represent emotions/feelings.

YOU'RE WELCOME FOR THE TIP

If you have not yet read Anaïs Nin's *The Delta of Venus*, we have a copy with all the good parts dog-eared.

FLOWERPOT: Domesticity and cultivating nature. The quality of caring and nurturing. On the other hand, this symbol might also point to substituting for the real thing; the flower in the pot is nature being controlled (and is therefore, in reality, a substitute for nature).

According to Freud: the symbol for women, as in Vase.

FLOWING: Drifting, not wanting to control anything, similar to River and Water. Are you living your life? Or are you swimming with the tide?

FLUTE: One of the oldest musical instruments, its sound is said to cast spells over people and gods (*The Magic Flute*). Harmony, accord, beauty, and tenderness. Let more joy come into your life. The flute is also a phallic symbol (Pan's instrument) and may sometimes indicate erotic self-absorption.

FLY: Overstimulated nerves. Resistance, nervousness, and slight irritation, as in Flea. May also point to Flying. Small things that can be very annoying.

FLYING: Overdramatization or fleeing from a problematic situation. Looking for clarification in difficult situations. Flying and Falling appear in Abyss, Elevator, and Trap, usually in nightmares; or as in Brook, Leaf, and, in part, Parachute, during very pleasurable liberation dreams. In case of teenagers: often a sign that too much is being asked of them and that they are being pressured to succeed. These dreams are often like being intoxicated, having a sense of being elevated, and a lightness: like being in love. Many ancient myths show the connection between flying and sexuality, and while flying today has become a commonplace activity, the old interpretations are still true (see *Fear of Flying* by Erica Jong). Now modern symbolic interpretations of flying include the image of worldliness, expansive ideas, and communications. Flying is also seen as a symbol of creative ideas. This image may also be a warning not to become too aloof and removed from reality through fantasizing. The dream may also be a challenge for either being too earthbound or taking flight into a greater dimension.

In ancient Egypt, dreams of flying were interpreted as fleeing from difficulties. In ancient Greece and Rome, dreams of flying were seen as passionate love.

According to Freud, they were dreams of sexual desire and erection (Freud dealt with this extensively). He saw dreams of flying exclusively as the desire for sex. Some modern dream experts interpret flying dreams exclusively as a desire to get away from problematic situations, or to cross one's own boundaries. Some researchers believe that in our dreams we go back to preborn states, make contact with the state of birds, and realize our innate ability to fly. Another contemporary dream researcher, Jack Maguire, believes that most dreams about flying are just a sign that we want to recuperate and refresh ourselves.

QUICK FIX

Yes, despite all of the above interpretations, the most accurate analysis of flying dreams is that they let us know we need to recuperate and refresh ourselves.*

*Source: The Gatorade Institute for Dream Analysis.

FOAL: Enjoyment of life.

FOAM/FROTH: This image is connected to the Venus symbol, Water and Air fusing emotion and intellect and representing redemption. The same symbol, however, might reveal a tendency toward unrealistic ideas and plans "the hot air merchant" indicating a tendency to blow things out of proportion, to exaggerate; or it may simply point to necessary cleansing.

FOG: Lack of orientation and lack of focus. Here, something needs to be explained more clearly and made conscious. Insecurity and deception. There is something you don't understand or that confuses you. The fog, however, also means creativity—something new is produced.

Astrology: A symbol of Neptune.

FOOD: Physical and emotional strength and energies. You are feeding the animal side in you.

Nourishment for body and soul. The kind of food you see is urgently needed for your soul. For instance, dreaming about Meat refers to drives and animalistic needs. Chocolate, on the other hand, or other sweets suggest being more open to love.

FOOD (STORED): Fear of deprivation, difficulties, and poverty, as in Savings, Coin, Counterfeit Money. You don't trust what you have, or are trying to protect it. But you have additional resources and energies at your disposal.

FOOL: Symbol of wisdom. Since the Middle Ages, the Fool has been the personification of sin. In some periods, he was even compared to the devil. The Fool is considered a symbol of carnal sin—a sex-crazed, lecherous person—with such characteristics as a weak will and an obsession with sexual drives. The Fool in early times was thought of as the counterpart and complement to the king. In the Tarot, the number of the card is zero, implying emptiness and at the same time completion. The wisdom of the Fool is the wisdom of the hour "0," of spiritual virgin land. It is the sense in nonsense. During a dream, the Fool often expresses a very strong loyalty to himself. So the message might be that you want to be able to laugh more—about yourself and others.

SECRETS TO MAKE YOU LOOK GOOD

Modern-day dreams involving a fool almost always point to the pain of watching your friends do karaoke.

FOOT: See also Leg. Your own point of view. Independence (to stand on your own feet). Always a symbol for being grounded, as in Basement and Floor.

According to Freud, a phallic symbol.

Astrology: Sign of the Fish (pisces).

FOOTBALL/SOCCER: Confrontation. The Ball expresses concentrated vitality and/or your own center. Here, the question is: Are you kicking *yourself*? Or are you bringing yourself into the game? It is important what position you play: quarterback, referee, fan, and so on.

FOREIGN COUNTRIES/ABROAD: The Other, the foreigner. The dreamer must deal with the confrontation of something new. A foreign country always is the "foreign land" within ourselves. A trip abroad and vacation when overworked. What does the foreign land symbolize to you?

FOREIGN LANGUAGE: The speech of Other; also the unknown part of ourselves. Something is not understood, or you are unwilling to understand it. Your task lies in the translation, and therefore the understanding, of the unknown and the foreign. Should you show more understanding? Or are you too understanding?

FOREST: See also Tree. A frequent dream symbol of the unconscious. Walking the forbidden path in the forest might cause us to be swallowed up and swept away by drives and instincts. The forest is a scary, potentially dangerous place where mysterious beings roam. It is also a place of transition (in Dante's *Divine Comedy*, for instance, a forest is found in front of the gates of the Inferno, as well as at the end of the Purgatorio and at the beginning of the Paradiso). On the other hand, this symbol indicates the attempt to make contact with the unconscious. See also Hiding Place.

SNAP OF THE FINGER

Have some fun online! Go to your favorite mapping Web site and get driving directions from the end of the Purgatorio to the beginning of the Paradiso. Should make for one hell of a printout.

FORK: Usually points to eating (particularly when you're actually hungry during your sleep). The devil and Neptune both carry a pitchfork (the three prongs are a symbol of the ancient trinity that represents Unity; see also Three). As a garden fork, to dig down into your own depth, grounding; also work.

As a "fork in the road," it is a symbol for your ability to make decisions and to differentiate.

As a tuning fork, it is a symbol of harmony (the right note) and orientation. Or—what or whom are you "forking" over?

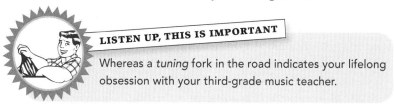

LISTEN UP, THIS IS IMPORTANT

Whereas a *tuning* fork in the road indicates your lifelong obsession with your third-grade music teacher.

FORT: See also Lodge. Protection, search for a home, and being indestructible. Memories of vacation, longing for relaxation. You want or *have* to protect yourself; or you are too protective, you are withdrawing.

According to Freud, a symbol for women and femininity in general.

FORTUNE: See Wealth. Abilities and talents.

FOUNTAIN: Beauty and harmony; a sexual symbol.

FOUNTAIN/WATERSPOUT: Water. Fertility, male sexuality.

FOX: A lover or lecherous person, a sexy female. Great instincts. Clever, cunning, calculating, and smart. The fox is considered our soul guide and companion on life's journey. It points to our childhood. A rabid fox means uncontrollable instincts.

According to the second century dream interpreter Artemidorus: bad reputation.

According to early Christianity, the fox is the devil.

According to Jung, a "foxy," cunning old man.

STRETCHING THE TRUTH

Fox is also a television network owned by Rupert Murdoch. Dreams of this nature are too terrifying to discuss.

FOXGLOVE (PLANT): Death and rebirth, medicine, and poison.

FRAGRANCE/SMELL: First, check to find out if you were smelling a real fragrance during sleep. Dreaming about fragrances is very rare. If you do, it is usually a sign that you are enjoying life and your sensuality. The type of fragrance indicates how you feel about the subject or object that gives off the fragrance (there are some smells we simply can't stand).

Fragrances are very effective in bringing back memories of places and people.

FRAME: Limitation or vanity.

FREAK: Behavior that is unbecoming. An outsider, as in Anarchist; broken. Unlikely romance. See also Fool.

FREEMASON: Good connections, power, and secrets. Are you searching for your own principles, or your own significance?

FREEZING TO DEATH: See Ice.

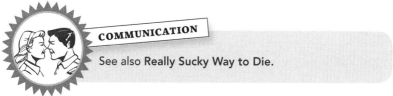

COMMUNICATION

See also **Really Sucky Way to Die.**

FRIEND: Favorable news, something lost has been found. Longing for social contact, similar to Companion.

Usually unknown aspects of your own personality. Wanting more support.

FROST: Suggests making peace with someone. It may be a warning that you are too cold, as in Ice.

FRUIT: First of all, the fruit of the life of the soul. Erotic sexual needs. A ripe fruit means being sexually balanced and enjoying life. A rotten fruit means an inferiority complex. A sign to eat more healthfully. The body needs fruit and vitamins.

When used in a derogatory way, insecurity about one's sexuality.

The erotic in adventure, success, and luck. A reminder of the sensual pleasures of summer. The first thing that you can and must pick—if you don't, you are missing your chance. That which is juicy and full. Fruit that is unpalatable or rotten points to problems—often illness and danger.

Ancient Egyptian dream interpretation: pleasant encounter. Classical interpretation: personal luck, when fruit is picked or collected.

According to Freud, women's breasts.

SECRET TIP

Also fruitcake, which indicates a repressed self-destructive desire to eat something hideous and frightening. (Usually confined to the holiday season.)

FRYING PAN: Domesticity, as with all symbols that have to do with food and eating.

According to Freud, as with everything that can be put on top of the stove, a sexual symbol.

FUNERAL: Frequent dream symbol. Something is supposed to die, to be put aside, to be completed to make room for the new, as in Baby, Birth. (Here, however, the emphasis is placed more on something "new" being about to happen). This symbol is similar to Abortion, Amputation. Differences are being buried; unrealistic wishes or tiresome, improper habits are being cast off. Possibly, a relationship is dying, as in Death, Divorce, Abortion, Good-bye. If it is your own funeral, it usually means that the "old you" is dying.

SNAP OF THE FINGER

Try to pay attention to what is being said about you at your burial. "You will be missed," for example, indicates that you are comfortable with how others see you, whereas "What a butt munch. I'm glad he's dead" may point to some unresolved issues.

FUR: Symbolizes nature and femininity (anima), desire to cuddle. See also Furs.

FUR COAT: Prosperity, luxury, as in Oysters, Champagne, and Aristocrat. Self-confidence, vanity, and need for admiration. Important to note what kind of fur it is.

YOU'RE WELCOME FOR THE TIP

If you dream about wearing fur enough times, you will sooner or later be accosted in your dreams by an animal rights advocate. If prepared, you can ask your subconscious to equip you with some pepper spray. If this does not work, steel yourself for the inevitable bucket of red paint hurled at you and your coat, your symbol of all that is wrong with the world.

FURNITURE: The dreamer's qualities, in the sense of the "internal furniture" of the soul and one's own identity. The type of furnishings and their condition are important.

FURS: If you know the animal the fur is from, it refers to the animal's character. If you don't know the fur's origin, then it means a longing for coziness and warmth.

According to Freud: pubic hair; according to Jung, the animal within.

FUTURE: Often a real foretelling when the dream takes place in the future. Also, a time when you are able to consciously experience intuition, fears, and expectations of the future.

LISTEN UP, THIS IS IMPORTANT

You may become alarmed if you dream of the future as a black, unimaginably deep void, but this is only because the truth is sometimes hard to accept.

GABLE (OF A ROOF): Good advice and security, as in Arch.

GAG: Restriction and lack of freedom, similar to Cage, Prison, Shackles. Restricted movements are particularly emphasized here.

GALLOWS: Hanging up your burden. Or, if you are being hanged, extreme danger. Ancient symbol for drastic punishment; however, it need not always be a nightmare. It could be a relief.

GAME: A suggestion to take life a little easier, not to be so serious. It is an image of the liveliness and the ups and downs of life. Communication, a warning against being too superficial. Longing for contact. See Ball (game).

GAP/OPENING: Female sexual organ, or a symbol of obstacles.

GARBAGE: Desire for cleansing. A need to discard internal refuse that is burdensome. Similar to Abortion. Much has accumulated and must be emptied: emotional garbage and everyday garbage. Suffering because of involvement with the environment (and yourself). You are making an important discovery: it is in the "garbage" that we find the gold of meaning; in the inconspicuous and rejected lies the chance for self-knowledge. As C. G. Jung has stated, in accepting the rejected shadow, we take the first step to individuation.

SNAP OF THE FINGER

"It is in the garbage that we find the gold of meaning." Save that one up for the next big argument with your girlfriend. It ought to at least stop her dead in her tracks before she realizes you're full of it.

GARDEN: See also Field. The garden is the place where our soul joins nature. It symbolizes longing, fertility, and a satisfying love life. A place of harmony and relaxation (as well as sin, as in the Garden of Eden), a place to become grounded and a place of civilized nature, corresponding to a "civilized" inner life. It is the domestic, fenced-in area, in contrast to the untamed Field, or even the Forest. Stepping into a garden is like retreating from the harshness of the outside world, looking for protection and relaxation. In Egypt the garden has always been the symbol for woman.

According to Freud, female sexuality.

GARDENER: Relationship to a partner or to one's own nature.

GAS: Influences that are trying to poison you. Something obscure (invisible) that creates fear. But there is a positive side to this dream image: you are becoming conscious of something you have been unaware of until now. What could it be?

GASOLINE: Physical and emotional energy, drive, nutrition. Impetus.

GAS STATION: See Tank. A place where you can fill up with new energy. Taking a rest.

GATE: See Door. A symbol of transition and a suggestion that something new is coming. See Threshold. According to Freud, if the dreamer is a neurotic person, the image has unmistakable sexual meaning (Vagina).

Astrology: A Saturn symbol.

GENITAL ORGAN: Its obvious meaning concerns sexuality. On the other hand, every actual sexual image points to the present situation of the dreamer. Often, other energies, like love, fear, power, and money express themselves in the form of sexual symbols. Freud makes a very clear distinction between genital sexuality and general sexuality. On one hand, he took a broader view: "First, sexuality is freed from a much too narrow connection to the genitals and seen in a much wider sense as a pleasure-seeking bodily function, which is only secondarily put to the service of procreation. Secondly," Freud continues in his *Self Portrait*, "sexual stirrings are all those merely tender and friendly emotions for which our language coined the many-faceted word 'Love.'" What this means is that, for Freud, sexuality is pleasure seeking, all encompassing, and expressed by the whole body, internally and externally. He was of the opinion that sexual urges and the tender feelings of love are connected, and that one part is not to be withheld at the expense of the other. In that sense, it is a question of "separating sexuality from the genitals," of sensuality, of saying good-bye to the notion of "always searching for one part only," when so much more is worth having. At the same time, Freud emphasizes the difference between general, unorganized sexuality and genital sexuality. It is only in the genital phase that "the full expression" of all drives/urges (and not only part of them) is achieved. See Erection, Intercourse, Sexuality.

BARE FACTS

Hey, listen, if you can't give Freud his props during a discussion of genital organs, when can you give Freud his props?

GERBIL: See Guinea Pig/Hamster.

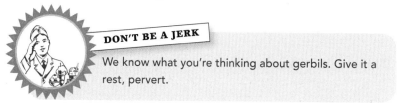

DON'T BE A JERK

We know what you're thinking about gerbils. Give it a rest, pervert.

GETTING LOST: Refers to the search for a proper solution in situations that are causing you great confusion. See Detour.

GHOST: Here, it usually means the so-called spirit of life, which makes up a distinctly human life. In addition, it might possibly point to unused or wrongly applied intellectual activities or actions. You are chasing a phantom. This is a warning against illusions and wrong insights. Creatures from the world of fairy tales are always somewhat frightening. They may be helpful or have bad intentions. Ghosts are often an expression of guilt feelings and pangs of conscience. If these images appear continually and are frightening, seek professional advice. The task connected with these dream images is often to find a better understanding and a more creative use of your intellectual powers.

According to Freud, they appear most often as women (in a white nightgown).

YOU'RE WELCOME FOR THE TIP

Sometimes, one might dream about visiting a haunted house, much like those that are set up in theme parks around Halloween time. These dreams should not concern you, as they feature totally lame-ass ghosts and are so completely not scary at all.

GIANT: An archetypal symbol of an overpowering father figure, but also of the universal beings that usually appear in the plural (they have no individuality). They are the antithesis of the gods, with whom they are in constant battle. They know only sensual pleasures and are greedy. See Monster, Dinosaur.

According to Jung, in a child's dream the giant represents adulthood. In that sense, giants are a symbol of future changes and growth that, in a young person's perception, appear "gigantic."

SECRETS TO MAKE YOU LOOK GOOD

Anything that is causing us anxiety can appear in giant form in a dream. There, don't you feel better about the one where you were being harassed by that two-hundred-foot-high wedge of Wisconsin cheddar?

GIFT/PRESENT: Relationships to the outside world should be improved. It is a matter of sharing joy and the joy of sharing. Life as a gift. See Birthday.

GIN: Tendency toward addiction.

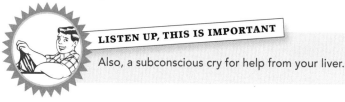

LISTEN UP, THIS IS IMPORTANT

Also, a subconscious cry for help from your liver.

GIRAFFE: That which is special, faraway, and exotic. You wish for a better view, to stand out among the crowd, or not to be treated as a child. But pay attention to the distance between head and body!

YOU'RE WELCOME FOR THE TIP

For example, if the distance between your head and your body is more than a mile, you could see yourself as "above it all," in which case why do you even need any advice from our lowly, humble little book, Sir Snotty?

GIRL: Often an erotic dream. In the case of women, it points to their feminine side or to childhood. What is addressed here is usually the lightheartedness of a child's life. In the case of both men and women, it symbolizes the feminine side of the dreamer. When the soul appears in a dream in the form of a girl, it usually points not only to the natural lively and innocent side of you, but also to the undeveloped and childish side.

GIVING UP/GETTING OUT: Fleeing or approaching something, as in Emigration. Not wanting to be part of something anymore, or not wanting to be doing something in a particular way. What's important is what you want to exit from, and what your feelings are.

GLACIER: See Ice.

GLADIATOR: Aggression and inferiority complex, compensated for with heroic dreams.

QUICK FIX

Take heart: Recent studies show that dumb-asses who overcompensate for their aggression and inferiority by having gladiator dreams are usually disemboweled by lions just before they wake up!

GLASS: The vessel of spirit. Transparent, clear, a sign of spirituality. Fragile and sensitive. Glass containers, glass, and a crystal goblet (the Grail) represent being conscious. A broken glass means injury and destruction of innocence—in the sense of Defloration—but also luck, as long as it is not a mirror. Occasionally, a glass is a symbol for frailty in the sense of impermanence and bewilderment. In alchemy, the stone of the Wise Men, lapis, is also called glass (*vitrum*), because it was seen as spiritual. See also Vase.

According to Freud, glass symbolizes female genitalia.

GLASS HOUSE: Greenhouse. Protection, as in Glass Wall. A message to be more open and transparent. Similar to the Container, in which transformation and growth takes place, in people as well as plants. Uterus. The glass coffin in "Snow White and the Seven Dwarfs." In mythological terms, a glass house is also seen as a sweat lodge, where the transformation of the prince takes place.

GLASS WALL: A frequent dream symbol when feeling cut off from others or objects; lack of contact. Something is seen as being unattainable. Reexamine your goals or ask if you have the necessary energies. In some instances, opposite image to Mirror.

GLOBE: See Atlas, Ball. Pleasure of traveling. You are looking for universal, global solutions.

GLOVE: Being detached from your actions. Reserve and an often exaggerated need for security. Fear of direct touch and danger of isolation. A frequent symbol in cases of the fear of AIDS.

Throwing a glove to the ground is an ancient sign of anger, and a provocation to fight.

GLUE: You want to put together something that has fallen apart. Something is being repaired. Are you being held by something or someone, or are you holding onto somebody tightly? The question of Liability and Responsibility in every form is being addressed here also.

GOAL: As in Target, this image refers either to very focused behavior, or to a necessary distance.

GOD/GODS: In the form of an actual image, these dreams are very rare. Rather, the feeling of a God-presence is a sign that a new state of consciousness has been reached. How are you dealing with authority?

GOLD: The sun of the soul and immortality, but it also might point to blindness, Greed, and materialism.

According to Freud, usually connected to feces. According to Jung and his successors, a symbol of whatever is most precious to the dreamer, his most prized possession, his higher self. See Money, Sun.

GOLDFISH: See also Gold. The special Fish. Life in the water of the emotions brings forth the true essence of your personality.

SNAP OF THE FINGER

And, like a goldfish, if the true essence of your personality dies, just flush it down the toilet.

GOLF: Wealth and competition.

QUICK FIX

Okay, so we meant wealth, competition, and stupefying boredom.

GOOD-BYE: Changes in the way you live and questions about your responsibilities. Separating from something important—a person, behavior, emotions—is imminent, has taken place, or is necessary. Compare this to Corpse, Death, Abortion, Sword, Divorce, or Funeral.

Folklore: A good sign, because you are letting go of something.

GOVERNMENT: On one hand, the image has the same meaning as Director. But attitudes toward authority are also implied. Do you want to control and govern your environment, or do you feel that you are controlled by it? See Ruler.

GRAIN: See also Rye. Grain in general symbolizes mental/intellectual and physical needs; but it may also—through an association with the Grim Reaper—point to the transforming power of Death. This may also address the question of personal productivity. See Field, Harvest. Bountiful harvest means self-confidence and health; crop failure, the opposite. A field of grain points to the "Fields of Life" and the "Field of

Experience." Here is a chance to find out what you have to work on. If you are a city person, the image of peace and quiet indicates a longing for a more natural life and relaxation. It relates to the idea that life bears fruit and brings maturity. Grain nourishes.

GRANDFATHER: See Grandmother. The all-powerful Father or the archetypal father, in contrast to the personal father. The father principle.

GRANDMOTHER: Very much like the symbol of Mother, but much more oriented to the past. The all-powerful mother, the archetypal mother (the mother principle) in contrast to the merely personal mother. Grandmothers, like Grandfathers, are often wise guides and advisers.

YOU'RE WELCOME FOR THE TIP

Grandmothers also put money in your birthday card every year. Bless their hearts; they don't need to know you spend it on beer and porn.

GRAND PIANO: Well-known symbol for harmony and Venus. See also Piano.

GRAPES: Naturalness, a productive life, fertile nature. See Fruit, Wine.

GRAPE WINE: A symbol of luck.

GRASS: Growth, connection to nature, groundedness. Something that is deeply rooted. The condition of the grass is important. Fresh green grass means health; dried-out, crushed grass means dissatisfaction, illness; grass that is too high and growing wild means unrealistic ideas. Also, as in marijuana, a longing for freedom, enlightenment, and relaxation.

SECRETS TO MAKE YOU LOOK GOOD

If by "enlightenment," you mean laughing at bad TV and getting the munchies.

GRASSHOPPER: See Greed, Loss.

LISTEN UP, THIS IS IMPORTANT

Also the nickname of the guy on *Kung Fu*. May indicate a repressed desire to snatch the pebble from someone's hand.

GRAVE/TOMB: Fear of life, resignation, and giving up. This symbol may refer to ancestors or to burial. What have you been burying? Or what is it that you should bury? Or should you unearth something? Also see Death.

GRAVEL: A dream of obstacles where it is difficult to get ahead. Gravel is part of the Earth, and points to matter and material.

GRAY: The color of something as yet unconscious and undefined, a colorless mixture where light emerges from the dark. Blending contradictions, as in Wedding, where it mixes black (female) and white (male), so it is archetypal. Gray borders between day and night, light and dark, and—in a dream—asks us to draw clear distinctions. Gray here may represent the unassuming; on the other hand, inconspicuous gray may also point to the conspicuous, the essential, and the real in life. See also Mouse.

SECRET TIP

A military connotation: Wearing your dress grays. Your dream may contain the phrase, "Do you call that a spit shine, maggot?"

GREED: Be more moderate. Or: you think you have been shortchanged. Repressed urges/drives, as in Miser. Also a hint that you are ravenous, which is a sign of unreasonable needs for gratification.

GREEN: Color of nature. Something is growing out of a state of immaturity.

GREENHOUSE: An artificially regulated and controlled space where aggression is not allowed ("People who live in glass houses shouldn't throw stones"). Are you isolating yourself in order to create a specific result? You may be able to do this successfully for a certain amount of time, but beware! Isolation must not turn into a prison. See Glass House.

GRENADE: Images of grenades, as well as bombs and accidents, according to Jung, appear only where the dream represents an actual experience. It is the attempt of the unconscious to integrate the shock psychologically.

GRID/BARS: Separation tendencies, confinement.

GRINDING STONE: A symbol for wanting to smooth out something. According to second-century dream interpreter Artemidorus, an encouragement to be more refined in your dealings with people.

GROOM: Longing for a permanent relationship. A need for connecting with the other side of the Self. See also Bride/Bridegroom.

GUARD: Defense and discipline, attention, and insight. See also Hermit, Dog.

LISTEN UP, THIS IS IMPORTANT

See also Mall Security, Nonthreatening, Ineffectual.

GUINEA PIG/GERBIL/HAMSTER: Emotional functioning and sexuality are made trivial, diminished, and viewed from a distance. As children are given guinea pigs as pets, and they build up a relationship with them, here guinea pigs represent the beginning stage of the development of emotional functions.

GUITAR: Passion and emotion. It often has a sexual meaning, as in Violin (female body). A playful self-portrait.

SECRET TIP

The guitar often represents a young man struggling with the notion that he will never get laid unless he starts a band.

GYM: Do more for and with your body.

BARE FACTS

While being looked at by the other weirdos on the workout machines.

GYPSY: The wild and adventurous person within. At the same time, one of the oldest images of the scapegoat in our culture. The term "Gypsy" discriminates against the Siniti and Roma tribes, branding them as outsiders and second-class citizens. This image in a dream often points to an immature masculinity.

HAIR: Baldness, Beard. A symbol of wealth and fertility. In mythology, cutting off the hair is the equivalent of castration. Samson was robbed of his strength when Delilah cut off his locks. Hair for men is a sign of freedom; for women, long hair is a sign of femininity. According to Robert Bly, wild men and wild women are always covered with hair. Those who dream about hairy beings are on the way to satisfying their own nature; longing for vitality. This longing for "the wild energies" to be set free is clearly expressed in the musical *Hair*, which depicts the mythology of the sixties generation.

Today, hair often appears in dreams in connection with wanting to create a certain image, one that we would like to present to the outside world. It also may refer to "splitting hairs."

According to an ancient Indian interpretation, hair that has been cut off means grief and sorrow.

Also, hair dreams are thought to be about close relatives. In addition, they may mean spiritual and intellectual property.

According to Freud, hair, as a secondary sexual characteristic, has phallic meaning. Also, according to Freud and Steckel in *The Language of Dreams*, dreaming of hair means castration.

In mythology, hair and beards play an important role. The chiefs of the Masai were afraid they would lose their supernatural powers when their hair or beards were cut. For many primitive tribes, hair was considered taboo. To be protected from danger means never getting your hair cut. Kings in Franconia (Germany) would lose their throne if they had their hair cut. Young warriors of Teutonic tribes could cut their hair and beard only after they had killed their first enemy. Hair, therefore, seems to mean power, strength, and magical vitality.

DON'T BE A JERK

Rock history contains a period in which "hair bands" flourished. Dreaming of this subject matter is seen as a harbinger of doom, as in a return to a time so embarrassing that we wish ourselves dead. Hair band dreams should not be revealed to anybody, lest you lose all credibility. And, just for good measure, go back and destroy all photos of you from this horrible period.

HAIRDRESSER: See Barber.

HAIRPIECE: See also Hair, Mask. An attempt to change part of the personality you would like to hide—and cover your "baldness."

LISTEN UP, THIS IS IMPORTANT

An unspoken desire to wear a badger-shaped merkin on your head.

HAIRPIN: A deadly weapon of Japanese women against their husbands in bed. The hairpin represents order and vanity, as does all jewelry. See also Hair.

HALL: Sense of community and communication; or a representation of your head/mind and its intellectual abilities. As a meeting place, the hall symbolizes your sharing and openness to the outside world.

Communication and action. Often it is part of yourself that needs to be opened up. The function of the hall is important, and who is in the hall.

HALLWAY: You want to escape narrowness and restriction.

HAMMER: Power, but also constructive endeavor. Vigor and drive, similar to Hand.

According to Freud, as with all tools, a symbol of masculine sexuality.

HAMSTER: See Guinea Pig/Gerbil.

HAND: Vigor and human endeavor, as in Hammer. Loss of or injury to a hand means you're not active enough. According to classical psychoanalysis, the right hand is masculine; the left hand, feminine.

According to Freud, a phallic symbol. (Each finger, in Freud's view, could also be a phallic symbol.)

LISTEN UP, THIS IS IMPORTANT

Since the right hand is masculine, you should pay particular attention to dreams in which the left, or feminine, hand appears as a phallic symbol. It could indicate some gender confusion and the need to start saving up for that expensive surgical procedure.

HANDKERCHIEF: Security and order. Crying. Grief. With a handkerchief on hand, you are prepared for all situations. It often represents something comforting that one holds onto.

STRETCHING THE TRUTH

Extreme cases of the need for order involve dreams of *Handkerchief Man!*, a superhero who, with his handkerchief in hand, is prepared for all situations! The dreamer often wakes feeling humbled, as Handkerchief Man soon realizes that when it comes to, say, a protruding knee bone or multiple bullet wounds, his handkerchief is at best laughably inadequate.

HANGING: As in hanging up clothes—cleaning, elevating, clarifying, and so on. If a person is being hanged, something must die. See also Abortion, Amputation. Something is suffocating or being strangled.

SNAP OF THE FINGER

Clothes drying on the line . . . a wistful image of simpler times, when Mommy took care of everything and all you had to do was play and get dirty. However, those days are now gone, and that hamper of yours smells like a Porta-Potti at a blues festival. Do the laundry, before someone dies.

HANGMAN: You must root out something—guilt feelings, for instance. Do you have to do something? See also Execution, Murder, Death.

HARBOR: Protection from the storms of life. Coping with life during difficult times or anguish. A need for security, as in Buoy, Anchor, Dam, and Family. Also, inhibitions. A frequent dream symbol in marriage, but also a place of adventure and "disrepute." When a harbor is visited for a short time only, vitality and self-confidence.

COMMUNICATION

The safe harbor is a frequent symbol in a *happy marriage.* For a different view, see also **Choppy Seas, Rocking, Nausea, Vomiting.**

HARP: Festivities, contemplation. A symbol for heaven. The kind of music that is being played is important. Are you playing the harp yourself or is somebody else? Are you harping on something, is someone else?

YOU'RE WELCOME FOR THE TIP

Or is the sound of the harp just indicating that you are going into a flashback? (Rare. See **Transition, Movies.**)

HARVEST: Desiring recognition, Success, and security, as, for instance, in Shares, Stock Market, and intellectual wealth. Here questions about your goals in life are raised. What is it you want to accomplish, to "harvest"? Short-term as well as long-term goals may be addressed here. If the dreamer is a city person, the image of an Ear of corn or Farm might mean a romantic longing for the country and the simple life. Crop failures usually point to inferiority complexes.

HASTE: In dreams, in spite of hurrying, we usually never reach our goal. You are afraid you're missing something; pay attention to your plans, stop for a moment, and deliberate. As with all dream images that have to do with time, remember that "time" is often only another word for limitation.

HAT: Points to intellect, but also to arrogance, as with all other symbols that have to do with the head. Vanity and self-expression, as with symbols concerning jewelry. The type of hat points to the personality of the dreamer. See Cap.

According to psychoanalysis, a hat is a phallic symbol. Today it is more likely a symbol of the condom.

HATCHET: Either bury it or excavate it. You have, or think you have, an axe to grind.

HATE: Repressed aggression, often due to a lack of boundaries. A lack of self-protection and a weak immune system. Are you afraid of confrontation? Or are you making your points too aggressively? It is necessary to find out what it is that you really hate. If a "hate dream" overwhelms you, and you have it often, consider consulting a psychologist.

HAWK: Fear of future loss, or of taking something that you are not entitled to. A symbol of aggression, like Falcon.

HAY: In the past it was in the hayloft that many people had their initial sexual experiences. Wealth.

HEAT: A symbol for passion and drive. You either need more heat or should cool down.

HEAVEN: The realm of spirits, thoughts, and intuition. Here, a person is confronted with two worlds, with head pointing toward heaven and feet planted on the ground. In that sense, this dream image points to the necessity of being more grounded, but it might also mean being in a good mood (heavenly feelings). The castle in the clouds is also pertinent, pointing to the conflict between fantasy and reality. Dark, cloudy skies symbolize depressive moods or lack of clarity about dreams and goals.

According to the *I Ching*, heaven represents the creative and powerful father. According to Freud, it is the place where wishes are fulfilled. According to Jung, it is the world in which one loses touch with the earth and with reality.

HEDGE: Isolation, obstacle, but also natural living space. The border between two worlds (in mythology, witches are said to sit on hedges, one leg in one world, the other leg in the other world).

HEEL: Your sore or vulnerable point, place of injury (Achilles' heel). Are you well grounded?

HEEL (OF A SHOE): Being grounded, which makes you appear taller. Losing a heel indicates the loss of being grounded—either the negative "living above your means," or the positive wish to live more simply and easily.

DON'T BE A JERK

Being downtrodden or prone to misfortune can also label you a "heel." However, your friends are starting to get tired of your promise that you will get back on your feet if they would only lend you several hundred dollars.

HEIGHT/HIGH: You are longing for excellence but are also afraid of overestimating your abilities. Or, don't be satisfied with mediocrity.

HELL: Archetypal symbol for sin, pangs of conscience, and guilt feelings that influence humans to this day. However, today the image of hell is connected to separation from self, a confrontation with the shadow, or unacceptable living conditions. Fundamental changes in situations—particularly improvement of financial situations—are predicted. And there is a warning not to "sell your soul." The positive aspect of the image of hell is connected to an image of fire inside the earth; this fire is the light that is born out of darkness. If the shadow is experienced in all its power and is endured, it turns to light and to truly mature experiences that can be integrated into your life, leading to a feeling of wholeness.

HELLFIRE: Repressed drives/urges.

HELMET: Protection of the head sometimes turns around and suggests that the head is the protector. But it also may mean a stubborn hardhead. Symbol for fear of war, as in Shot, Bomb, Bayonet, Jet, Siege, Rifle.

HEN: Feminine, maternal feelings, as in Mother, luck, honesty, and domesticity, Baking, Roast, Frying Pan, and Cooking; also Flowerpot, Porcelain, Apron, and Iron. Fertility and fear of pregnancy, as in Egg.

HERB: According to Jung, herbs are always connected to healing. The herb is the alchemist's elixir, the universal medicine.

LISTEN UP, THIS IS IMPORTANT

Also that one guy *named* Herb, who just sort of creeps you out.

HERD: Are you following your inner voice or that of the general population? Symbol for community spirit or opportunism.

HERITAGE: Inheritance; precious quality. Talent and/or a task that has to do with the preservation of what has been handed down.

HERMIT: Recluse; danger of losing contact with other people. Self-realization, purification, internalization, fleeing from the world; or self-determination and autonomy.

HERO/HEROINE: A well-known desire for acceptance and validation, even if you are the hero or heroine yourself. If you see a hero, it would indicate that you are hoping for help, but pettiness is involved. Adventuresome, craving for admiration, exaggerated and immature masculinity and femininity; but also vitality and the ability to succeed, similar to Hammer. It may also mean the opposite—that you feel like a failure—or that you must be in control of everything. Dreams about heroes usually belong to so-called big dreams, which take place in a person just prior to puberty, during a midlife crisis, or before dying.

According to Jung, the hero is one of the important archetypes.

SECRET TIP

Hero dreams during a midlife crisis are often accompanied by hair extensions, obsessively Googling old girlfriends, and the purchase of a Camaro.

HIDING PLACE: A symbol of the unconscious. Repression and flight from problem situations. Need and desire to find and to be found.

HIGHWAY: On life's journey, are you moving along fast, or are you stuck in a traffic jam? Are you rushing or taking a leisurely trip? As a traffic symbol, as in Driving a Car and Auto, it almost always has sexual undertones. Is the highway crowded (I must defend myself against many rivals) or is it empty (I am going my own way)? Are there any complications during the trip, like accidents, breakdowns, or difficult traffic situations? This would always correspond to problems in the present.

BARE FACTS

Are you carefree, zooming along the highway at sixty-five miles per hour, the breeze blowing through your hair, with wide open lanes for miles and miles? You are definitely dreaming.

HIKER/HIKING: A peace walk, under your own power, moving ahead slowly but steadily. Being on a hike also refers to life's path—the pilgrimage where we learn and move closer to our goal. On the other hand, it implies distancing—the hiker moves away from his point of origin, or moves away from something else.

HILL: Small obstacles, good perspective. A female sexual symbol. A corn or callus, aging, and experiencing pressure. A hardening.

HIP: Usually refers to being grounded. The hip is the connection between the upper and lower body—between the conscious and the unconscious.

HIPPOPOTAMUS: Physical urges and emotional energies that have not yet been developed and are in need of differentiation. It could also mean encountering the massive and devouring energies of the unconscious, particularly physical urges and emotions.

The devouring mother or woman; the devouring unconscious, animalistic but also comic.

According to Jung, the monster, the evil, that wants to swallow you up.

YOU'RE WELCOME FOR THE TIP

Hippos are traditionally slow, dull creatures. A hippo dream can point to your utter disbelief at the moronic drone your ex-girlfriend got with right after she dumped you.

HITTING: Aggression. Energy shift and exchange. Desperate need for touch and an attempt at greater closeness. Immediacy and simplicity of method.

HOLE: Female sexuality. During fertility rights in honor of the Great Mother, a phallic-shaped loaf of bread was baked and buried in a hole in the ground. In Rome, money was thrown into a hole in the ground that was a symbol of fertility. A deep hole also symbolizes loss, insecurity, and fear of the future. The hole might also represent a blind spot, that area within us (and sometimes in others) that we cannot see.

Mystical place of death and rebirth (lion's den). Graves as holes in the ground.

According to Freud and Jung, it is an obvious female sexual symbol.

STRETCHING THE TRUTH

Men have often wondered why women go to the bathroom in groups and why they are always gone so long. It is because they are baking a phallic-shaped loaf of bread and burying it in a hole in the ground. And you thought she got pregnant because of those stupid fertility drugs?

HOME/APARTMENT: Area of life. A longing for a relationship that will bring security and a feeling of belonging.

A new home or apartment points to a new area in your life. It is a symbol for the inner Self.

HOMELAND: Security that originates from a particular place in the world that you have either searched for or found. This image is often related to Parents, and is similar to Parents' House. However, with increasing maturity, one usually dissolves the link to homeland and parents. Longing for quietness and a feeling of belonging.

COMMUNICATION

See also Homeland Security. You dream of repeatedly taking your shoes off to go through the X-ray.

HOMELESS SHELTER: See Asylum/Exile.

HONEY: An ancient symbol for rebirth. Wealth, food; and, from antiquity to modern times, it has had a special sexual implication. (Mick Jagger's "I Am a Honey Bee," for example.) Honey stands for the term "loved one." This symbol represents, in addition, sensuality, pleasure, luxury, well-being, and a general feeling of satisfaction. But it may also point to much work ("busy as a bee") needed to collect honey. It may also be a sign of wellness, particularly in connection with milk, as in Paradise—the "land of milk and honey."

SNAP OF THE FINGER

Somewhere in the above paragraph is a subliminal message designed to make you download the entire Rolling Stones back catalog. Can you find it?

HONEYCOMB: See Honey. Symbol of the desire of love.

HONORING: Recognition, as in Applause.

HOOK: To get stuck on something and be unable to get away. A frequent dream symbol in cases of addiction. You feel emotionally imprisoned, as in Cage, Prison.

HOOKER/PROSTITUTE: As in Bordello, only more active. Your physical urges are clamoring for attention. This dream symbol appears particularly often when one's principles are too rigid. Desire for wild sex during times of involuntary isolation. Points to the difficulties the dreamer has integrating love and sexuality. The symbol appears frequently in the dreams of "confirmed" bachelors and men with strong bonds to their mothers, as well as in the dreams of girls who have had a particularly sheltered upbringing. Acknowledge your urges and have the courage to be who you are.

According to Jung, it points to problems with one's shadow. According to Freud, repressed cravings in connection with living out one's sexuality.

STRETCHING THE TRUTH

It may seem shocking that folklore bypasses repression and sexual guilt in favor of interpreting prostitution dreams as signs of winning the lottery. However, we must take into account that, from the twelfth to the sixteenth centuries, "winning the lottery" was a euphemism for a urinary tract infection.

HORSE: Vitality, energy, mobility, and honor. It may mean speed, power, potency, and drive. Dynamism. According to second-century dream interpreter Artemidorus, luck in love. Other classical authors saw in the horse a symbol for the woman the dreamer would love to possess physically. In late medieval books on dreams, hitching horses to a carriage meant that one had many love affairs.

According to Freud, a life as well as a death wish.

HORSESHOE: Well-known symbol for luck. Travel.

According to Freud, the outline of the horseshoe represents the opening of the female sex organ.

HOSPITAL: You feel in need of help in times of emotional trouble. In rare cases, also a sign that you resent the type of help you get because it could be harmful. The hospital also stands for the dreamer himself. If you are the sick person, the type of illness will give insight about the problems you face. If you are the physician, your role as helper is addressed.

According to Jung, the hospital is the place where people are being taken care of, a symbol of mother.

HOST/HOSTESS: In dreams, a host is often a friendly person who mirrors how the dreamer feels he is being accepted by others and how well he accepts himself. He also personifies the talent for creating a home in the world. Longing for social contact, as in Friend, Companion. Wanting to be more socially acceptable and engaged.

In ancient Egypt, great tasks are ahead. Pay more attention to the people around you and to your friends. However, the task may also be to be kinder to yourself and to be, in a way, your own guest.

SECRET TIP

If you have ever tried to get a table at a pricey restaurant, your host/hostess dream may not be such a positive experience. (See also **Stuck Up, Attitudinal, Sun Shines Out of His/Her Ass.**)

HOTEL: Symbolizes real or emotional changes; stations on the journey through life, a transitional period. Adventure and restlessness. Hotel personnel symbolize some of our own internal entities. People in the hotel show us sides of our own unconscious.

BARE FACTS

Pay attention to the type of hotel you are staying at in your dream. A luxury room indicates a need to be pampered, while a room in the Hotel Scuzz indicates a need for something else entirely. (See **Hooker/Prostitute.**)

HOUSE: The emotional and physical constitution, characteristics, and body of the dreamer. A place of protection and security, the shelter of the soul. Individual rooms symbolize the different emotional functions. It is important to determine if Door and Window are open or closed and what the condition of the house is. The house is also a universal female sexual symbol.

Compare this to C. J. Jung's 1909 dream in which—while exploring a house—he finds a flight of stairs that leads to the basement, where he discovers bones and human skulls. This dream was important because it led to Jung's idea of the collective unconscious: attics and basements are places that hold what we repress; rooms in the upper part of a house provide perspective and vision; bedrooms indicate sexual content; the kitchen is the place where alchemy provides transformation; the bath is the place for cleansing; a workroom is the place for everyday situations.

STRETCHING THE TRUTH

In a rare bit of precognition, Jung's historic dream also involved his wandering into the TV room. This was important, because it led Jung to yet another area of the collective unconscious: a place where the mind turns to mush and we sit and wait for the fat cells to collect around our arteries.

HUNGER: Physical, emotional, and mental deficiencies; wanting or being in need of Food in any form (usually emotional food).

HUNT: This image is an obvious reference to pursuing your own goals. In Greek/Roman mythology Artemis (Diana), the goddess of the moon and a feminine archetype, is also the goddess of the hunt and, therefore also a masculine archetype. In the past, the symbol of the hunt referred mainly to the masculine side of a woman. Today it is more a matter of emphasis on masculinity, self-worth, and connection to nature. Or you are feeling pressured and under stress. Are you being chased in the dream or are you chasing somebody? If you are chasing someone or something, then it would not be a sign of stress, but rather a reminder that life needs to be more exciting.

HUNTER'S LOOKOUT: Overview or warning of self-elevation and arrogance.

HURRICANE: Wild times, but they will pass.

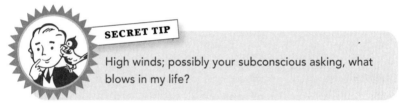

HUT: Like House. Looking for security, comfort; alternatively, poverty.

ICE: You are too cool, too distant. Frozen emotions, emotional coldness, isolation. In rare cases, there is also the suggestion that the water (of the soul and the emotions) can be carried. Falling through the ice—danger that emotions are going to crash.

One of the most difficult dream symbols to analyze, since an emotionally cold person is too emotionally cold to understand that they are being told in a dream that they are emotionally cold.

ICEBERG: Great strength through discipline. Distance, as in Ice.

In addition, represents a craving for lettuce. Hence, the "iceberg" dream is only one tier of this type of dream. Equally as common are the "romaine" dream and the "red leaf" dream. Then, there is the rare but extremely symbolic "mixed baby greens" dream, which can point to a likelihood that you will soon have lunch with a bulimic actress.

ICE CREAM: Sexual pleasure, summer fun, relaxation.

If you think "relaxation" is driving to Orlando for ten straight hours looking for a place to stop for said ice cream, with the kids screaming at you because they need to pee, except you're so mad right now they can go on the upholstery for all you care! Yeah, I got your "summer fun" right here.

ICE SKATING: See Flying. You are stepping on Ice. Are you prepared to take that risk? Trust in your own body and elegance of movement, smoothly gliding over the surface.

ICICLE: Happiness and satisfaction or emotional coldness, as in Ice.

IDIOT: Fear of mental overexertion, longing for a simpler, childlike life. A warning to live unconsciously. Also, "idiot" in ancient Greece meant the "nonpolitical" common man—in other words, those who were thought to be negative because they didn't care about the community. In addition, today we use the expression "the idiot savant," which raises the question: what does the idiot know?

QUICK FIX

See also **Your Boss.**

ILLNESS: Inner, personal arguments point to a heightened need for self-protection, or could mean self-injury. Such a dream should be analyzed very thoroughly, because it can provide valuable information about the condition of the dreamer.

IMMUNIZATION: Warning about illness. Also a well-known sexual symbol (penetration). See also Thorns.

INDEX FINGER: The finger used for scolding; or a phallic symbol.

INFANT: See Baby.

INFIDELITY: See Marriage.

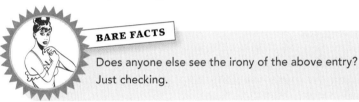

INFLATION: Psychological overexertion or in rare cases an expression of fear or poverty.

INHERITANCE: See also Heritage. Your own assets and resources need to be put to better use. You have much that you can fall back on. You want money that you don't have to work for.

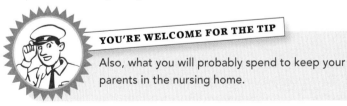

INJURY/WOUND: Feeling of hurt and being injured, vulnerable, and weak. Often a reference to old injuries that want to be healed.

INK: Symbolizes a responsibility that cannot be changed. What is the color of the ink?

SECRET TIP

Black Ink: You will one day die. Blue Ink: You are sad that you will one day die. Red Ink: Internal bleeding.

INSANITY: Emotional and senseless action that requires more clarity and insight. Pay attention to the reality of everyday life. Often reveals a distrust of Self. See Fool, Door, Stairs.

INSTITUTION: A symbol of ability and cooperation of diverse interests, which points to intellectual energies. To agree with others or with the different sides within yourself. Herd instincts, as in Uniform.

BARE FACTS

Where you will end up if you suffer from the previous entry two back from this one.

INSULT: Dissatisfaction or arrogance, but frequently directly connected to actual insults, either received or given. In most cases, there is a hidden longing for understanding and new insights.

INSURANCE: Well-known symbol for safety, which may point to emotional rigidity. Be more courageous and stand by your feelings!

INTERCOURSE: Desire for, or fear of, intercourse. Climax and relaxation. The image of one's own personal, physical sexuality that often points to sex as an end in itself. What is addressed here is not only sexual lust, vitality, and depth, but also a challenge to find your Self, which is only possible through intense communication with the Other. Symbolic meaning of sexual climax reveals (not only in dreams) how we can become centered and engage our personal strength and passions. Other interpretations, as in alchemy and analytical psychology, include a sign of contradictions acknowledged and overcome.

COMMUNICATION

Of course, there is the non-sexual meaning, that of simple "social intercourse," but it's pointless to bring up because everybody just giggles.

INTOXICATION: Warning about illusions. Clear awareness is necessary. Or, it points to a great deal of rigidity and an aversion to eroticism.

INVALID: Loss of independence. Loss of room to maneuver. Somebody or yourself needs support. Inferiority complex, self-doubt, and anguish. You feel you have been injured. In spite of the obvious meaning, this image has a positive side: it is a reminder that we are also allowed to withdraw from normal activities. In this sense, the dream image often points to being one-sided in relation to work. For instance, you do not have to do everything yourself and always be the best. It is important to accept and to admit helplessness. On the other hand, there is a belief that invalids are unable to act, which might indicate that you are asking too much of yourself.

DON'T BE A JERK

The connotation not only of being an invalid but of feeling invalid, as in "invalidated." Are you seeking validation in your life? If so, don't you hate it when you go to get your parking ticket validated and you say you need validation and the dork behind the counter says something like "Okay, I'll validate you . . . You're a really great person!" They really think you've never heard that joke before! God, don't you just want to smack people like that?

INVITATION: See also Loneliness, longing for social contact. Or you are inviting a part of yourself.

YOU'RE WELCOME FOR THE TIP

Could also indicate something more concrete—such as how you never get invited to weddings anymore, even though you offered to pay to get the barf out of the bride's dress.

ISLAND: Isolation and loneliness that you suffer from, or that you desire. This image often appears when you are frustrated at work. A longing for harmony and peace, wanting to leave the world; vacation.

As the "island of dreams," this image is a symbol of self, pointing to a self-directed life, autonomy, and independence. Also, a symbol of the unconscious.

Astrology: A symbol of Aquarius.

BARE FACTS

Not all island images indicate a need for peace and tranquility, especially since the advent of spring break. Nowadays, an island dream could simply signal a need for doing body shots off some clueless hottie.

IVY: Old relationships are getting stronger. Also, warning of false friends. You can be smothered (parasites on the plant). Compare this also with Vampire. Also steadfastness and stamina (ivy is evergreen.)

SECRET TIP

Don't forget poison ivy. Are you "itching" to get something out? What is it? Go ahead, let it out. I'm sure the statute of limitations is up.

JACKET: The image you would like to present to the outside world. Similar to Shirt.

JADE: Something not highly valued, but still important and precious. Points to too much vanity or to a bright personality. According to Chinese understanding, jade is a lucky stone that keeps you healthy.

JELLYFISH: Uncomfortable feelings or, in rare cases, a hint that you entertain addictive thoughts. Memories of vacation.

JET AIRPLANE: Speed of thought, fear of war, as in Helmet, Bayonet, and Bomb, but more impersonal and technical. Aggression. Such dreams often appear when the airplane noise is real.

JEWEL: See also Jewelry. Emptiness, vanity, and often a suggestion of the treasures inside of you. Temptation, because of the glitter.

JEWELRY: Well-being. Beauty for women, honor for men, or vanity; but it also implies that an inner Treasure has been discovered. Also a desire for acceptance and affection. According to Freud, the symbol of the person one loves.

Vanity or pleasure in one's own attractiveness.

JOKE/JEST: A joke works because it shows situations in a new perspective. Perhaps you should reexamine your rigid perspective. Don't take life quite so seriously, and let the soul be a source of joy.

YOU'RE WELCOME FOR THE TIP

Do you know how many dream analysts it takes to screw in a light bulb? Three. One to analyze the dream, one to say it's about a penis, and one to say it's about a vagina. (That killed at the shrink's convention.)

JOY: Inner equilibrium; or you need more fun in your life.

JUDGE: A symbol for the superego that is a warning against bold undertakings. Also the desire for justice. See also Court.

STRETCHING THE TRUTH

Also plural, **Judges.** Panels of said judges common to early twenty-first-century phenomenon "reality TV."
See also **Trio of Washed-Up Celebrities.**

JUDGMENT: At issue here is the attitude toward a very important matter and justice. Earlier dream interpreters believed that the conscience was speaking. Court, Attorney, Confession.

JUGGLING: Are you trying to juggle life by keeping all the balls in the air? If you juggle balls in your dream, it means that you need to keep your energy in motion, be more playful, and keep your goals and desires in balance. On the other hand, this image might also symbolize a fear of making decisions; you are too often undecided.

KETTLE: Where cooking takes place and where life is renewed. In the mythology of the Mabinogions (medieval Welsh lore), the kettle was where dead soldiers were brought back to life. The kettle, just like any of the containers in alchemy, is where transformation of matter takes place, and for that reason it is reminiscent of the uterus or the center of the earth. The kettle is almost always a sign of creative energy. Figuratively speaking, it is the kettle where the vitality of the dreamer is transformed into something new. It is the blended pot where emotional energy and the power of the soul are blended together to create the individual personality.

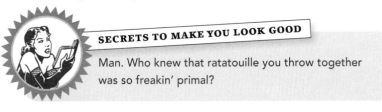

SECRETS TO MAKE YOU LOOK GOOD

Man. Who knew that ratatouille you throw together was so freakin' primal?

KEY: See also Lock. You have the right attitude and are posing the right questions, in the sense of how you are using your personal qualities. Ideas and new experiences.

Locking something up indicates a fear of relationships and a fear of getting involved.

According to Freud, the symbol of the key/lock stands for sexuality. The key is the phallus, the lock the vagina, and the function of locking means intercourse.

COMMUNICATION

Scientists and philosophers have for centuries been on a quest to "unlock the secrets of the universe." And they would have found out what those secrets are except, ironically, they are also the people who never get laid.

KING/QUEEN: Lover. Archetypal symbol for father/mother, dependency on father/mother. Also symbolizes the dreamer himself.

See also Ruler. May also represent the Great Father and Great Mother. The Great Father is the symbol of an aware and elevated consciousness. You are standing with great awareness in the world. In fairy tales, as well as in dreams, the self usually has a royal beginning, from which it is separated in order for it to master the adventures in the world. The king also means wholeness and completeness.

The Great Mother is symbolized in the dream as a queen, always representing the image of wholeness. In the end she represents the integrating power of nature. The image of the queen as the fertile mother always addresses the self of the dreamer. Implied here is the idea that we should rely on our own abilities, care for ourselves, and find a Home within ourselves.

Kings and queens also represent one's masculinity (animus) and femininity (anima). Such archetypes not only are persons of authority, but also represent the image of a loved one (idealized and elevated masculinity or femininity). According to Freud, often the symbol of parents who are seen as overly powerful.

STRETCHING THE TRUTH

Inevitably, images of royalty become trivialized and so may have less dream significance than we might assume. The term "queen" has come to mean an overtly homosexual fellow, and the word "king" is casually tacked onto retail establishment names to indicate large supply and great savings. It is entirely possible that the modern dream of royalty involves a drag show in a mattress store.

KISS: Uniting, connecting, and good luck. Intimate closeness, intellectual communication, desire for closer contact, maybe making up after a fight. Rarely is a kiss a sign of betrayal (the kiss of Judas).

YOU'RE WELCOME FOR THE TIP

You may be dreaming about the "kiss of death" (especially Mafia informants).

KITCHEN: See also House. Refers to housewife. Change and transformation of emotional energies.

KNEE: Erotic symbol. Also, agility or rigidity of one's own point of view. Unbending pride or humility. An injury to the knee is often part of a nightmare, particularly in situations of running away.

Astrology: Relates to the sign of Capricorn.

KNIFE: Seeking power. Aggression and symbol for masculinity. However, the knife may also point to security and protection. Often internal suffering and passions are being addressed, pointing out innermost secrets that you want to hide. Ask how to call up the unconscious strength that could bring results. Are you able to show your wounds and acknowledge your injuries? Can you see that acknowledging your vulnerabilities could make you more human and likable? To acknowledge pain eliminates your fear of weakness, making aggressive action to protect yourself unnecessary. According to psychoanalysis, in the case of women, the desire for total abandon.

Analysis and differentiation, as in the Sword in the Tarot.

According to Freud, a phallic symbol; but today it is rarely seen in that context.

SECRET TIP

In movies (which are themselves dream-like), a knife is that thing that is always placed within easy reach on the counter, when there is a mysterious attacker in the hero's apartment.

KNIGHT: Adventurous, with an immature masculinity, but also responsible and honest. In a psychological sense, you are protected by the armor and are unreachable, which can make sense but also cause problems.

KNOT: Symbolizes complications, unsolvable problems, and entanglement. Warning of being emotionally tied in knots. Undoing knots means the end of entanglements (Gordian knot).

LISTEN UP, THIS IS IMPORTANT

You are so totally emotionally entangled . . . KNOT! (A bit more dream analysis humor. Sorry, we don't get out much.)

LABORATORY: The place where we experiment with life. This symbol represents the way we deal with our emotions and where we do our emotional work. How do you deal? Is your life too planned or deadened by too much technology?

BARE FACTS

The laboratory is a place where mad scientists create Frankenstein-like creatures. Perhaps you see yourself as about to unleash something huge. (Men only.)

LADDER: Overly organized development. A symbol of the connection between the unconscious (below) and the conscious (above). May point to Jacob's Ladder, leading into heaven. Are you confronted with new tasks? Are you climbing up or coming down? How many rungs does the ladder have? See the symbolic meaning of numbers. Some people get dizzy when they climb too high. According to Freud, the rhythm of the motion of climbing up and coming down is symbolic of intercourse. See also Stairs, Career, Step.

LAKE: See Water. In the *I Ching*, the lake is the symbol for a happy and cheerful youngest daughter.

LAMB: Purity in the sense of patience and gentleness. See Victim. Easter. The Easter lamb also points to a new beginning.

LAMP: This is an object often found in fairy tales. The hero or the dream-self is emerging. Light is about to be shed on a problem, which will then be solved. Trust your own insight!

LANDSCAPE: Freud saw this image as a symbol for the human body.

LANTERN: See Lamp. Symbol of the light of awareness; it usually points to the need for taking a closer look at your problems. In rare cases, it also reflects the electric power of love. A light shining in the dark attracts attention, like a moth attracted by a light.

LAP: Return to mother, longing for one's childhood, or fears from childhood.

Could also refer to the modern practice of the lap dance. Lap-dance dreams usually involve your rationalizing it as not cheating.

LARGE: Anything that grows in size during a dream should be paid attention to.

QUICK FIX

Some of these just write themselves.

LARK: Singing bird. Good perspective, because the "lark" flies high in the air. Joy.

LAUGHING: Usually seen in a very difficult situation, where laughing is the last thing that you'd like to do. Laughing is a form of relaxation. Sometimes it is also an expression of the search for freedom and emotional peace within your self.

LAUNDRY: White laundry and white clothing are considered the symbol of innocence and purity. White laundry is, according to Freud, a symbol of femininity.

Folklore: Quarrels, separation, and loss.

LAVA: An important dream symbol, pointing to inner, psychic energies. Uncontrolled release of tension.

LAVENDER: A symbol of femininity.

LAWN: See also Grass, Meadow. Hope and well being.

LAWYER: See Attorney.

LEAD: Physicality, heaviness (clumsiness), but also relative softness; it is durable, but melts and mutates easily. Lead is poisonous and has been associated with a curse ever since antiquity. Are you "poison" for somebody, or has somebody been malicious toward you? Also, weighing down, complaint, center of gravity/main focus.

Astrology: A symbol of Saturn.

LEADER: Symbol of authority, as in Father and Wise Man. One who is free to move, a symbol of freedom.

LEADING: Motivation to pursue advancement. Or loneliness. Life needs to be better organized. This is a dream that almost always calls on your inner guide, or how you are guiding others. Can you lead and still let others lead you?

LEAF (OF A PLANT): Being subjected to changes, or Letting Go. Similar to Abyss, Brook/Stream, and sometimes Parachute, only in more playful terms. A wilted leaf means troubles. A green leaf means rejuvenation, fulfillment of a wish.

LEAF (OF PAPER): Are you being challenged to take note of something or express something? In what sense do you see yourself as a blank piece of paper, and in what sense as a piece of paper that has writing on it?

LEAK: Emotional isolation and separation is breaking up.

LEATHER: Symbolizes toughness—tough as leather—aggressive tendencies, fetishes, but also soft, "smooth as silk," indicating tenderness.

LEATHER CLOTHING: Isolation and promiscuity, but also a search for invulnerability and sensuality. See also Animal.

DON'T BE A JERK

The appearance of a black leather jacket on a person in your dream often indicates someone who entertains the fantasy that they are some kind of bad-ass, when they usually are not. If it is you wearing the leather jacket . . . well, we rest our case.

LEAVES: Emotions and thoughts the dreamer has. The condition of the leaves is important—what time of year is it? Green leaves mean joy, fun, and growth; dead leaves mean disappointment and failure, but also, in time, maturity and insight.

The interpretation in antiquity was Joy.

LEAVING (ON A TRIP): Wanting to leave, often because of stress, overwork, and marital conflicts. Desire for irresponsibility. Also a sign that, having assumed power in order to move out of the situation, you have freed yourself.

LECTURE: As with everything that is performed publicly, it refers to a portrayal of the Self, as in Theater and Concert. If the dreamer is the speaker, it indicates a desire to make a statement. The task is to serve the interests of all the listeners and to find and make clear to them your point of view. There is a desire to solve present situations intellectually. See also Puzzle. As far as the speaker is concerned, the issue is to combine emotion and logic, intellect and consciousness. This dream symbol almost always includes aspects of self-understanding. It might also encourage you to become a better listener, as in Ear and Mouth. And lastly, this dream symbol also represents your inner voice.

STRETCHING THE TRUTH

As rebellious children, we resented being lectured by our authoritarian parents. "Smoking is bad for you." "Finish high school or you'll never amount to anything." "Don't marry the first person you fall in love with." When these admonitions turn up in your dreams, it could be your subconscious dealing with the fact that you never listened to them. And now you are living in a double-wide with a double-wide spouse, working overtime at the slaughterhouse, and concerned about that X-ray, in which your lungs look like a chimney sweep's hankie.

LEECHES: Feeling of disgust for your own body. The feeling of being sucked dry, as in Vampire.

LEFT: The side where the heart is, the emotional area of the dreamer, and also the feminine aspect. It rarely has political meaning. Sometimes, it is injustice. According to Freud, it is perversity. See also Right.

LEG: Foot. Symbol for setting things in motion on your own initiative, in contrast to being in a vehicle—Auto, Car. It is also a symbol of your attitude toward life and, particularly, to being grounded.

In psychoanalysis in the past, the leg was considered a sexual symbol: a beautiful leg meant satisfying intercourse; a broken leg was a symbol of adultery (today this is probably less appropriate).

LEMON: See Fruit. You are "sour" and/or feeling funny. This might also point in part to the body's need for more vitamin C. On the other hand, it may refer to an intrinsic worthlessness, as in the car that is a "lemon."

LEOPARD: Vitality, elegance, drive. In case of danger, a leopard points to your fear of erotic entanglement. See also Cat.

LETTER: Being connected with a loved one, news, communication with the outside world. A message that has not yet reached your consciousness.

BARE FACTS

Nobody dreams about letters anymore. Text messages and Tweets, maybe.

LIBRARY: Symbol of intellectual life, as in Book; great knowledge. A warning of too much one-sided intellectual activity, as in Balcony. Often a challenge to look for a more holistic education and character formation.

YOU'RE WELCOME FOR THE TIP

Libraries contain, of course, librarians—who, when they take off their glasses and let their hair down, become suddenly attractive. (Movies only.)

LIFEBOAT: One way to extricate yourself from "oceanic emotions" and/or escape from the storms of life.

LIGHT: See also Lamp, Lantern, Lighthouse. Symbol for consciousness, intellect, reason, clarity, hope, and joy. The image of the center of life—as the sun is the center of the universe—the spark of the soul and the longing for a much sought-after object. The light is the opposite of depression, doubt, darkness, and illness. Light means creative spirit. However, keep in mind that light and darkness contradict as well as enhance each other. Negative meaning: Blinding, bright, or dying light.

LIGHTHOUSE: See also Lamp, Lantern. Helpful for orienting oneself in difficult situations. Problems that you are not aware of are made conscious. Well-known phallic symbol.

LIGHTNING: A sudden idea. On November 16, 1619, Rene Descartes had a dream and, among other things, saw lightning, which showed him that he had found his own method of understanding.

Lightning as a natural occurrence indicates a repressed effect, denial that wants to be expressed or lived out through sudden aggressive action; an uncontrolled release of great energies. Fighting ("lighting into somebody").

According to Artemidorus, the second-century dream interpreter, a good omen.

According to Freud, a phallic symbol. Jung also stated that everything that strikes something has to be interpreted as a phallic symbol.

LILAC: Love, tenderness, and romance. Also warns against arrogance and witchcraft.

LILY: A symbol of purity, innocence, and naturalness. In France, a symbol of power.

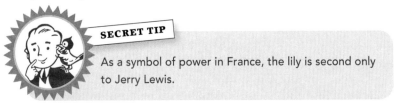

SECRET TIP

As a symbol of power in France, the lily is second only to Jerry Lewis.

LIQUID MANURE: Inferiority complex, disgust; less often, fertility.

SNAP OF THE FINGER

Yes, we know, we've just put the image of "liquid manure" in your brain, and now it will be stuck up there like a song you can't get out of your head all day. No need to thank us.

LIQUOR: Relaxation or trouble.

LIVER: First, make sure that you do not have real, physical complications involving the liver. If you don't, this symbol refers to restlessness and irritability—something is galling you. Also, it is a symbol of vitality and productivity.

LIZARD: Usually a harmless miniature Dragon will bring you luck.

LOCK/PADLOCK: This is the image of inner, psychic tension between openness and retreat (isolation), between risk and security.

LOCK/SLUICE: A symbol for regulating the level of Water, meaning the emotions. Here the level of the water is adjusted to the needs of the traffic, and in that sense it raises the question of the need to regulate and adjust your emotions to the needs of everyday life. Are you holding your emotions in check, or allowing them to flow? What is restricting you?

LOCOMOTIVE: See also Train. Collective psychic energy; life's journey as seen through the eyes of society/community. Moving forward with energy and power, or being pulled forward.

LODGE: Town. Power and isolation, but also the symbol for the center. As a Mother symbol, protective, inclusive, or nurturing.

According to Freud, castles, lodges, and forts are always female symbols.

LONELINESS: Inner longing for social contact, as in Invitation. You let yourself down (become unfaithful to yourself). Tendency to become too self-absorbed. Independence; you must stand on your own two feet.

LOOK: See also Eye. Perception. At what should you take a closer look? Who do you wish would look at you more often?

LOOM (WEAVING): Time and fate, the thread of life. Longing for a "simpler life." Often a sign that much spiritual work is being done.

LOSS: Fear of loss, or joy over separation.

LOTTERY: This image warns against risks of any kind. You have wishes and desires; take a good look at them.

LOUSE: Lack of cleanliness; leech, as in Vampire. Disgust.

LOVE: You are longing for love. A desire to be able to love as well as to be loved. Pay special attention to the quality, emotions, and circumstances in the dream.

LOWER BODY: Be sure that no actual stomach problems exist. See also Sexuality, Toilet, Stomach.

BARE FACTS

Sexuality, Toilet, Stomach. Bet you never thought you'd see those three words together in a sentence.

LUGGAGE: See also Suitcase, Pocketbook, Backpack, Package, and Box. All symbolize a burden (everybody carries his own baggage) or, less often, energy and making plans. Energy reserves. Possibly a reference is being made to a dowry and inheritance, which could be a burden as well as an opportunity. What talents are at your disposal? What tasks are connected to them?

According to Freud, a symbol of sexuality.

SECRET TIP

Also, as mentioned, baggage, or what the two of you have so much of that this relationship was doomed from the start.

LUNG: Feeling restricted, needing more space and Air, as in Cage and Elevator (Lift). A symbol of power that has been achieved through clear thinking and personal judgment.

LYING: A symbol of falsehood; it often points to a bad conscience. You are leading a double life. You are not honest. However, if you discover in your dream that you have been lying (including to yourself), you are now aware and have gained important insight. Be glad that you have found the capacity for self-criticism.

COMMUNICATION

Somehow, the important insight gained in a dream about lying has historically eluded politicians.

MACHINE: Lack of meaning in your work; stupidity. The type of machine is important. Is the dreamer a machine (a robot)? Also, it may be an image of the internal work your soul is undertaking.

MADONNA: The big woman. Release from guilt and pain; self-elevation or self-denial. Also a sexual symbol and a symbol of self-sufficient, independent femininity. The image of the madonna may also be pointing to sexual repression and a bad conscience, because of the dreamer's attitude about his or her own sexuality and/or femininity.

BARE FACTS

Also, a successful woman in the music industry, who somehow keeps reinventing herself as a different kind of slut.

MAGGOT: Greed and laziness.

MAGIC/MAGICIAN: In the past (but still relevant today), the image of supernatural power that you wish you had. This dream symbol frequently appears when one is feeling worthless. Today, it refers more to the dreamer himself and his magical qualities. A magician represents the integrated whole and the individuality of the dreamer—that's the reason why the magician in the Tarot was assigned the number one. This integration and uniqueness is what makes him magical. The message here might be that the dreamer ought to concentrate on his "magical powers" and know that they contribute to success on his life path. But no personal magic will make itself known unless the dreamer chooses to pursue his own path. If he doesn't do that, everything will seem jinxed. He will not get ahead and a multitude of obstacles will get in his way. On the other hand, this symbol may also point out that too much emphasis is being put on the individual at the expense of the collective. See also Witch.

COMMUNICATION

Are you the magician in your dream? Is there someone bothering you whom you would like to make "disappear"? If so, what's the problem? You can't scrape up the cash to have it done professionally?

MAGNET: Strong force of attraction and personal success. Sometimes a symbol for one's own center, Love, and a lover. Pay attention to what is fascinating to you and what is attracting you. To paraphrase the theorist and teacher G.I. Gurdjieff, great danger may lie in the powers that are attracted to you.

MAGPIE: The Bird that combines black and white, as in Birch in the plant world. Light and shadow are to be integrated in your inner life, as in Marriage, Intercourse, and Bride/Bridegroom. The magpie is a thief; something is being taken from you, as in Burglar.

MAILMAN: See Post. Carrier of information, communication.

SECRET TIP

Since ancient times, a symbol for "sustainer of dog-bite injuries." More recently, a symbol for someone who seems to be taking his sweet time weighing that lady's package when you've got somewhere to be and there's only one other stinking window open.

MAN: See also Companion. In the case of a woman, this dream may be pointing to a father figure or ego ideal. A strange man in a man's dream always means his own unknown side, the shadow. An older man represents the father figure in dreams of men as well as women, or he may represent the dreamer himself. A naked man means openness.

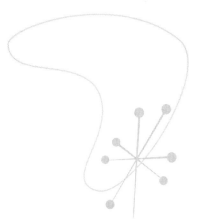

MANDALA: A symbol of wholeness, aiding us to find our center. Points to personal development.

MAP: See also Atlas, Book. As in the case of Crossing, this image points to finding direction in your life. A plan for your life.

According to Freud, it depicts the human body.

SECRETS TO MAKE YOU LOOK GOOD

Something a man will only consult at the very last minute, when you're already totally lost.

MARBLE: Steadfastness, luxury, but also toughness (biting into stone). A sense of beauty, but also a lack of feeling, up to and including frigidity.

YOU'RE WELCOME FOR THE TIP

A common slang for going insane is "losing one's marbles." However, if you dream you have lost your marbles, it means you are still sane enough to maintain a distance from the act of losing your mind. It's all the other times when you *don't* dream about losing your marbles that you have to worry about.

MARMALADE: Enjoying life—the sweet life—or "preserves."

MARRIAGE: Union of contrasting parts of yourself (often your feminine and masculine sides). Longing for a permanent bond.

MARRIAGE RING: Separation or longing for a relationship.

MARRIAGE/WIFE/HUSBAND: Compensation and reconciliation of differences, melding of male and female energies. Usually, the dreamer's own characteristics are indicated. Longing for partnership, particularly in a divorce or separation situation; or fear of commitment. Are you able to accept the Other? Are you able to preserve the space between yourself and the Other, experiencing it as positive? You also have to ask yourself if you expect your partner to fulfill all of your desires, or are you willing to work for them yourself?

MASK: That which we would like to present to the world around us, or what we would like others to view as being real. A weak sense of self, inferiority complex. Hiding from the truth. But also fun, lust, and erotic adventures. Being misled, false impressions, and temptations. If the mask in your dream is visible, this is also a sign of your ability to look behind the scenes (including your own). See also Curtain.

MASSAGE: Enjoying erotic and relaxing experiences. This image in a dream often expresses the need for more bodily contact, or a need to "save one's own skin." If bodily contact is present in the dream, it may point to emotional contact.

SECRET TIP

If the massage dream progresses to the "love you long time" dream, then you have obviously paid extra.

MASSES (OF PEOPLE): Often a fear of social contact and agoraphobia. Here, you find the social contact you need and a place where you see yourself apart from—and also a part of—a larger whole. So in a sense, this dream image poses a question about your social adaptability on one hand, and on the other, your sense of what is yours and what you have taken on from the outside world. Do you have contact with many people, or none? Do you feel socially overwhelmed, or accepted? Does your dream express a need for liberation?

MAST: In psychoanalysis always a phallic symbol.

MASTER: See Chief.

MASTER OF THE HOUSE: One who has provided well, who keeps order. A frequent dream symbol for the conscience. Often points to the fact that you should take better care of body and soul.

MATCH: See also Fire, Flames, Light. Did you set something on fire? Or have you burned your fingers?

MATTRESS: See also Bed. Eroticism, sexuality. The place of birth and death.

Thus, in the mattress, we see how the erotic is so inextricably linked with birth and death. If you would like to avoid such dark thoughts during lovemaking, simply go at it on the kitchen floor.

MAY: Youth, eroticism, and growth; a productive time; and a favorable outlook.

MEADOW: A large meadow points to growth and joy. The condition of the meadow is significant.

MEAT: See also Sausage. Physical, usually sexual, energies. A frequent image when you force yourself to follow a vegetarian eating style before you're ready for it.

Raw meat points to raw physical power, passion, and creative power. Cooked meat points to addiction to pleasure. Rejecting meat indicates chastity.

According to the Indian tradition Jaddeva, lust for power, or the desire to have many offspring.

BARE FACTS

Sure, rejecting the meat indicates chastity. But let's face it, ladies, with most guys, it usually just indicates your good judgment.

MEDAL: Competitiveness and being externally oriented. You want to be praised, accepted, and rewarded. Also a symbol for wanting to belong to a certain group—almost always a group made up of men.

MEDICAL ASSISTANT: Erotic, helpful woman.

MEDICATION: Apothecary, Pharmacist. Fear of illness, need for help, bitterness, emotional or physical neediness. Fear of disappointment, pain, poverty and/or old age. Often a hint that one can heal oneself. You have to "swallow" something.

MELON: Erotic symbol, luck in love.

MEMENTO: A hint that something needs to be remembered. Do not repress your feelings. Remember vacations or other memorable events.

MENOPAUSE: Primarily a woman's dream, pointing either to menopause about to take place or to other general and long-term changes.

MENU: Important is the symbolic meaning of the foods that are listed on the menu.

MESSENGER/CARRYING A MESSAGE: Are you playing the role of an intermediary? Are you satisfied with that role or would you rather take care of your own affairs? What message do you have to transmit? Is the messenger coming to you—are you receiving an important message? In any case, important news.

METAL: Success, prosperity, wealth, consistency, and toughness. Also, iron will, weighed down by fear. See also Gold, Silver, and Fire.

SECRET TIP

See also **Metal, Heavy**. Betrays a desire for a truly righteous and awesome song with killer guitar riffs.

METAL WORKER: What has been close to you is opening up.

METEOR: Brainstorm, idea. A messenger from heaven.

QUICK FIX

For more on "messenger from heaven," see **Pizza Delivery Man**.

MICROPHONE: Challenges you to internalize something. You need to speak your mind, announce something publicly. Also, self-talk.

MIDDAY: See Light. Awareness, midpoint of life.

MIDNIGHT: The darkest hour and the hour of ghosts. The beginning of a new day.

COMMUNICATION

Also the time when you might as well turn off Letterman and go to bed (unless they haven't gotten to the top ten list yet).

MIDWIFE: Wishing for a child or fear of pregnancy. Desire to bring something to light or fear of its coming to light. A new phase in life or a new idea or behavior needs help in order to be accepted.

MILITARY DUTY: Self-affirmation, possibly also self-punishment, authority, fleeing from an inferiority complex, immature masculinity, and repressed aggression. In women's dreams, often the desire for aggressive sexuality and devotion.

MILK: See also Cow. Food, security; a symbol for the original mother. Paradise is where milk and Honey flow. Something needs to be nourished with milk—with femininity. It might point toward regression. Drinking milk means to increase knowledge (alma mater, the nourishing mother is the name for the university attended). Sour milk means trouble and uncertainty. According to ancient Norse mythology, the cow is one of the oldest beings; it nursed the ancient giant Ymir.

LISTEN UP, THIS IS IMPORTANT

You will note above that milk has a connection to alma mater, the nourishing mother, in this reference to where we went to college. Yet, what we drank in college was as far from milk as you can get, and it most likely destroyed more brain cells than we ever actually nurtured there. Such ironies are the stuff dream books are made of.

MILL: Working, daily grind, but providing well and success.

MILLET: Grain.

MINE: Depth of body and soul; highly self-absorbed; but also good news.

MINISTER/CLERGYMAN: See also Priest. Father figure and guide for the soul. Indicates too much or too little self-confidence. It points to good support, a perfect disposition of life, and an accepted portrayal of the Self to the outside world. Be more open, not only in matters of faith, but also in matters that deal with society in general.

MIRROR: Insightful intellect that reflects reality. A common allegory for self-observation. We are looking into a mirror in our dreams in order to confirm our identity. If, in a dream, we are looking into the mirror and see not our own but somebody else's image, it is always a sign that we are living in a fantasy world. It is also possible to see an actual person in the mirror.

The mirror is considered an attribute of the Fool, always pointing to vanity as one of the classic seven sins. Fools have often been depicted with mirrors. The image of a mirror in a dream is a very important event, and should be analyzed in detail. For the Greeks, a mirror appearing in a dream meant the death of the dreamer, since what he saw in the mirror was considered a look-alike. In fairy tales, a mirror represents hidden and future events, and the image of the soul.

According to Jung, the mirror is usually considered magical; it is "a knowing mirror," as in "Snow White and the Seven Dwarfs." Using a mirror often transforms us into a mythical state. In Lewis Carroll's *Through the Looking Glass*, Alice enters another world through a mirror. In Cocteau's film *Orpheus*, the mirror is the entrance to the underworld. The image of a mirror also points to a tendency to inflate emotions and lose touch with our grounding.

MISCARRIAGE: Abortion. May point to what is actually happening in the body. One is letting go of unproductive qualities. Or something new you started is not working out—this may be a warning dream.

MISER/TIGHTWAD: Might be a suggestion to be more generous, open, and flexible. Or can you never be satisfied because your needs are not met? See also Vulture.

MIST/HAZE: Lack of clarity, as in Darkness, only less severe. Other than that, see also Fog.
  Astrology: Symbol of Neptune.

MISTAKE: Usually points to the need to deal with mistakes made during waking hours. Something is missing.

MISTLETOE: A symbol of the Druids and of consciousness. According to English custom, everybody is allowed to kiss a person who is standing below a sprig of mistletoe. The mistletoe stands for the healing power of love.

MODEL/FASHION MODEL: Conflict with conventional norms, accommodation, and vanity. Due to an inferiority complex you are trying to create ideal beauty; or emotional certainty about your own beauty.

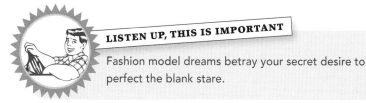

LISTEN UP, THIS IS IMPORTANT

Fashion model dreams betray your secret desire to perfect the blank stare.

MONEY: Rarely connected to financial problems. Dreaming about money points to your behavior in matters of love. It is probably the most frequent symbol of sexuality and power. A coin generally points to success and security. Are you always weighing every situation and thinking through a plan for every situation? Are you afraid of losing control over yourself or over a situation? Often such a dream is telling you to open yourself up to life and allow your wild side to surface. Passion for life is suggested here instead of control.

According to Freud and Jung, money is a symbol for the libido—silver coins indicate an attraction toward women; gold coins, an attraction toward men. For some modern psychoanalysts, it is a symbol of creative power.

MONK: Discipline, self-restraint and self-determination; but also losing oneself. See also Abbey, Hermit.

MONOTONY: See Boredom, Uniform, Rhythm.

MONSTER/MYTHICAL CREATURE: Beast. Your animal nature is becoming too strong, too frightening, meaning that you are afraid of your own strength and drives. It could also indicate a person (Father or Mother) who appears overly powerful.

Talk to the frightening monster in your dream, have it out with him and observe him.

Mythical creatures, like dragons and ocean monsters, point to moral conflicts that may cause personality disturbances. Seek therapeutic help when these images appear often and include a great amount of fear.

MONUMENT: Success, reward for efforts or trouble, seeking power—as in Sword, but not that aggressively.

MOON: Femininity, mother, and woman. In a woman's dream, it is her own femininity that needs to be accepted. Mood, moodiness, and emotions. In Greek and Roman times: Luck with a beautiful woman.

According to Freud, the symbol of the buttocks (particularly a woman's buttocks). According to Jung, the moon is the "place of departed souls." He also sees it as the shadow side or the unconscious, a symbol of the libido. See Cat, Night.

MOOR: See Swamp, Mud. Physical desires that are being repressed, that are dragging you down. Fear of death or fear of life. You are unable to move forward, and are being held back—pulled back—into the unconscious through fear of the feminine. On a positive note, the wild side of the character can be helpful in healing.

MOOR/HEATH: Prudish restraint, emotional tension. Naturalness and asceticism.

MOPED: As in Motorcycle, only less powerful.

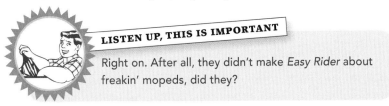

LISTEN UP, THIS IS IMPORTANT

Right on. After all, they didn't make *Easy Rider* about freakin' mopeds, did they?

MOSAIC: See Picture. A mirror of the experiences of life; many parts create a whole. See also Concert, Puzzle.

MOSS: As with all plants, the vegetative in human beings; quiet, and equilibrium.

According to Freud, the symbol for pubic hair. An erotic symbol.

BARE FACTS

Moss is a particularly evocative symbol of the vegetative in human beings, since it is what grows on you while you are watching *Three's Company* marathons.

MOTH: Subversive emotions and feelings. See also Light.

MOTHER: Your own nature, the archetypal feminine—life giving, nurturing, devouring, protecting, that which is fruitful and fertile. When the mother is your mother, she indicates a bad conscience because of past behavior toward her. When the mother refers to the internal mother, it points to a desire for psychological support that is often not provided by a partner. The mother in a dream, as well as in fairy tales, is often the helper whose strength, in a negative as well as positive sense, reaches beyond death. She is the Witch, the Wise Old One, who gives correct advice, the Earth and the goddess of the earth. The symbol of the mother also addresses the task of self-discipline. Be a good mother to yourself and thereby become productive.

According to Jung, the mother is the archetypal symbol of "the secret, the hidden, the dark, the abyss, the temptation, the poisonous, and the inescapable."

COMMUNICATION

So your mother is the archetypal symbol of "the secret, the hidden, the dark, the abyss, the temptation, the poisonous, and the inescapable"? Jeez, no wonder she gets so bent out of shape when you never call.

MOTOR: Energy, power, and mobility.

MOTORBOAT: Moving powerfully through your emotional landscape. See Water, Ship.

MOTORCYCLE: Getting ahead and doing it alone. Individualism, the Self, psychic energy. Sitting on the "hot seat" represents vitality and drive.

MOUNTAIN: See also Hill. Protection and consciousness. Overview, standing above a given situation, as in Bird. A difficult time in life's journey is beginning. Romantic notion about nature and solitude, flight from the city and culture. Climbing a mountain is facing an important problem. Encountering obstacles or troubles on the way points to actual difficulties. What did the mountain look like?

According to Freud, the mountain is a symbol of the male sexual organ.

MOUSE: A symbol of control and lack of control that you have over the small things in life. The "small" or unimportant things can also mean those that are invisible.

Mice are often "signs of death" (Death is meant in the sense of completion). They are symbols of nagging thoughts and a nagging conscience. When they become a plague, they are a bad omen. In Goethe's *Faust*, mice appear in the form of ghosts that nibble at the Pentagram that is supposed to ban the devil. Gray and black mice in a dream point to bad luck. The gray and the black mouse may also be a symbol of the shadow, since gray and black are shadow colors.

The positive meaning of this symbol lies in the fact that parents sometimes call their children "little mouse." It is also the language of lovers who use such endearments.

According to Mohammed, the mouse represents the "little sinner," the adulteress. When Faust dances with a witch, a mouse jumps out of her mouth. White mice are believed to be the souls of children and of the poor, and also fever demons.

According to Jung, the mouse is the animal of the soul, the image of a difficult-to-understand reality, the relationship of the dreamer to sexuality, fertility, and the devil or witch.

SNAP OF THE FINGER

Are you a man or a mouse? is a threatening question often put to men who seem unwilling to act on their aggression. The modern, sensitive man may wish to reply, "I refuse to give in to your narrow definition of the paradigm of manhood," before getting the tar beaten out of him.

MOUTH: Contact and communication, erotic kissing and relationships. According to Freud and Jung, it represents the female sexual organ.

MOVING: Changes.

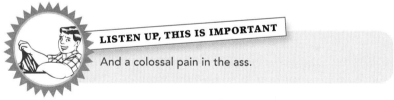

LISTEN UP, THIS IS IMPORTANT

And a colossal pain in the ass.

MOVING OUT (OF HOME): Like Emigration, Giving Up/Getting Out, and Foreign Country.

MUD/SLUDGE: Fear of sinking and of stagnation. Being a mixture of water and earth, this image refers to emotions flowing and needs realized.

MUG, CUP, BEAKER, GOBLET: First try to establish if, in your sleep, you are really thirsty—see Drink, Water. That which is giving, that which is mysterious. But also zest for life, advances, and luxury, as in Oysters, Balloon, Champagne. A warning sign of alcoholism. What is the goblet made of? What is in it? Possibly something poisonous? The next question would be what kind of poison.

Classical symbol in depth psychology for female sexuality.

SNAP OF THE FINGER

Why not compose a moving love poem to female sexuality using your new-found knowledge about the classical symbols of depth psychology? (Sample below.)

My darling, you are like a beaker
I must establish whether or not I am, in fact,
Are you a poison? If so, what kind?
Are you a warning sign of alcoholism
. . . (etc.) You can take it from here.

MUMMY: A long life. You want immortality and have a tendency toward grandiosity. The mummy may also indicate an age-old burden, something that died long ago but still influences and fascinates you.

MURDER/MURDERER: See also Funeral. Warning: A very important part of your emotions have been severed: unused talents, relationships to other people, the ability to love, and so on. These are frequent dreams during depression, and reveal repressed drives, as in Ashes and Abyss. This, however, is only one, although it is the most important, interpretation of this dream symbol. On the positive side, it is very healing that you are "murdering" something in the dream and thereby putting a radical end to it. You are standing by your aggression and thereby expressing a very important part of you. As in a detective story, murder can be stimulating as well as tragic and have a purifying effect.

DON'T BE A JERK

It is crucial that you do not allow the symbolic nature of a murder dream to influence how you look at waking life. For example, "Your Honor, I was standing by my aggression and expressing a very important part of me," will likely not fly, nor will, "Don't you find, Judge, that my heinous crime has a stimulating as well as a tragic and purifying effect?"

MUSEUM: Usually represents the dreamer. What is being exhibited?

STRETCHING THE TRUTH

Below are some painters in your museum dream and what they represent:

Pablo Picasso: You seek a woman with a nose growing out of her cheek.

Vincent van Gogh: You see yourself as a tragic, undiscovered genius. Leave the ear alone, big guy; you're not in his league.

Thomas Kinkade: Please, please, cut off your ear.

MUSHROOM: Something is growing out of the depths. It may be poisonous or nurturing. Drug-induced, ecstatic, religious, or sexual experiences. In addition, a symbol of the hidden energies of the earth and the importance of things that are very small.

According to Freud, a phallic symbol.

MUSIC: Emotions, feelings. Important are the feelings that come up when listening to the music. Are there words to the music?

In ancient Egypt, music meant a joyful heart.

MUSSEL: A female sex symbol. A closed mussel means virginity or frigidity.

MUSTACHE: See also Beard, Hair. Symbol of creative power.

SECRETS TO MAKE YOU LOOK GOOD

See also **Village People**. A 1970s phenomenon that could not have happened without the large mustache.

MUSTARD: Sharp; hot; spicy intellect, irony, cynicism.

YOU'RE WELCOME FOR THE TIP

As of the early twenty-first century, intellect, irony, and cynicism are now available in a handy squeeze dispenser!

NAIL: Similar to Needle, or "hitting the nail on the head."

NAIL FILE: Something needs to be smoothed out. Vanity. According to Freud, male genitals.

LISTEN UP, THIS IS IMPORTANT

Sure, a lousy little nail file may have symbolized *his* male genitals.

NAKED: Often the dreamer fearing the truth. Or, naturalness, honesty, and openness, but also poverty and impertinence.

YOU'RE WELCOME FOR THE TIP

Dreams of being naked may point to a desire to join a nudist colony. However, you may want to reconsider, because for some reason it's always the saggy, gross people who like to walk around nude all the time.

NAVEL: Center, or egoism. The center of the person or the body. In the case of men, often bonding with the mother.

BARE FACTS

Also in the case of men, an endless supply of good lint that must be excavated and inspected.

NAVIGATION: This is usually a reference to the kind of life the dreamer is living. Also a symbol for the mental task involved in orientation.

NECK/THROAT: When dreaming about a sore or painful throat, make sure that you are not being bothered by a real health issue, like a cold. Other than that, people you deal with, or annoying situations, may give you a "pain in the neck."

As the neck is the connection between your body and your head, you are either too intellectually engaged or not engaged enough. The throat is the place where "words get stuck."

A sexual connotation may also be indicated, when people are "necking." Or the idea of a close finish—as in a horse race: neck in neck.

SECRETS TO MAKE YOU LOOK GOOD

As noted above, a neck dream can mean you are either too intellectually engaged, or not engaged enough. Given the public schools, we'd put money on it being the latter.

NEEDLE: Emotional and physical pain. Sometimes a symbol for an awareness that is driven to an extreme. It may also address "sewing together" single parts of what the consciousness is working with. It could also be—and not only according to psychoanalysis—a phallic symbol. See Thorns.

NEIGHBOR: Suggests the usual characteristics of the dreamer, of which he or she is relatively aware. Here are the parts of the ego that are fairly close to consciousness. Or, responsibilities and sympathy toward others.

SNAP OF THE FINGER

In the case of noisy neighbors, see also **Murder**.

NEST: Motherhood, protection, longing for security, family, and home. Also, a projection for every type of positive feeling about life.

NET: You want to catch somebody or understand something. Loss of independence, temptation, and possibly something threatening about sexuality. Also, systematic entanglement of emotions and needs, thoughts, and insights. Points clearly to networking and, in that sense, a meaningful connection to others.

DON'T BE A JERK

More modern interpretations point to the net as the Internet, where a "meaningful connection to others" consists of pleas for help from dignitaries of Zimbabwe. (Usually something like "Dear Sir or Madam, You may find this case of worries for you, but I ask your help in money situation which can keep my family from being victims in poor funding violence plus you will get all dollars back twice as much when investment gets big.")

NEW BUILDING: A challenge to find new directions.

NEW YEAR: A new beginning and fun.

NEWSPAPER: Often a suggestion to pay more attention to the outside world. Emotional news.

NICHE: Secrets, or a chance.

NIGHT: The unconscious and unknown—the other world. Often that which is frightening. Similar to end of the workday, Darkness, Evening, Moon.

NIGHTINGALE: Harmony. Hoping to be lucky in love.

NINE: With the number nine, you have reached a level of completion, which is also expressed in the nine-point configuration the enneagram, the system that explains the world, according to theorist and teacher G. I. Gurdjieff. In all Indo-Germanic languages, the number nine is connected to the adjective "new." Nine refers to renewal.

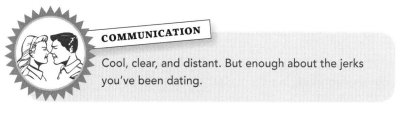

STRETCHING THE TRUTH

Sorry to disappoint you, Mr. Smarty-Pants G. I. Gurdjieff, but we already have a nine-point system that explains the world. It's called chocolate.

NOISE: It might be real noise that is reaching you in your sleep. But it might also be that you want to create excitement or that you do not have enough excitement in your everyday life.

NORTH: "Top" of the map—therefore, the intellect, cool, clear, and distant.

COMMUNICATION

Cool, clear, and distant. But enough about the jerks you've been dating.

NOSE: A phallic symbol—probably the reason why the long nose of the Fool is so popular. To have a good nose means to have rank and fame, intuition, and instinct. It is also a symbol for being nosy—sticking one's nose into other people's business.

NOSEBLEED: Loss of strength and a symbol of injured sexuality. In the dream of a woman, it symbolizes the loss of a partner; or it may be a menstruation dream.

NOTES: Pay close attention. Remember what came into your mind and remember your feelings.

NOTES (MUSICAL): See Music. Sensuality, desire for harmony and accord (particularly in relationships). See also Concert.

NOTICE-OF-INTENTION-TO-MARRY: Positive friendship or longing for a solid relationship. See also Bride/Bridegroom. Looking for understanding and security, as in Anchor, Family.

NOVEL: The title and content are important.

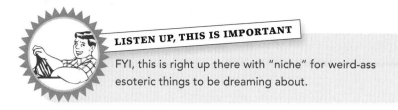

NUMBERS: When dreaming about numbers, pay attention to their symbolic meaning—often the sum of the digits is meaningful. Numbers always represent an ordering principle in the world of the dream. Jung suggests that when dreaming about numbers that have no noticeable meaning, you think about whether they might refer to a year or any other time or date.

NUN: See Virgin. Chastity and disappointment, the longing for a spiritual life. Problems with one's shadow and repressed desires.

NURSE: Femininity and motherliness. Either you need help or you don't want be helped.

NUT: A symbol of wholeness. Also represents the Head and brain and thus thinking. Points to toughness. Ancient Egyptian interpretation: Expect a gift.

If there are two, see Genital Organ.

SNAP OF THE FINGER

If there are three, see **Supplemental Sideshow Income.**

NUTSHELL: Narrowness, protection, and security.

NUT TREE: Strength, fertility, wealth, and abundance.

NYMPH: See Virgin. Similar is nymphomaniac, with sexual limitations.

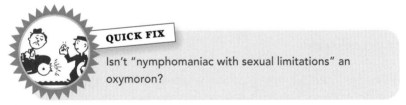

QUICK FIX

Isn't "nymphomaniac with sexual limitations" an oxymoron?

OASIS: An erotic symbol. Relaxing after the troubles of the day, wanderlust, or memories of travel. According to Jung, it is the place that has water in the ground, which he interprets as contact with the unconscious and the possibilities of redemption.

BARE FACTS

May represent a person. Indeed, some people seem to us like an oasis: calming, nurturing, refreshing, waiting there to give us whatever we need. Who are these people, and have you told your spouse about them?

OATH: Truthfulness. You want to have willpower and be dependable in times of (inner) insecurity. Relationship and commitment to something.

OATMEAL/GRANOLA: Health and strength, new energies. You would like to eat healthfully. Also associated with soul food and "alternative" ways to eat on a daily basis.

YOU'RE WELCOME FOR THE TIP

Often accompanied by open-toed suede sandals, tie-dye, and women who don't shave their underarms. Hell of a price to pay for lowering your cholesterol.

OATS: Grain. High spirits. "Feeling your oats" means you should show the world what you can do! "Sowing your wild oats" points to pleasure, usually sexual and promiscuous, after which time, presumably, you "settle down" to a more responsible lifestyle.

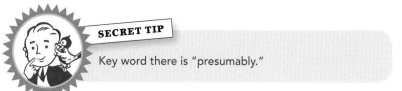

SECRET TIP

Key word there is "presumably."

OBEDIENCE: An indication that more discipline is necessary, or the opposite.

OBELISK: Phallic and power symbol.

COMMUNICATION

Toughest dreams to tell your loved ones about. People tend to tune out after "and then, there was this obelisk . . ."

OBSTACLES: Obstacles in life. Resistance to obstacles that need to be overcome. The positive side of this symbol is that unknown obstacles are made clear and become conscious, which is the prerequisite to overcoming them. The type of obstacle is important.

OCEAN: (Latin: *mare* = Maria = Mother). Emotions, archetypal energy, power, food. It is a symbol of the collective unconscious. Traveling across the ocean represents courage, new beginnings, and new Shores. A longing for freedom and independence.

LISTEN UP, THIS IS IMPORTANT

The ocean is also the lair of the great white shark, which, if The Discovery Channel is any indication, still scares the sh*t out of people.

OFFICE: Professional activity, work, feeling of comradeship. One's own office points to your working habits; somebody else's office may refer to the fact that you are looking to others for guidance in your work.

QUICK FIX

Okay, we'll own up to it. When we mentioned that "professional activity" and "feeling of comradeship" stuff, we were talking about someone else's office.

OFFICE (BUREAU): Dreaming of holding an important position expresses the desire for achievement. Are you too ambitious—or should you be more ambitious? Rigidity, stubbornness, and social protocol. Cooperation, need to be more factual.

OFFICER: For man and woman, a symbol of authority and masculinity.

OLIVES: A sexual symbol, erotic adventures, or travel memories.

LISTEN UP, THIS IS IMPORTANT

Though the olive may appear in your dream as a happy symbol of travel memories, please don't take that as a sign that we want our inboxes clogged with the 250 jpegs of you and your honey's trip to freaking Machu Picchu.

ONE: Unity. See also Ball. That which is indivisible, the self.

ONE-WAY STREET: Being one-sided. Also, a sense of feeling trapped, and a sign of focusing on a goal.

ONION: Vitality and health, but also false tears. The onion is the hot spice of life.

YOU'RE WELCOME FOR THE TIP

Warning: Only as a dream symbol is the onion the hot spice of life; do not include eating onions as part of foreplay. You will only have to get up to gargle, which is a total buzz kill.

OPAL: Life that glitters in many colors! Opals also have the reputation of being unlucky.

OPEN HEARTH: See Fire. Domesticity, protection, as in Parents' House. See also Cooking, Baking, Roast.

According to Jung, transformation process in alchemy; something wants to transcend.

COMMUNICATION

Yes, we know, there was never an "open hearth" in your parents' house. No, your emotional growth was stifled by an environment of condemnation and guilt. Blah, blah, blah; get over it.

OPENING (OF AN EXHIBITION, ETC.): Well-known symbol for new beginnings, as in Baby, Birth, and Child.

Is it a store or art gallery that is opening? What is being shown or sold? The kind of objects that are on display point, symbolically, to the kind of new beginning that is to come. A bookstore, for instance, might point to education and intellectual subjects; an art exhibition might point to creative/artistic self-development.

STRETCHING THE TRUTH

If you are at an art gallery opening in your dream, can you explain what that one so-called painting is supposed to represent? Honestly, a child of four could come up with this crap, and they want how many thousands for it?

OPERA: A warning of too much vanity, pathos, and self-absorption. Danger of overdramatizing, but also joy and vitality.

LISTEN UP, THIS IS IMPORTANT

Also **Opera Fan.** Symbol of a sexually ambiguous older man wearing a velvet dressing gown and living among bronze busts and teak.

OPERATION: Emotional problems and their elimination. The type of operation is important. It will show what is disturbed and how it can be remedied.

SNAP OF THE FINGER

See also **Malpractice Suit.**

OPTICIAN: Clear insight and objectivity are suggested. The way you see things is being questioned. See also Eyeglasses, Eye.

ORANGE: A sexual meaning. When dreaming about two oranges or two apples, they symbolize women's breasts. See also Fruit, Sun.

BARE FACTS

When dreaming about Billy having five oranges and giving one to his friend Suzy who has nine oranges, you are having the sexiest dream about a math problem you may ever experience.

ORANGE JUICE: Usually a sign that you are actually thirsty. See also Orange.

ORCHESTRA: Usually points to a desire for harmony in relationships or with people at work. You would like to unite many voices within yourself, or you experience many voices and run the danger of losing yourself. See Concert, Mosaic.

ORGY: Points to boredom or undefined sexuality. This insight is only the beginning of the process of forming your own erotic sexuality.

ORIENT: Longing for beauty and to possess wealth. A symbol of that which fascinates us, but also that which we do not understand. Secrets and eroticism.

ORIGIN: Purification, composure, prayer, devotion, and deep emotional feelings.

OVAL: You are approaching the Circle and completion.

YOU'RE WELCOME FOR THE TIP

The dream may be a sign that you will one day occupy the Oval Office. (Rich, connected people only.)

OVEN: Heat, urges. You are "cooking" something up; something is brewing internally. Romantic flight into the so-called good old days.

Warm feelings. A cold oven refers to emotional coldness. Points to the state of your relationship.

According to Freud, female sexual symbol, uterus.

OWL: Symbol of wisdom. Owls can see in the dark and for that reason are said to have greater perception. One feels found out.

OX: Energetic, stubborn, and clumsy. When stifled and overwhelmed, a search for relief and a lighter workload.

OYSTERS: Luxury, social advancement. Desire for material excess. According to classical depth psychology, a symbol of female sexuality, and often seen as an aphrodisiac.

PACKAGE: Troubles, worry, and burdens that you have to carry, but also gifts. The image of opening a package often has to do with self-awareness.

PACKAGE (LARGE): See Package, Container. Often points to the unknown or to repressed emotions, obstacles, burdens, and complications that you carry with you. See Gift.

BARE FACTS

Okay, we left "package" alone. But then they go and put "large package" right under it, and they want us to stay quiet? Man, where's Freud when you need him?

PAGODA: Wanderlust, travel experiences. You are looking at your own body and soul as a temple.

SECRET TIP

If your partner wakes up in a cold sweat complaining about having another of those horrifying pagoda dreams, you may want to start seeking thrills outside the relationship.

PAIL: See also Container that wants to be filled or that has been filled. A full bucket always indicates that you have much to give. Female sexual symbol. Something is being ruined, thrown away into a pail!

DON'T BE A JERK

A full bucket may also indicate that your stomach rejected the combination of Cajun jambalaya and Red Bull.

PAIN: Being sensitive or overly sensitive. It points to either the necessity of grieving or a new beginning.

PAINTBRUSH: Stupid person. Art and harmony. In psychoanalysis, a sexual symbol.

PAINTER/ARTIST: Creativity and a sense of beauty.

PALACE: An archetypal symbol for Mother. Emotional security or imprisonment. Compare this to "castle in the air."

Your own self as well as your own body; megalomania and freedom. According to Freud, this image symbolizes the female.

PALENESS: Fear, illness, or being blasé.

PALM: A phallic symbol, and one of friendliness and peace. Exuberant vitality. In a man's dream it may also indicate an unsatisfactory sex life.

PAPER: Book. Something you are aware of, which is long overdue, needs to be resolved. A clean, white sheet of paper also symbolizes innocence as well as "empty consciousness." In a positive sense this could mean a creative emptiness. In a negative sense it indicates a lack of awareness. It is also a symbol of the spirit. Paper with writing on it is the same as a book, meaning you need to pay attention to the text.

According to Freud, paper is a symbol of femininity.

PARACHUTE: Not a dangerous fall; letting oneself fall gently. Sexual connotation, as in Falling, Brook, and Leaf. You are letting yourself glide through the air, which symbolizes an associative, creative, and playful intellect. This dream symbol also points to more general situations where you are letting yourself go, and you will like it. When in fear of Flying, the parachute usually does not open.

PARADISE: Possibly a symbol of running away from difficulties, or a "big dream" that points to important life goals and desires. A desire for quiet, relaxation, and peace—to be enjoying life and productivity. A conscience that is at peace with "God and the world" and that has recognized the Self. Release of what was repressed. See Bird, Parrot, Hell.

YOU'RE WELCOME FOR THE TIP

You might need to ask yourself, what is paradise to me? If your answer involves line dancing or a mechanical bull, you may need to expand your horizons.

PARALYSIS: Feeling handicapped in a mental or emotional area. Feeling the need for quiet and rest. Should you be less active? See Illness, Invalid.

PARASOL/CAP: See also Umbrella. Old symbol for power, protection, and keeping your distance.

According to Freud, phallic symbol in the process of erection.

SECRETS TO MAKE YOU LOOK GOOD

Suddenly, "Let a smile be your umbrella" takes on a whole different meaning.

PARENTS: Father, Mother. You are seeking help from the outside, as in Physician, Medication, and Pharmacist; however, the danger is not that great. Often an expression of considerable immaturity in adults.

"Dream parents" are a hint that you need to be a good father or a good mother to yourself. Are you a mother to yourself? Are you a loving father to yourself?

PARENTS' HOUSE: Separating from Parents, a new beginning (particularly when leaving home). Security in the Family, Notice-of-Intention-to-Marry, Sidewalk, and Bureaucrat. Suggestion of helplessness. In this case, ask yourself how you experience your childhood. How are these feelings connected with your life today? In addition, the question of parenthood comes up. What do you want to bring into this world?

COMMUNICATION

You know what? Parents get a bad enough rap. We're not going to add fuel to the fire by suggesting that some silly dream could be a sign that they have screwed you up for life. No way.

PARK: A symbol of nature controlled; pointing to the dreamer's repressed wildness. At the same time, however, it is also a symbol for culture, beauty, and graciousness. It points to the connection between nature and intellect.

SECRET TIP

It also points to the connection between pigeons and that weird old lady on the bench.

PARKING: Coming to rest, becoming rigid, standing in one place. But also having found a goal and purpose.

PARLIAMENT: Points to your social abilities and desire for advancement. An indication of coming to terms with other people and the voice inside you. It is a symbol of governing and points to the need to coordinate your own qualities. How are you putting together your emotions and intellect? How do you "rule" yourself and others?

PARROT: Highly confidential secrets are being given away by close friends. An eccentric person glittering in many colors. Either dependency and immaturity, or a challenge to be more unconventional, exotic, and colorful.

BARE FACTS

To parrot is to simply repeat verbatim what has worked for others, even if there is no real feeling behind it. Such as, "Honey, I'm sorry; you were absolutely right."

PARSLEY: Strengthens the heart. Success.

SNAP OF THE FINGER

Now that you know it strengthens the heart, maybe you'll actually start eating this useless garnish.

PARTY: Pleasure after work is completed, social exchange, and communication. Well-being, fun, and joy in the dream, as in life, always mean to search for or to have found your center. Your personal characteristics are getting stimulated and recognized, and that is the meaning of "party," too.

YOU'RE WELCOME FOR THE TIP

You don't need to keep dreaming about that party and the underwear-on-the-head incident. Let it go. As dreams inform you, you were just finding your center.

PASS/PASSPORT: The dreamer himself. Wanderlust; often also saying good-bye to old habits. In addition, it may mean fleeing from something, or indicate an inferiority complex, because you have to legitimize your identity.

PATH: As in Street; a frequent symbol of life's path. See Wagon. Your personal path is laid out for you. You are walking your own life's path. Or, difficulty on the path.

PAYMENT: If you receive money, you are receiving energy. If you have to give money, energy is lost. Always make sure that you pay attention to the direction of the flow of energy: where it is coming from and where it is flowing to. Of course, in addition to the symbolic meaning, this dream might also represent an actual financial situation that might cause apprehension.

PEA: Female sexual symbol (clitoris). Easily irritated, or positive sensitivity (as in the fairy tale "The Princess and the Pea"). In another fairy tale is the incident of "counting peas," which could mean either pettiness and being a stickler for details or being precise and careful when dealing with small items.

PEACH: An erotic symbol. Romantic relationships. According to Freud, a symbol of the female breast.

PEACOCK: Vanity. A symbol of narcissism and arrogance. But at the same time it may represent the beauty of the soul and the diversity of one's own personality. In alchemy it is a symbol that points to changes in life. Also, a symbol of rebirth. See Phoenix.

QUICK FIX

We think of the expression "proud as a peacock."
Examine your own life. Are you too proud? Because,
really, you have no reason to be, from what we've heard.

PEAR: Symbol of female sexuality (as with all fruits); possible dream at the beginning of pregnancy.

PEARL: A symbol of the mature soul and completeness of the emotional experience. Also a female sexual symbol (clitoris), and a general symbol of women, loved ones, something precious and complete. Pearl also refers to domestic help and "the good soul." If a pearl necklace breaks, trouble and worries due to a loss.

SECRET TIP

If a pearl was really a symbol for the clitoris, then
men . . . Oh, never mind.

PENCIL/FOUNTAIN PEN: News, notes. Appears often in dreams when something is in danger of being forgotten that needs to be remembered (better write it down).

According to Freud: phallic symbol (particularly a fountain pen filled with ink).

PENIS: Symbol of masculine power. See Genital Organ.

What we want to know is, if almost everything else in a dream represents a penis, why can't a penis in a dream represent a mountain, or a fountain pen, or the Space Needle? It would certainly help when you don't feel like telling your friends that you dreamed about a penis last night.

PENITENTIARY: A dream about obstacles, as in Prison, Cage—only more severe.

PENSION: Quiet and relaxation.

PEPPER: Refers to "hot stuff."

PERFORMANCE: Publicity, end of secrecy, vanity, and superficiality. Show your colors. You may be getting too worked up about something, showing off too much. See also Arena. What is playing at the theater/movies?

PERFUME: Wanting to look good and be seen in positive terms, loved, and accepted. Addresses the power of attraction and subtle radiance. Like the fragrance of a perfume that evaporates quickly, your understanding of yourself and others is difficult to maintain. On the other hand, making a definite statement (with a fragrance) about your presence, the scent of the perfume expresses sexuality and fantasies.

PERIOD: See Rhythm, Haste, Step, Nosebleed.

PERSON: Any person in a dream can represent you yourself. Particularly when important persons—like father, mother, lover, and children—are recognized clearly in the dream, it is truly yourself that you are dealing with. In addition, every person in a dream may point to some of your own characteristics and tasks in life, or may symbolize something impersonal. Less often, a person in a dream might be a reminder of another similar person.

PEST/VERMIN: A symbol that points to unmet sexual desire or fear of unwanted pregnancy. In antiquity it was a symbol for foolish gambling.

According to Freud, it often points to children or siblings.

PESTILENCE: Emotional disturbance and, at the least, great insecurity.

PETS: Either "back to nature" or damaged nature. The tension between the animal and civilized nature.

PEWTER: See Metal.

PHARMACIST: See Alchemist.

PHOENIX: See also Peacock. According to the most widely read book of the Middle Ages, *Physiologus*, the phoenix of India is more beautiful than a peacock. After five hundred years, and at new moon, the phoenix flew to Heliopolis, presented itself to the priest, and then burned itself on the altar. What remained was a worm from which wings began growing, and the phoenix was reborn. A symbol of resurrection, rebirth, and transformation.

PHOTO/PHOTOGRAPHY: The past of the dreamer, memories of past events (also in the sense of wanting to hold on to them and idealization). Playing with Light and Shadow (with so-called light and dark places), which means seeing life according to your own imagination. You want to focus on seeing clearly and recognizing what you see. You are working with the camera lens, which is a hint to be more objective.

PHOTO-COLLAGE: Photography, but with the main emphasis on creative aspects. Here, it is a question of putting together the puzzle of your own life. It is important what is being assembled, and in what way.

PHYSICIAN (MALE OR FEMALE): Comfort, sympathy, fear of pain, Illness, and Death. Anticipating problems ahead and looking for a way out, for advice and help. May also stand for general improvement and stabilization. A symbol of masculinity, of a wise man, wise woman, or an emancipated female. Authority and wealth. Try—in the dream—to talk to the physician and ask questions about the situation. The answers can serve as an important clue, not only to your health. If the dreamer is the physician, he or she wants to have control over life and death.

According to Freud, also a symbol for eroticism. The physician is a person that we stand before naked.

BARE FACTS

Actually, we usually stand before a physician in a paper johnny, which is even more embarrassing than being naked.

PIANO: The scale of emotions, intensive feelings, culture, and harmony. Being spiritual and intellectually alive.

According to Freud, because of its rhythm when being played, it is a symbol for intercourse.

As with all musical instruments, according to psychoanalysis it symbolizes the body of the woman. See Grand Piano.

PICKAXE: A symbol of aggression in a sexual context, but also, the other side of the axe—used to loosen and penetrate hard surfaces.

PICNIC: Eating always points to the natural and intimate.

YOU'RE WELCOME FOR THE TIP

Whereas eating *outdoors* always points to the paper plates flying away in the wind and the flies landing on your hand, trying to suck the mayo out of your tuna salad sandwich.

PICTURE: Portrait. Not the real thing! Being either egocentric or self-reflecting. Search for a relevant worldview or your true self.

PIE: Enjoyment.

PIG: See also Greed. Sexuality demanding to be freed, but also rejection of physical sexuality. Symbol of luck, natural sexuality, intellectual power. Fertility. According to Moses and the Koran, pork is a forbidden food. It represents the low and primitive—"casting pearls before swine"—laziness, wallowing in dirt; but also comfort.

According to Freud, a sexual symbol (in the *Odyssey*, Circe transformed men into swine; she frees their animal side to bind them to her).

In the East, a symbol of the unconscious.

PIGTAIL: This image refers to taming.

PILL: Bitter truth, illness, but also searching and finding. Fear of pregnancy. Uppers: a suggestion that you have to find happiness in yourself and not expect it to come from the outside. Downers: You need to "work" for relaxation and not expect it to come by itself. Drugs: You are seeking deeper spiritual insights, but in a regressive way. One has to learn to find experiences of freedom without drugs. Birth control: The dreamer is longing for sex, but there is fear involved.

PILLAR: Support. According to Freud, a phallic symbol.

PILLOW: Rest, relaxation and domesticity, as in Baking, Roast, Cooking, Flowerpot, Iron, Porcelain, Apron, Hen.

PINEAPPLE: Being a juicy and sweet Fruit, it is a sign of self-confidence, enjoyment of life, and sexuality. It is a female sexual symbol (as are all fruits, except bananas).

PINECONE: Phallic symbol.

PIRATE: Freeloader. Longing for freedom and independence and living out the masculine in man and woman. Opposite, and a complement to, Admiral.

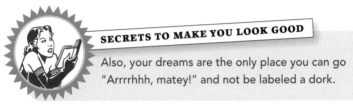

SECRETS TO MAKE YOU LOOK GOOD

Also, your dreams are the only place you can go "Arrrrhhh, matey!" and not be labeled a dork.

PISTOL/GUN: Masculine sexual symbol, and a symbol for aggression always connected to power and achievement. The dangers and the potentialities of self-determination are emphasized here. It also means: come to the point; hit your target—or better not hit it—and conclude something or begin something new.

SECRET TIP

Be aware that most dreams have a very powerful gun lobby in place to insure your right to dream about small firearms.

PLACE: Often your own center, especially if the place is round or square. Or, in a public place, becoming aware of something.

PLAIN/PLATEAU: Boredom, but also being in balance. Good foresight and perspective, similar to Bird.
   Folklore: Material rewards.

PLANE/SLICER: A very focused attempt to create order, smoothing things out at any price. This dream often indicates a process of elimination.

In its connection to "airplane," see also Flying and Parachute. Also, may indicate a concern with how people judge you and how you want to be seen.

PLANET: For an interpretation of the meanings of planets in dreams, look up books on astrology, or better yet, read Greek mythology. A symbol of your own Star.

SNAP OF THE FINGER

Translation: Can't you people do anything for yourselves?

PLANT: See also Tree, Flower. A plant often represents a part of the dreamer. It symbolizes growth, naturalness, but also that which is slow and logical. This dream image often suggests the need to plant something, pointing to the development of the dreamer's talents and abilities.

PLASTER: Stabilizing, bonding medium. Being steadfast or stubborn. Heat that needs to cool down.

Getting stuck, being glued to something (such as relationships, work, etc.). Something may be smoothed out with plaster, as in Ironing. Plaster is used to make a copy of an original. What are you copying? Falsehood.

Folklore: Being wrongly accused.

PLATE/DINNER PLATE: Social advantage or hunger for life.

PLATEAU: Perspective, as in Skyscraper/High-Rise, Hiding Places, and Bird.

PLATFORM (AT THE TRAIN STATION): See also Railway Station. The symbol for taking a trip and for waiting. Also, meeting other people.

COMMUNICATION

As you wait for the train, do you have a moment of thinking how easy it would be to step off the platform, into the path of the oncoming locomotive? And if yes, is your first thought how much your death would inconvenience all the other passengers? Congratulations! You have explained codependence for the rest of us.

PLAYING CARDS: Happenstance, luck, and skill.

PLIERS: Are you feeling squeezed? Often a hint to be more decisive in a given situation; or, are you trying to force something? This dream often points to a complicated situation, perhaps catch-22, and requires your finding an alternative approach, another level of communicating, a different attitude.

PLOW: Changing and loosening up one's lifestyle. According to Freud, and also most other dream interpreters, plowing means intercourse (see also Furrow). Plowing, as well as Sowing, is one of the many late-medieval sexual rituals. See Fools.

YOU'RE WELCOME FOR THE TIP

Note to drunkards: Telling everyone you got really plowed last night could mean a little more than you intend it to.

PLUM: A female sexual organ. In the Orient, it means luck, and is also an erotic symbol, suggesting domestic bliss.

PLUMBER: This image refers to Pipe (water); in other words, guiding the emotions. In addition, the matter of sexuality should not be dismissed, since the plumber does install a pipe.

LISTEN UP, THIS IS IMPORTANT

As far as plumbers go, there may also be something sexual about "paying through the nose." When we figure it out, we'll let you know.

POCKET/BAG: See also Container, Suitcase. Indicates the ability to carry a load and, if necessary, the ability to take action. It is a symbol of that which we carry around with us (purse, attaché case, etc.), that which we own. It is also a symbol of what we are made of (what is in our pockets symbolizes what is in ourselves—what moves us—because the pocket is inside our clothes).

According to Freud, female genitals. The apron pocket, according to Jung, is the "pocket" the woman or girl carries within her body. In the case of a man or a boy, the pocket refers to the region from which sexual desires arise.

POCKETBOOK: Property. A female sexual symbol that appears frequently in women's dreams. On one hand, a pocketbook stands for personal Luggage (or burden). On the other hand, it points toward a notebook, as a symbol for memory.

POET: Longing for creative activity, fantasy, and inspiration. The belief that creative work is the result of suffering is an often quoted meaning of this dream symbol. In the end it comes down to condensing one's existence, compressing it, intensifying it, and living in a more focused way, according to one's personal essence.

DON'T BE A JERK

Don't try any of that fancy artistic stuff in your dreams. Poetry's supposed to rhyme, damn it, and that goes for your subconscious, too.

POISON: Cruelty and aggression. Often, poisonous thoughts and feelings. It may represent everything that is a contradiction within the dreamer or, on rare occasions, medicine.

POISONOUS SNAKE: See also Snake. Well-known symbol for a deceptive woman. Dangers in matters of the heart and erotic issues. See also Enemy.

POLE: See Rod. Masculine sexual organ, and not only according to Freud.

YOU'RE WELCOME FOR THE TIP

Unless all the guys who scrawl stuff on men's room walls are *quoting* Freud.

POLICEMAN: Father figure, authority, and person of respect—in short, a symbol for the superego. A feeling of oppression and dissatisfaction, possibly a sign of immature masculinity. This dream image points to the danger of an impersonal and abstract consciousness. It challenges you to find out if you have a mind of your own or are strictly submitting to an authoritarian direction. Does law and order play a big role in your life? Or would you rather be a friend and helper? Maybe you should bring more of your own personality and opinions into the game. Take a chance, be more liberated and more responsible.

STRETCHING THE TRUTH

Many test subjects report having the "buddy cop" dream, in which they are a grizzled veteran of the force and must contend with a new, young renegade partner who doesn't play by the rules. Eventually, the two cops come to respect each other, just as the grizzled veteran dies in a shootout two weeks before he was due to collect his pension.

POND: Stagnant water, often symbolizing erotic feelings. If the surface is calm, a balanced emotional life. As indicated in the saying "Still waters run deep," it is also a symbol of deep feelings. If the water in the pond is cloudy, it is often a symbol of sexual conflict.

POPE: See Bishop.

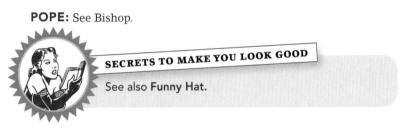

SECRETS TO MAKE YOU LOOK GOOD

See also **Funny Hat.**

POPPY/FLOWER: Intoxication; more awareness is demanded. Losing oneself as either a dangerous or a positive sign.

PORCELAIN: See also Marriage. Domesticity, culture, and lifestyle, as in Iron, Flowerpot, Hen, Pillow, Apron, Baking, Cooking. Sometimes, but very seldom, it points to luxury.

PORTER: Someone who is carrying the burden for others. Is it you or is somebody else carrying your burden for you?

PORTRAIT: You are getting a clearer picture about yourself or somebody else. Calls for creative vision and actions instead of logic alone. Portraits almost always show characteristics of the dreamer. Every picture is a self-portrait and a reflection of one's personal or broad and universal attitudes. See also Picture.

POST/POST OFFICE/POSTCARD: Sending or receiving important information from the unconscious. Increased awareness, communication.

POST/STAKE: A post driven into the ground is a symbol for intercourse and it starts a spring flowing.

POT: Container. A symbol for virginity. Pouring liquid out of a pot points to devotion. See also Frying Pan, Soup.

POTATO: The food of the poor, particularly in the nineteenth century, which thereby connects this image to fear of social decline—note van Gogh's painting *The Potato Eaters,* for example, where dark and somber colors convey the mood of poverty.

At the same time, the image of the potato refers to groundedness, since it grows underground. As a root plant, the potato addresses the rootedness of the dreamer. As a tuber, the potato has a peculiar androgynous shape: it could represent a phallic symbol as well as typically feminine shapes. As one of the basic food forms, the potato also represents the nurturing female as well as the power of Mother Nature.

POTTER: Shaping life. Creating a way to express emotional energies. Romantic longing for an activity that is perceived to be simple.

POWDER: See also Mask. Inferiority complex, disguise. You want to pretend you're something that you are not. On the other hand, completion, the final touch.

POWER: The game of power is always playing with fire. This image points to your passionate vitality. At issue here are the energies that are available to you and how they are being used. The image of power addresses your shadow as well as your strength. How are you using your power? Against others? Or is somebody's power being used against you? Are you feeling powerful or powerless? See Ruler.

Indicates luck and health, or it may be pointing to weakness. More important is how the energy is being expressed—through the heart, the soul, the mind, the body, or the character.

COMMUNICATION

Don't forget a "Higher Power," as in "one who delights in biting you in the ass when you get too cocky."

PRAYER: Often points to a dreamer's childlike behavior. Often a hint to become more active, or to turn more inward. On the other hand, praying is also connected to the practice of asking and receiving.

PRECIOUS STONE: The treasures within you, the higher self. Points to the fact that something very precious has been growing within you. Steadfastness, faithfulness, dependability, but also pride. The shinier the stone, the greater the emphasis on pride and vanity. Pay attention to the color and the type of stone. Stones that are damaged have a negative symbolic meaning.

PREDATOR: "Every woman at some time dreams about a predator." So it has been said in the past, but the same holds true for every man. Points to sexual feelings, animalistic ones that could be enjoyed or that you are trying to repress.

SNAP OF THE FINGER

Points to one of the least sucky Arnold Schwarzenegger movies.

PRESENTATION: Showing something off, as in Undressing. Wanting to be cultivated or sophisticated or at least appear to be. Self-portrayal, as in Arena, Performance.

PRICE/PAYMENT: You must pay for everything. Or do essentials come as a gift to everybody? May or may not have to do with transformation of energy.

PRIEST: See Minister, Bishop, Professor. Ancient Egyptian interpretation: You are offered a prestigious position.

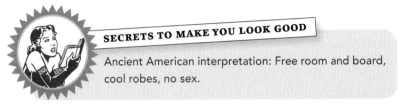

SECRETS TO MAKE YOU LOOK GOOD

Ancient American interpretation: Free room and board, cool robes, no sex.

PRIMEVAL FOREST/JUNGLE: A place that is generally inaccessible, representing the unconscious and physical drives. A symbol of strength and vitality, but also the danger of falling prey to drives and urges. It may point to more discipline, or challenges to live out physical urges more clearly.

PRINCE/PRINCESS: Always you yourself. Often refers to your own magical spiritual dignity—either negative or positive—new emotional independence, and ability to express yourself.

PRISM: Points to a situation that has many facets, as in Crystal and rainbow, Multiplicity. A symbol of unity and of collecting what is scattered.

PRISON/BEING IMPRISONED: May symbolize restrictions and dependency in many forms. Usually, it expresses a need for more space and freedom, as in Crowds, Shackles, and Cage. You feel limited (often because of a relationship or situations at work) or awkward. In rare cases, it refers to a "blind spot" or a sore point you're saddled with.

Freud dreamed in his youth about a prison in the shape of a Box, which to him was the symbol of a Uterus.

SECRET TIP

Freud would have been somebody's bitch in a heartbeat.

PRISONER: See also Prison. Strong guilt feelings, to the point of feeling unconscious restriction. But by recognizing this feeling of apprehension and imprisonment in the dream, you can change it. Often this image recognizes that it is not necessary to punish yourself.

PROFESSOR: Intellectualization and advancement. Or, life is too one-sided intellectually. Somebody who pronounces something publicly, defends, and teaches. See also Minister/Clergyman.

PROSTITUTION: Men or women who sell themselves. Repressed drives, as in Breaking Up, Attack, Electricity, Defloration, Flames, Violence, Greed, Harem. Also see Skin Rash and Wire (High-Tension). The dreamer is dissatisfied. In the case of a woman, a symbol of courage and independence, but also of senseless and thoughtless sexuality. This dream symbol often points to an aversion toward sexuality and everyday life.

BARE FACTS

This image is rarely complete without torn fishnet stockings. Well, for some of us, anyway.

PROTEST: Self-determination and establishing boundaries.

PUB/SALOON: Restaurant.

PUBLIC: Self-portrayal or lack of it, depending on whether, in the dream, you have an audience or you are the public.

PUBLIC TRANSPORTATION: A limited but sensible way of moving about collectively, not individually. See also Train.

QUICK FIX

Some see a limited but sensible way of moving about collectively; others see a haven of disease and a conveyor of strange people who communicate by barking.

PUDDING: Is what you eat unhealthy? Do you think you are too heavy? See Ice, Cake, Jellyfish.

PUDDLE: Dirty Water and emotions.

PULLING TEETH: Something that you cannot or are not supposed to have. ("Getting the information is like pulling teeth.")

PUMP: Sexual symbol, fertility, flowing emotions.

PUNISHMENT: Bad conscience and masochism. Moral problems, similar to Confession. It is also possible that you will be asked to consider taking responsibility for somebody, or that you need to forgive somebody.

PUPPET: Numb, childish, dependent, insensitive (a child projecting its psyche on the puppet). It is important to look at how these symbols are connected. They may point to a rediscovery of childlike emotions, or to the necessity to say good-bye to them.

If you are the puppet, you see yourself as without a soul, as only a pretty plaything.

Until the late Middle Ages, the puppet was considered a defense against evil ghosts or as possessing magical powers. Such beliefs are still mirrored in the practice of having mascots.

PURPLE: Purple is the color at the border of the visible spectrum. You are seeking awareness and transcendence. This is a symbol of conservative religion (the aristocratic cardinals in the Middle Ages wore purple). It is also symbolizes royalty and female emancipation.

PURSUIT: A dream symbol that appears rather frequently. Something that you have repressed is trying to make itself known. Subconsciously, sexuality is perceived as bad.

According to Freud, drives and urges are haunting you. But in contrast to Freud, this dream may indicate that the dreamer is pursuing that which is rightfully his, which are his ideals.

In so-called chase dreams, according to Jung, something is trying to reach you. What has been split off and repressed wants to be united again. If this is the case, don't put up defenses, rather invite in what is trying to reach you. If the dream suggests that a good-bye is necessary, resist what is chasing you.

PUTREFACTION: In alchemy this image is part of the process of blackening and a symbol of total unconsciousness, of decay. A frequent symbol in nightmares. The decay usually points to your own characteristics that have died and that you need to either let go of or revive. Fear of illness. Challenge to be more self-critical and more self-confident.

PUTTY/CEMENT: Holding together (against the outside world).

PUZZLE: See Riddle, Mosaic.

PYRAMID: According to Jung, the graves of kings who were honored as gods are a symbol of the idea of resurrection. Egypt is not the only place with pyramids; they have also been found in Mexico and in China, where the idea of resurrection is expressed through the choice of the place where they were built, between mountain and valley. A pyramid stands between heaven and earth. Pyramids also refer to wanderlust and travel experiences. Also, they are signposts. The pyramids served as enormous mirrors, due to their polished surfaces, making them a source of light. Given their foundation, they are also a physical mandala. Know your own light—your strengths and talents. The pyramid stands for those who elevate their own fire and light, growing beyond their personal world. See also Square, Triangle.

PYRE/STAKE: Guilt feelings have piled up.

QUARANTINE: Warning of isolation and illness. Something is troubling you and you are dealing with it in the emotional arena.

QUARREL: Inner conflict and contradictions.

QUARRY: Is your rigid attitude crumbling? Is your heart—that seems to be made of stone—softening?

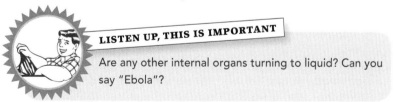

QUARTER/DISTRICT: This image is always a part of the dreamer himself.

QUEEN: See King/Queen.

QUICKSAND: Getting lost in emotions. Treacherous dangers, lost insights, insecure emotions. See also Dunes.

YOU'RE WELCOME FOR THE TIP

You are sinking . . . about to be pulled into an unpleasant, even life-threatening situation . . . You are going home for Thanksgiving.

RACE: This image almost always refers to career issues, addressing primarily the question of winner and loser, because such dreams usually deal with emotional energies. Are you running ahead? Are others behind you? Or are you running behind the pack? Different people taking part in a competitive race in the dream represent the many different sides of the Self.

STRETCHING THE TRUTH

Many test subjects report anxiety dreams about having a track announcer cover the race among their many different sides ("and Never Got Hugged by My Mother is gaining fast on Beat Up in High School, with Overachiever Father still very much in this . . ."). Terrifying indeed.

RACING: Wanting to reach the goal in a hurry. Haste. That holds true for your external as well as internal goals. Racing—whether it is a marathon, an auto or horse race—is always connected to stamina and not "getting out of breath." This dream symbol appears often during stress situations. On the other hand, racing is also an image of ecstasy.

RADIO: Communication, information, messages about emotions, internal dialogue. To listen to a radio in a dream is to listen to your own voice.

RAGS: Desire for advancement, or fear of poverty, as in Charity, Asylum, Beggar. Also a romantic desire to let things go and break with convention. A protest against success and self-portrayal.

RAILROAD CAR: See also Railway Station, Platform. A frequently appearing symbol for travel. What is important is whom you meet in the railroad car.

RAILWAY STATION: See also Train. A frequent dream symbol. Changes in the present life situation. At the train station, we often find out where our life's journey is taking us. Also an image of rushing ("It's high time"). Waiting for something or "being thrown off track."

The conductor might be a symbol for our better-informed self. Is the train coming, are we on the right train, where and to which train are we changing, the waiting room: all these symbols can easily be a reflection of our own emotional situation.

In depth psychology, the train represents our unconscious, which is trying to get us on the right "track."

BARE FACTS

The latest update is that the 9:45 train to your getting everything you want out of life is delayed indefinitely.

RAIN: See also Clouds. Longing for deep relaxation. A symbol of fertility. Also, a longing for mental/intellectual inspiration.

RAINBOW: A symbol of wholeness. The Fire of the sun and the Water of the rain come together; contradictions are united. The connection between desire and will. The rainbow has also been a Christian symbol for the bond between God and human beings. Today, it is often a symbol for creativity and fantasies.

According to the Talmud and kabbala, we are not allowed to look at a rainbow, because it leads back to God. In some African mythology, the rainbow is a devouring animal. According to Jung, it is the bridge leading into the next life.

A rainbow can also be seen as a Circle; it contains every color and meaning, every quality.

SECRETS TO MAKE YOU LOOK GOOD

We may think of the song *Over the Rainbow*, which presents a longing for a more exciting life. Of course, Dorothy's farm was in black and white, so her criteria for "more exciting" was probably pretty flexible.

RAISINS: Money, but also romantic feelings.

YOU'RE WELCOME FOR THE TIP

Can also resemble rodent droppings. (Adolescent pranksters only.)

RAM: See Buck.

RANGE/COOKING RANGE: See Oven. In the past, the central place for family events, eating, motherliness, woman, and marriage. Similar to Cap. Today, a range does not display an open flame; but the transformation of food from a raw to a cooked state is emphasized more. The oven, like the Kitchen, is one of the most frequent symbols of transformation. Danger lurks when the fire is going out.

According to Freud, the symbol for women and the female body.

STRETCHING THE TRUTH

There was an '80s band called Bruce Hornsby and the Range, wherein, as near as we can tell, Bruce's backup band was an oven.

RANSOM: Emotional expenditure; an attempt to free oneself.

RASPBERRY: See Berries. Happy life.

RAT: Warning signal in a dream—nagging thoughts and doubts. If this is a frequently occurring dream and is accompanied by fear, it would be a good idea to seek therapeutic advice.

RAVEN: See also Bird, Crow. Supposed to mean bad luck, or a messenger of bad luck. At the same time, however, the black bird is a symbol of creativity and femininity. In Germanic mythology, the raven is the bird of death. According to Mohammed, a raven represents sinners.

RAZOR/RAZOR BLADE: Analytical thinking, the need to smooth something out.

RED: A positive color, representing vitality (fire) and activity, love and passion. Red, however, can also be a sign of aggression, rage, and vengeance. According to alchemistic tradition, red is the color of the spirit, of gold, and of the sun. It is a warning of danger. For the Hindus, red means vitality and expansion. For the Mayans, red meant victory and success. For the Chinese, red is the color of luck. In alchemy, red is the color of emotions, of Blood, and Fire. The colors of heaven and hell are red. Red is the color of overwhelming emotional upheaval and in a dream often points to a situation that is packed with intensity.

REDUCTION: See also Telescope. Inferiority complex, devaluing the Self. Taking small things too seriously. Possibly a suggestion to expand your frame of reference, and grow in awareness. See also Lewis Carroll's *Alice in Wonderland.*

REED: Be careful—quagmire and mud. Either it is difficult to get ahead or the reed points to protection; you can hide in the reeds, and you can also cover your roof with them.

REFEREE: This image refers to fairness in contact and dealings with the world and the Self. The image points to the inner, psychic authority of the Self that judges you as well as others. It suggests you take on a more neutral and detached attitude toward life. Observe your own "games" a little more closely.

REFRIGERATOR: Hiding place for physical drives; repression and isolation. What do you want to preserve? Or are you expressing here a need for "staying cool" or for "clarity"?

BARE FACTS

The refrigerator is not only a hiding place for physical drives; it is a hiding place for that dish of congealed, pudding-like toxic matter that you have been too afraid to deal with for the past six months.

REJECTION/REFUSAL: Longing for closeness; or distance. Feeling of social isolation, of being closed off or refusing to face up to something, or refusing to take action. Often, however, the opposite meaning—being accepted, though fearing rejection.

RELATIVE: Usually points to sides of the dreamer himself, such as well-known characteristics and qualities. When a relative is rejected in the dream, a side of yourself is also rejected. According to Freud, sexual organs.

QUICK FIX

Okay, Freud, now you've gone far enough. We have enough problems dealing with our relatives without them representing sexual organs. Give it a rest, Sigmund!

RENT/TENANT: Using something without owning it. Everything we use we must pay for.

REPORT CARD: See also School. Expression of old fears of failure or failure of performance. The dreamer is evaluating his own life, his actions, and his performance. It is either validation and acceptance or a reprimand and criticism.

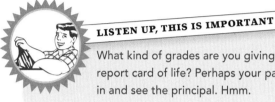

LISTEN UP, THIS IS IMPORTANT

What kind of grades are you giving yourself in the report card of life? Perhaps your parents need to come in and see the principal. Hmm.

REPTILE: See also Snake. According to Freud, male sexual symbol.

RESPONSIBILITY: Are you overtaxed? Do you feel you need more balance and more appropriate tasks?

REST/QUIET: You are usually longing for it.

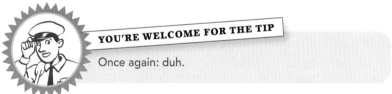

YOU'RE WELCOME FOR THE TIP

Once again: duh.

RESTAURANT: Enjoying contact and communication; but there is also superficiality here. A longing for social contact and diversion. Eating and feeling comfortable in public points to either being open or a lack of a private space.

See also Food, Eating. It is important what type of restaurant and what is happening there. How do you feel being there?

RESURRECTION: Developmental process. Something has to die,
needs to be let go of, as in Ashes, Funeral, and Phoenix. A new beginning, perseverance. For Christians, this image is always connected to
"The Last Judgment" (fear of death, overcoming death).

RETIREMENT HOME: See Harvest. This dream symbol is often connected to an invitation for self-acceptance—to just be, and to pursue
appropriate goals.

REVOLUTION: See King, Government.

REVOLVER: See Pistol.

RHYTHM: Your own vibrations. Rhythm in a dream often has to do with scheduling time. Are you following your own rhythm or are you feeling pressured?

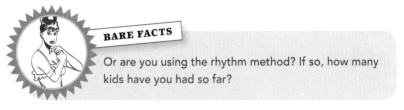

BARE FACTS

Or are you using the rhythm method? If so, how many kids have you had so far?

RIB: According to the Bible and Mohammed, this is the symbol for woman.

RIBBON/TWINE: Connecting, restricting. Also, untangling a situation in one's life, as in ball of yarn.

LISTEN UP, THIS IS IMPORTANT

Possibly domestic pet related. Remember that a cat can make a delightful game out of unraveling a simple ball of twine. And your girlfriend can use up all the memory in your digital camera photographing the stupid thing.

RICE: See Grain.

RIDDLE: Search for an answer, search for freedom.

RIDING/HORSEBACK RIDING: Controlled (reined-in) eroticism and energy, power, and movement.

According to Jung, a symbol for intercourse, especially in women's dreams.

SECRET TIP

A man's dream of bouncing up and down on a horse might be more erotic, except his testicles hurt too much.

RIFLE: The dreamer wants to impress others through power and strength—or may be intimidated by it. Fantasies of omnipotence are a symbol for aggression. It may also be an expression of fear, as in Helmet, Bomb, Bayonet, Shot. By far the most famous sexual symbol in classical psychoanalysis. It retains that meaning to this day.

SECRETS TO MAKE YOU LOOK GOOD

Actually, in classical psychoanalysis, the rifle just got trumped as the most famous sexual symbol by the plasma screen TV.

RIGHT: The masculine side. Being active. The logical and rational side. What is right, correct, fair—in contrast to the left (unfair).

According to Freud, "the normal," in contrast to the left or perverse sexuality. Possibly a political symbol. See Left.

RING: A symbol of commitment or a bond; a symbol of wholeness that points to vanity.

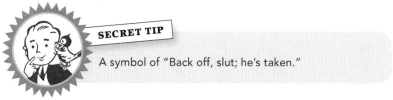

RIOT: Changes and action; fear of political unrest. See also Assassination.

RITUAL: On the surface, it points to habitual behavior, even though rituals are important and bring deeper meaning to life. This symbol can be pointing to something that has become rigid, as well as to something lively and meaningful. See also Rule, Wealth.

RIVAL: Usually the enemy within.

RIVER: Stream, Water. In the stream of life and time, Flowing. A trip on a river often symbolizes your life journey. A raging river predicts difficult obstacles connected to physical urges and bothersome emotions. Pay attention to how the water is moving!

YOU'RE WELCOME FOR THE TIP

Confront your fear of the raging river in your dreams by going on an unguided, level 5 white-water rafting excursion. You will die, and what you're dreaming about will no longer be an issue!

ROAST (AS IN OVEN): You are planning something at work and it has to be successful. Desire for domesticity, as is frequently the case with symbols like Eating, Baking, and Feast. Often an expression of lifestyle and enjoyment. But be careful: Don't let it burn!

SNAP OF THE FINGER

Oh, let it burn, for God's sake! Jeez, every other entry in the book is about wanting to be more impulsive and free. Why not sacrifice one burnt pot roast to the cause? Booyah!

ROBBER: See also Thief/Stealing, Pirate. What has been stolen? Have you been robbed, or are you the robber?

According to Freud, fear of sexuality.

ROBOT: See also Computer. What is missing is a lively spirit. A repressive atmosphere has taken over. On the other hand, a robot is also doing work for us.

BARE FACTS

From what we hear about your sex life, a robot would be a step up.

ROCKET: Courage; fleeing from life and everyday burdens. Sexual symbol. In danger of losing the ground under your feet, or of wanting to lose it.

ROCK MUSIC: Lively, erotic movement. Business, star-cult. Possibly also emancipation of the unconscious and expression of the "wild side" of the dreamer. Who is singing? What song? What message? What emotions?

LISTEN UP, THIS IS IMPORTANT

Here are a few rock song titles and what they mean in your dreams:

"Lucy in the Sky With Diamonds"—Consume fewer mushrooms.

"Suspicious Minds"—You are on the threshold of gaining weight and wearing rhinestone-studded leotards.

"Stairway to Heaven"—There's a bustle, apparently, in your hedgerow.

ROD: Well-known phallic and power symbol (a rod of the chieftain, the magician, the king, or emperor). It points to a search for personal freedom.

The shepherd's rod refers to the responsibility for drives and physical urges. The animals that the shepherd is guarding are the symbol for the animal side. See also Fishing Rod.

RODENT: Usually points to nagging problems. Less often, it points to domesticity and fertility—as with all small animals.

ROOF: Security, protection, head, and intellect. Area of conscious mental activity. We are talking about having "a roof over our heads," and very often "roof" is a metaphor for a higher intellectual capacity. Are you asked to gain more new insights? Roof also stands for the whole House.

QUICK FIX

The roof is the traditional landing point for Santa Claus, who never visited the likes of you because you were always naughty. That and daddy drank the present money away.

ROOF TILE: Security, protection, as in Roof, Gable, and Arch.

ROOM: The room of your soul, the dreamer's inner space.
According to Freud, points to woman.

ROOSTER: Dreaming about masculine vitality. Ever since the Middle Ages, the Buck and Rooster have been considered symbols of lechery, at the same time as they have meant a desire to be taken care of. On the other hand, a symbol for maturity in the sense of awareness and dependability.

COMMUNICATION

This is the only time in the book we can legitimately talk about a cock, so we just decided to go for it.

ROOTS: See also Tree. Being grounded and rooted. Ancestors. Possibly a symbol for a lack of decision and a lack of ego-identity.

ROPE/CABLE: Reliable help that, if received often, is an aid when descending from a tower or a high building. Aid when one is fleeing. But also a symbol for bonding as well as being tied up. Dreams about a rope always have something to do with security, similar to Anchor and Buoy.

BARE FACTS

Indeed, we have all heard the expression "enough rope to hang yourself with" (see below). And that's just what you'll have if those pictures of you being tied up in rope leak onto the Internet.

ROPE/CORD: Obstacle dream; or desiring or needing to connect with somebody/something. Despair (the rope that you hang yourself with, the rope of the gallows).

ROPE (NAUTICAL): See Cord. Connection and security.

ROSARY: Comfort. See also Prayer. Praying the rosary means comfort.

ROSE GARDEN: The garden of the soul, representing great beauty, but also thorns, which represent work. The rose garden is the image for paradise on earth, a place of mystical transformation, magic, and wonder. See also Paradise, Heaven.

ROWING: Heavy work, moving under your own power. See also Ship, Boat.

RUBBER: Smoothness and adaptability.

RUDDER (IN THE SENSE OF STEERING): You need solid direction, a goal. Determination.

RUIN: Pay more attention to your health. Or, the sign of a new emotional beginning—from ruins grows something new.

RULE: Here lies the tension between habitual and pioneering thinking. Are you making up your own rules? Or are you following the rules others have made? Do you follow them or break them?

RULER: Self-determination and self-rule. To be the ruler in your own home. See also Leader, King/Queen.

RUST: Impermanence, a sign of the times. What is rusting?

RYE: See Grain.

SABER: Repressed aggression. According to Freud, it is a male sexual symbol, as are all weapons that penetrate the body.

SADDLE: Being upright and well established (sitting securely "tall in the saddle").

SAFE/SECURITY VAULT: Security. Fearing for the safety of possessions, or being locked up either too tightly or not tightly enough (from the Self and others).

SAILBOAT: You are driven by intellect (the wind) and are carried by Water (emotions).

Often, you are driven by hubris (the beer) and end up plucked from the water (the Coast Guard).

SAILOR/VOYAGER: Male sexuality, restlessness and wanderlust; also adventuresome and immature masculinity.

SALAD: Longing for nature and health. Sometimes also a hint to eat more healthfully.

Also **Salad Bar.** An unlimited supply of salad. Allows you to eat eight times as much as you normally would, thereby defeating the initial reason for eating salad.

SALAMANDER: A magical animal. See also Snake. Symbol of the movement of the unconscious.

SALMON: May be a phallic symbol, but, as with all fish symbols, it usually points to the attitude of the dreamer toward his emotions.

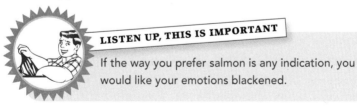

If the way you prefer salmon is any indication, you would like your emotions blackened.

SALOON: See Pub/Saloon.

SALT: Intellectual spice. Grounding ("the salt of the earth").

SALVE: See also Medication. In a dream, also emotional injuries.

SAND: This image represents the transitory—as in the hourglass—and the fear of getting stuck and sinking into the sand. The saying "throw sand in people's eyes" means deception. However, the sandman also throws sand in people's eyes so that they can get a restful night's sleep. In addition, sand also points to the element of earth (in a more delicate form), and in that sense again points to the dreamer being grounded.

In the form of sand on the beach, this image points to vacation and relaxation and, in addition, the gentle waves of emotions that over time smooth out that which is rough and tough (stone). If this dream takes place in a sandbox, your unconscious wants to give you a plan that you can use in your everyday life.

COMMUNICATION

How your unconscious wants you to implement a plan involving plastic shovels and child-size buckets is anyone's guess.

SANITORIUM: The place for health.

SATAN: See also Devil. Symbol for logic, but without a soul. Also undefined nature. An archetypal symbol for darkness, but also a symbol of creativity and resistance.

YOU'RE WELCOME FOR THE TIP

See also **Your Dog**, when he stares like that.

SAUNA: Cleansing, as in Bath and Shower. Openness and eroticism.

SAUSAGE: See also Meat. A phallic symbol, specifically the sausage in the hand of the Fool.

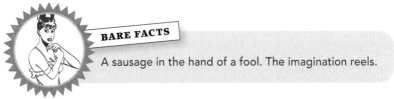

BARE FACTS

A sausage in the hand of a fool. The imagination reels.

SAVINGS: Energies that you can reach back for (in the sense of reserves and inner strength). It might also imply that you are withholding energies that could be put to better use. In addition, savings could mean hoarding as well as keeping a thrifty, good house. At times it might be connected to fear of poverty, as in Asylum and Beggar. However, here it is not so negative, and more like Food and Coins.

SECRETS TO MAKE YOU LOOK GOOD

Maybe you are literally saving someone's life. For example, saving them from drowning, or from a life of crime, or from asking a woman if she's pregnant when she isn't.

SAW: Something drastic is happening. A well-known symbol of differentiation (analysis) and intellectual work. The saw is changing something rough into something more precise that the dreamer then can use. In many instances, this dream image has something to do with willpower that can be used to bring success.

SCAFFOLDING: New beginning, helping yourself, support.

SCALE: Power of judgment. The dreamer's weight in terms of personal influence and significance. Assessment, judgment, balance, and order. Where is the center of your life? What is important? Vocal complaint about life's ambiguity and what is unknown and unclear.

SCAR: Great misfortune and injuries from the past, which can now be overcome.

SNAP OF THE FINGER

Everything that injures our psyche leaves an emotional scar. Here's a fun project you can do at home: Every time someone you love crushes your ego, draw a scar somewhere on your body to illustrate the insult. At the end of the week, whoever has the most unexposed skin wins—or loses, depending on how you look at it!.

SCHEDULE: Working efficiently; order and discipline. Also often refers to the feeling that thoughts and work have become inflexible; you are "caught in a cubby hole mentality" (organizational blindness). See Rhythm.

SCHOOL: Learning, as in School Work and Tests.

SCHOOL WORK: See also Test. Something you still have to do.

SCIENCE: Indicates feeling intellectually or mentally secure. What does knowledge mean to you? What does knowledge do for you? What are you doing with the knowledge you have? See also University, Temple.

LISTEN UP, THIS IS IMPORTANT

Have you made the most of the knowledge you've accumulated in your life? That depends on how many different ways you can say, "Please pull forward."

SCIENTIFIC INSTRUMENT: See Laboratory. On one hand, a place for the unnatural and artificial; on the other, the receptacle for intellect, or the place where connections are made. In alchemy, a reference to the uterus.

SCORPION: Sexual danger, death, and rebirth. In dreams, the scorpion represents a powerful positive symbol for the transformation of vitality, relating to the Phoenix.

But also, the scorpion is considered a negative symbol. Dreaming about one almost always suggests that something old that has caused suffering is being dissolved to make room for something new. The body of the scorpion is very delicate. At the end of its body is a poisonous sting used not only for sudden attack, but also to kill itself. This dream image always refers to life with all its tensions, sufferings, death, and liberation. Are you willing to let go and open yourself up to something new?

SCOUNDREL: Dishonesty, a warning against taking financial risks.

SCREAM: Warning dream. Desperation, but also experiencing and waking, as opposed to the image of Sleep.

SCREEN/MOVIE: The symbol for your inner screen, the soul, which is a mirror of your internal and external situation. You are asked to look at what is playing on the stage of life.

SCREW: Sexual symbol. Here the relation between two people or two situations is emphasized. What has to be connected here? Or, experiencing increasing pressure.

SCULPTOR: Creatively accomplishing something in the face of obstacles. Negative: Shying away from accepting oneself and things as they really are. Maybe fear of not presenting a good "image." Positive: You are working to get to the core of things and to find the essence of yourself.

SCYTHE: Ability to achieve. Harvest, aggression, and Death.

SEA: See also Ocean. Is the sea calm or stormy? What are the weather conditions? Sometimes a symbol of obstacles.

SEAL: "Under the seal of secrecy"; or, you are locking up something, closing off something (usually yourself). You are taking yourself very seriously.

SECRET TIP

We also have the animal seal, which can balance a ball on its nose. Dreams of this nature may indicate a desire for balance in your own life—or a desire for that stud in the khaki shorts who does the seal show at the aquarium. Rrrowrr.

SEAT: Resting and relaxing. Whatever you do, take your time.

SECOND STORY/SECOND FLOOR: See also Attic, House. Awareness and perspective. A frequent symbol when your life is too one-sided and you are engaged intellectually either too much or too little. According to Jung, the intellectual area and consciousness are challenged.

SECRETS: Denial of the truth or, just as likely, a hint that we also need our own secrets.

COMMUNICATION

We're not supposed to tell you anything about this one.

SEED: Psychic energy, creativity, and productivity. See also Rain.

SERPENT, COSMIC: In the lore of many cultures, this serpent laid the eggs out of which the cosmos grew. It points to the unconscious and the need to organize energies. Here the dreamer is made aware of the importance of life's energies and vitality (the Kundalini "serpent"), and suggests that the dreamer pay more attention to physical drives and urges.

The Indian god Vishnu, after having concluded the creation of the world, rests on the back of the cosmic serpent and watches over the preservation of the cosmos.

LISTEN UP, THIS IS IMPORTANT

That Vishnu was wack, homies.

SERVANT: As in Chauffeur, points to the fact that either you must be more humble or orderliness is lacking. Symbol of one's own reason and intellect; or a sign of laziness.

SEVEN: A holy number that connects the masculine with the feminine, since it is a rational number (masculine), which is needed to explain the irrational number pi (female) as $^{22}/_7$.

According to Jung, seven always characterizes time.

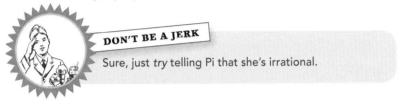

DON'T BE A JERK

Sure, just *try* telling Pi that she's irrational.

SEWAGE/WASTE: Going with the flow, but there is a certain amount of stain connected to it, in contrast to the image of Brook, River. Often a symbol for the shadow or underworld (as in underground sewage pipes). Need for cleansing (see Toilet). It may also be a sign of concern for the environment (see also Environmental Pollution).

SEWING: Fertility, growth, emotional and intellectual maturity. Traditionally, sewing symbolizes intercourse.

SNAP OF THE FINGER

Even *sewing* symbolizes intercourse? Well, darn my socks, baby!

SEXUALITY: Often unfulfilled desires. Generally, a symbol of meaningful contact and development of Self. The male animus and the female anima are what the dreamer needs or wants to be connected with. Sexuality in dreams often refers to the secrets of life, such as birth, marriage, death (also life and the Devil). One of the strongest symbols of creativity.

SECRETS TO MAKE YOU LOOK GOOD

Animus, anima, whatever. As long as it's in a thong.

SHACKLES: Usually points to a situation at work or with your partner. You are bound to something or somebody and are unhappy about it. On the other hand, shackles also hold something together, keeping you from running away immediately.

SHAFT/WELL: A symbol of the level of the unconscious, and for descending into the world of the mothers and the past, into one's own darkness. A vaginal symbol, according to Freud.

COMMUNICATION

No matter what Freud said about Shaft, he is, ultimately, a complicated man who no one understands but his woman.

SHARES (STOCKS): See also Bank, Money. Are you taking too many risks? Are you looking for great riches and easy money? Are you looking for security (See also Family, and Sidewalk) that is not necessarily available? Or do you want to be part of something? What is it that you want to (or feel you should) be part of?

SHARK: Vitality and aggression, brutal violence. Projections of all kinds of fears (as in the devastating film *Jaws*).

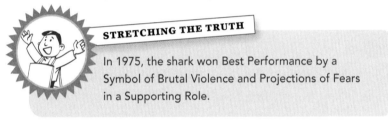

STRETCHING THE TRUTH

In 1975, the shark won Best Performance by a Symbol of Brutal Violence and Projections of Fears in a Supporting Role.

SHAWL: Warmth, protection, and deep devotion.

SHEEP: Patience, stupidity, romanticism about the country, but also devotion and innocence. The Wool of the sheep refers to warmth, protection, and the need for loving care. See Lamb.

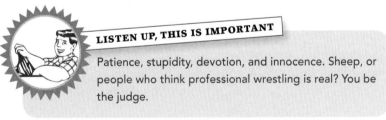

LISTEN UP, THIS IS IMPORTANT

Patience, stupidity, devotion, and innocence. Sheep, or people who think professional wrestling is real? You be the judge.

SHELF: Storing. You are hanging too much on something.

318

SHELL/SKIN: Superficial and tough, but something soft is hidden underneath the toughness. See also Person.

SHIELD (PROTECTIVE): Protection. Something behind which one can move freely and organize an attack. It is also a place to which the soul can retreat.

SHIP: See also Boat. If you are in the boat, you need to rethink the direction you are taking. A distancing from emotions: you are not in touch with the Water. Also, if the ship is far in the distance, a longing for femininity. Different types of ships characterize your personality.

According to the Koran and the Bible, the ship is a symbol of rescue. According to Freud, it is a symbol for woman.

STRETCHING THE TRUTH

Indeed, seafaring men always refer to their vessel as "she." Many longtime ship captains have even reported that their ships could stand to lose a little weight on the starboard side.

SHIRT: The image that you project to the outside world—how you would like to be seen. This often indicates your economic state—the garment you wear when you're dead and being laid out; or losing your shirt—meaning all you had left has been taken away.

Combat your fear of dreaming about the shirt you will wear when you are dead, by picking out the shirt you would like to wear when you are dead and sleeping in it each night. One day, fate will make good on your advance planning.

SHOE: Being grounded and protected against the powers of the earth. It also points to the place where the dreamer is standing.

According to Freud: putting on a shoe symbolizes a sexual act. Compare this to River.

SHOEMAKER: See also Shoe. Being grounded.

SHOOTING: On one hand, a reference to your setting your sights on a goal. Are you meeting your goal? On the other hand, aggression and a hunter's instinct. See also Arrow, Pistol.

SHOOTING (MURDER): Something is being killed (violently): a relationship, an emotion, an unused talent, or any number of things. On the other hand, just as often, it may mean a courageous act of liberation that is freeing emotional energies. A frequent dream symbol to have at the end of a depressive phase, because now, after being liberated, you can search for a new beginning. Such dreams always set in motion something symbolic and by no means refer to the real danger of death.

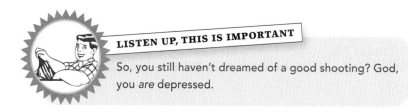

SHOP: The place of the emotional, spiritual, and libidinal work of creativity and production where energies are mobilized, where things are exchanged. You want to be served and choose the right thing. Can you serve yourself? Serving oneself always refers to self-sufficiency. Are you buying or are you selling?

According to Jung, this is the place where you get something that you don't have and that you have to pay for. See also Businessman, Cash Register.

SHORE: "Land in sight," and everything will be better soon. The shoreline is the seam between land and water and, in that sense, the connection between body and soul.

SHORELINE: The intellect that guides and thereby limits emotions, in contrast to Water, the emotions. The shore is sometimes the image of the outside reality, while water represents the emotional reality. What condition is the shoreline in? Reaching a new shore often represents new insights.

SHOVEL: Repressed feelings or memories need to be uncovered; something needs to be remembered; it is necessary to do some work.

YOU'RE WELCOME FOR THE TIP

The shovel also enters into college dreams, particularly final exam essay questions, in which breaking out the shovel is usually a necessity.

SHOWER: Desire for cleanliness, as in Bath, Soap, Sauna, but the sense of not being clean is not as negative as in Abortion, Abscess, or Sewage/Waste. It is more a desire to gain new energy and more zip (emotional rejuvenation). Relaxation.

See also Rain, Fear.

SHRINKING: A frequent symbol when the dreamer is feeling inferior. As in the story of *Alice in Wonderland*, shrinking means entering a new reality. A suggestion to become smaller.

SIBLINGS: All are different parts of self. According to Freud, this is very often a symbol for genitals. Older siblings, according to Jung, point to more developed parts of the self, that which is wanted and admired.

SICKLE: See Scythe, Moon.

SICKNESS: See Illness.

SIDEWALK: Almost always indicates security that one is longing for in order to get ahead, as in Shares, Bureaucrat.

SIEGE: Confinement and narrowness, as in Amber, Trap, Elevator, Village, Cage. Fear of war, as in Bayonet, Shot, and, more specifically, Atom Bomb. What reserves are at your disposal during the time of siege?

SIEVE: Something is draining away, but what counts remains.

SIGN/NAMEPLATE/ADVERTISEMENT: The meaning of the image depends a great deal on what is written or depicted on the sign. If there are names on the sign, pay attention to the writing: small letters, elegantly written letters, ornate letters, or letters written in color. If the sign has a picture, look up its meaning.

SIGNAL: Advice and help.

SIGNATURE: If it is about the dreamer's own signature, it points to his identity. What was signed and what effect did the signature have? If it is the signature of somebody else, get to know that person better.

SIGNPOST/CROSSROADS: The crossroads is a place where one must decide which way to go. It points out to the dreamer which road should be taken in life. See Cross, Fork (as in fork in the road), Division.

SILK: Ruler; well-being and luxury. See Caterpillar.

SILVER: See Metal. Emotions, a symbol of the moon and femininity.

SINGING: Emotional release, peaceful times, harmony, balance, and unburdening.

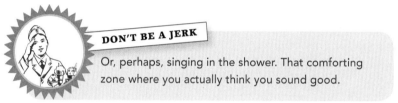

DON'T BE A JERK

Or, perhaps, singing in the shower. That comforting zone where you actually think you sound good.

SINKING: Fear of sinking into the world of the emotions and/or instincts that need to be dealt with. An opportunity for self-knowledge. See Submarine, Swamp, Diving.

SIX: Usually a symbol of sexuality.

SKELETON: Clear thinking, lack of emotion, asceticism, and death.

SKI/SKIING: You are doing well, everything in life is going smoothly.

COMMUNICATION

Clearly, this dream was analyzed by someone who has never actually *been* skiing. (See also **Knee Surgery, Torn Rotator Cuff.**)

SKIN: As a mirror of the soul, the skin points to the state of the dreamer's nerves and emotional condition. Isolation from the world around you. A person's protection.

SKIN RASH: Emotional tension, repressed urges, and aggression. The external and internal states are out of balance. The boundaries to the outside world are not intact.

SECRET TIP

Plus, everybody thinks you got it doing something funky.

SKIRT: See Clothing.

SKULL: A reminder of Death and the meaning of life. This symbol often points to a feeling of spiritual emptiness. On the other hand, it also addresses the shape, structure, and essence of spirituality and, in that sense, of life itself. (See the skull of Yorick in *Hamlet*.)

SKYSCRAPER/HIGH-RISE: Usually the same as House. Great perspective, loss of restraint, individuality—but also elevation.

SLAP IN THE FACE: Carelessness, punishment, and lack of appreciation.

SNAP OF THE FINGER

Or, pleasure, if you're into that sort of thing.

SLAUGHTERHOUSE/BUTCHER: A place where your animal side is killed. The symbolic meaning of the animal being slaughtered is important.

STRETCHING THE TRUTH

One test subject dreamed of his animal side being killed in a slaughterhouse, and when he woke up, his Hummer was gone.

SLAVE: Dependency.

SLED: The image of letting go with abandon, in a positive sense, as in Brook, Leaf, Parachute, and in part also in Flying. It might also express aggression.

SLEEP: Something important is not being understood. A lack of clarity and consciousness, avoidance of problems. The need for rest.

SLIPPERS: Domesticity in all its different meanings. Sluggishness and insecurity.

According to Freud, female genitals. See also Shoe.

SLIPPING: Behaving badly or not being centered. Fear of falling (due to lack of attentiveness), or a desire to have "a slip," to *want* to behave badly. Not behaving like everybody else but rather finding one's own way of being. Have courage to live according to your beliefs. See also Fool.

Falling suddenly in a dream often happens when there is too little or (rarely) too much humility.

SMELL: See also Fragrance. A bad odor symbolizes aversion ("I can't stand the smell of ____"). Pleasant smells symbolize affection. Furthermore, the expression "having a nose for news" may play a role in this image, pointing to the fact that either you can trust your intuition (do you "smell a rat"?) or you should trust more.

SMITH/BLACKSMITH: A symbol for great misfortune or stroke of fate; or of becoming the master of transformation. See also Anvil.

SMOKE: Something dark; but also something light rising out of your unconscious. Where there is smoke there is Fire, transformative power that comes through your energy. Dissipating smoke indicates relaxation.

SMOKING: A frequent dream symbol when the dreamer has stopped smoking. Otherwise see also Smoke.

STRETCHING THE TRUTH

Recent studies reveal that even more harmful than the smoking dream is the secondhand-smoke dream. This is the reason that nobody smokes in dream bars and restaurants anymore.

SNAIL: Retreat, being overly sensitive, inhibition and lack of contact. This dream symbol appears often when one's shyness collides with the desire for an energetic lifestyle. Are you facing risks with courage? Or retreating into your shell? This dream symbol is also a challenge to make life a little easier and to follow your own Rhythm. According to Freud, a sexual symbol.

COMMUNICATION

The snail is, of course, trying to get you to slow down. So that, like them, people can step on you, squish you, and kill you. Well, that's one interpretation, anyway.

SNAKE/SERPENT: See also Poisonous Snake. More than anything else, this is a symbol of fear. It is also often a sexual symbol, and a symbol of wholeness, transformation, and rebirth. A symbol of the dark feminine and deception, it also represents wisdom and cunning. Almost every woman dreams about serpents at least once in her life, which could mean fear of a rival or of the male gender. The serpent stands for physical drives. If something is not right in that area, snake dreams appear. The image of the serpent may also refer to the "water of life," since it comes from inside the earth where the healing springs originate. The Caduceus, the staff of Aesculapius, a symbol of the healing arts, shows two serpents winding around it. In the sacred temple of Aesculapius, serpents crawled on the floor of the sleeping halls. They were said to induce healing dreams.

According to second-century dream interpreter Artemidorus, dreaming about serpents indicates healing and the return to vitality. It is also a symbol of immortality (shedding of the skin—rebirth). The "Midgard-serpent" and the "Ferris wolf" in Norse mythology threaten the gods as the world comes to an end.

The serpent is also the symbol for secret wisdom and the revelation of the hidden. Snakes are quick, attracted by fire and the birth of energy. A snake steals from Gilgamesh (hero of the Sumerian epic) the herb of immortality, while he is taking a bath in a pond. In Greece, Gaia, the goddess of the earth, produces two half-serpents called Titans, who do battle with Zeus. For the Gnostics of late antiquity, the serpent symbolized the dark, deep, and unfathomable side of God. The serpent is also a symbol of Kundalini (the yogic life force). In ancient Greece, serpents were even honored publicly, because they were believed to be ghosts of the dead.

Snakes appear suddenly, out of the unknown, creating fear. It is impossible to have a meaningful communication with them; they are secretive and fear inducing, as is the unconscious. Their poison is sin, their wisdom transformation and deliverance. According to Early Christian imagination, when a snake was attacked, it would only protect its head.

According to Freud, a phallic symbol. According to Jung, the image of the snake means that something important is taking place in our unconscious; it may be dangerous or healing.

STRETCHING THE TRUTH

Obviously, there are as many meanings of the snake in history as there are ancient civilizations. The most intriguing is that of the ancient Greeks, who saw snakes as the ghosts of the dead. In more modern mythology, snakes represent only the ghosts of dead lawyers, specifically the ones who advertised on television.

SNOW/SNOWING: See also Ice, Cold. Emotional coldness, feeling of security, but also punishment, Virgin. White snow also symbolizes the Leaf of innocence. Customary and sharp distinctions lose their significance; the snow turns everything soft and white. In that sense it points to liberation from conventional attitudes and to a new orientation.

YOU'RE WELCOME FOR THE TIP

Snow is a term for the static image on a television—or, what you know as the first thing you see when you wake up from your bender.

SNOWMAN: See also Snow. Either emotional coldness or playfulness.

SOAP: Symbol for cleanliness, as in Bath, Shower, and Sauna.

SOCCER: See Football.

BARE FACTS

Could be a sign of something that will never quite catch on in America.

SOLARIUM: See Light. Devotion, warmth, and relaxation.

SOLDIER: Aggression, but also camaraderie. If a man dreams about a soldier, it often expresses a longing for connection with other men. See Military Duty, War.

SON: This image refers either to the actual son, or to future ideas, creativity, and something new. The son, according to Jung, is the absolute substitute for the father, guaranteeing the immortality of the father. Also, pay attention to the similarities between the words "son" and "sun."

SNAP OF THE FINGER

And for heaven's sake, if you're going to be with your son for very long, wear your *sonblock*.

SONG: Happiness. The text of the song is important.

SOUP: Whatever you have cooked up you must and should be allowed to eat. This is a reference to consequences. What we have "cooked up" is composed of what we have created through our actions, influenced by emotions.

Soup is also a symbol of strength and nutrition. The soup pot is a symbol of fusion and integration. See also Kitchen.

SOWING: Well-known sexual dream in the widest sense —the urge to impregnate or be impregnated. The need to accomplish something. It frequently appears when the dreamer is feeling unproductive. May also be interpreted as a longing for a simple life in the country.

SECRETS TO MAKE YOU LOOK GOOD

Ah, the simple life in the country, where decent people can have sexual dreams in the wildest sense, where ordinary folk can have the urge to impregnate or be impregnated, and ain't nobody gonna know about it for miles around.

SPACE: Inner space.

SPADE: Sexual meaning; attempted grounding.

SPARK: See Fire, Flames. The so-called spark of the soul, the divine in us.

SPARKLING WINE: See Champagne.

DON'T BE A JERK

There again, comparing the two is just plain insulting.

SPARROW: Secrets that are being given away. See also Bird.

SPECIALIST: Estrangement; intellect, but also stature. This symbol warns against one-sidedness of emotions and spirit. It is often a suggestion to become a specialist in your own important matters.

SPEECH: Emotions and/or needs are vocalized. The content of your soul is made conscious, expressed, and vocalized to the people around you. The content of the speech is important.

SPEECH (GIVING A): A need to communicate, get somebody's ear, convince somebody. Usually a sign that you are justified in expecting recognition. Fear of appearing in public or public speaking. Wanting to arrive and be liked (see Applause, Approval). If a politician is giving the speech, it—almost without fail—is about lying and egotism.

SPEED: A typical symbol of stress. Take more time, or move faster in order to take advantage of your chance. However, it seems that stress can also be overcome with speed.

SPHINX: That which is mysterious. It was Oedipus, the hero, who solved the riddle of the Sphinx.

SECRET TIP

Yeah, and we all know what Oedipus got up to in his spare time.

SPICES: Sharpness, in the sense of intellect and wisdom. Emotional irritability, but also extravagance and finesse.

SPIDER: The image of an aesthetic or artistic person. One's own dark side. Intrigues are planned. In a woman's dream, indicates conflicts with the mother.

According to Freud, the fertile mother or fear of mother incest.

SECRETS TO MAKE YOU LOOK GOOD

In certain cultures, the spider represents that which weaved a place into existence—which would go a long way to explaining the street plan in Boston.

SPIDER WEB: A certain subject has to be approached with great care. You are feeling trapped.

SPINE: The support that brings everything back into order. Honesty and civil courage. See also Stairs, Tower, Skyscraper/High-Rise.

SPIRAL: Emotional dynamics and development.

SPIT: You ought to spit out something, or has something overwhelmed you?

DON'T BE A JERK

Or are you just a disgusting pig in your dreams, too?

SPLINTER: Are you feeling injured? Inconsequential things are getting you upset. (In the Bible, one often sees a splinter in the eye of a neighbor, but not in one's own.)

SPONGE: See also Water. Squeezing out and soaking up. Let go of something.

SPORTS: Ambition, performance, and physicality. In a dream it is often a suggestion to be more playful in everything you do; or are you taking things too lightly?

LISTEN UP, THIS IS IMPORTANT

Hey, guys, painting yourselves blue and/or waving foam-rubber fingers ain't exactly taking things lightly.

SPRING (SEASON): Generally well-known symbol for virility, fruitfulness, and Youth. Easter.

SPRING (WATER): Symbol of fertility. In fairy tales it also symbolizes virginity—the dreamer's emotional energies. Positive psychic energies, dedication. Expressing purity. Fairy tales and myths also tell about clouded and poisoned springs; in that case, go back to the origin of the problem and work with your karma in order to clean up old burdens. See also Water, Bath.

COMMUNICATION

Could also be a symbol of bottled water, and your frustration at paying two bucks for what is probably tap water with a mountain on the label.

SPY: See Agent, Detective.

SQUARE: A symbol of wholeness. You are on the path of individuation and self-awareness. You are grounded and emotionally balanced. The idea of being grounded was particularly emphasized by Plato, who considered the square the original symbol of Earth, since the angles of the square are an expression of permanence, in the sense of its structural shape.

SQUIRREL: Fast, shy, smart animal that symbolizes ideas, plans, and hope. Longing to be in nature.

BARE FACTS

Could well be a symbol of your family coming to visit for Christmas, as in you're gathering nuts for the winter.

STAB: See Needle, Sting.

STABBING: Shooting, Murder. Clearly there is a sexual component here, since it points to penetrating (the skin), Thorns, and Blood. The sting, as in the fairy tales "Sleeping Beauty" and "Snow White," points to the awakening of consciousness. One is opening oneself and something of oneself (blood) flows out. Such a dream often points to the dreamer having been injured. Where is your wound? Could you protect yourself from injuries? Were you stabbed or did you stab someone? How did it happen? From the front, in the back? As is the case with Shooting, this dream is also a symbolic reference to your inner strength, and never has anything to do with a real danger to your life.

SNAP OF THE FINGER

So pay no attention to those times you've woken up to find your spouse straddling you and holding an ice pick.

STAGE: Points to an important position at work or position in life. A desire to be more in the limelight, as in Arena. Are you outgoing? Do you share of yourself? What role have you played, or what mask have you been hiding behind? What piece have you forgotten?

STAINS/SPOTS: Dark spots in the soul, being soiled and feeling guilty. Often combined with being embarrassed. There are also "erotic" spots, which, however, appear seldom.

STAIRS/SPIRAL STAIRCASE: Changes and transformation start from below (the unconscious) and come to the surface (consciousness), or vice versa. A frequent symbol in fairy tales and movies, suggesting personal growth. The landings in a staircase correspond to the dreamer's energy centers (the chakras). Are you going up the stairs or coming down? According to Freud, going up symbolizes sexual union.

STALL: An image of one's drives that have become domesticated.

YOU'RE WELCOME FOR THE TIP

Also bathroom stall, where men who are traumatized by the urinal experience can get a little much-needed privacy.

STALLION: Horse. Increase in strength, but also taming one's own strength.

According to Freud, a symbol of sexuality, particularly of repressed drives in men and women.

STAMP (AS IN RUBBER STAMP): Putting your stamp on something. Desiring a higher position.

STAMP (LETTER): The value of communicating with the outside world. The value is important, as well as what is depicted on it.

STANDARD: Which flag did you see? Under which flag did you join? The way the flag acts in the wind might possibly be a hint about your sex life.

STAR: See also Light. The inner core, the image of guidance and hope. In dreams and fairy tales, this is always connected with the fate of the hero (he was "born under a good/bad star"). Just like the hero, you are following your star, or your inner desires and longings in order that life may be bright and shiny. To follow your star means to be clear and to know your own needs. Following your own desires, longings, and needs presupposes the courage to be unconventional, which in turn will bring about new insights and a more fulfilled life.

When the sun—the symbol of consciousness—has gone down, stars appear in the heavens, so in a real sense stars are the "light" in the darkness.

According to an old Native American dream interpretation: illness.

A falling star in a dream means birth. A star often points to the birth of an important person.

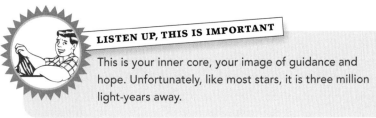

STATUE: Who does the statue represent? If necessary, look in the encyclopedia to get information on the personage. Or is it a representation of yourself? In that case, this symbol is a warning about an addiction to approval and self-elevation.

STEALING: Greed and dissatisfaction.

STEEL: See also Metal. Toughness ("hard as steel"), determination, and will.

STEERING WHEEL: Independence and determination.

STEP: Something new is arriving. A Threshold (obstacles) that needs to be overcome. Usually a sign of growth. See also Heel, Stairs.

STEPS (STAIRS): Reaching a stage of advancement—social and conscious. Often, stopping in order to gain a better view. Stairs also represent an interim stage between above and below—between head and belly, emotions and intellect, heaven and earth.

COMMUNICATION

Or, in the case of a fifth floor walk-up, between normal breathing and an impending heart attack.

STEP/TREAD: Fear of social decline, opponents, and enemies.

STING: The sting in our flesh symbolizes obstacles in our life that need to be removed, or may be a symbol of our desires. Other than that, the meaning is similar to Splinter and Rose (with thorns).

STOCK MARKET: Risky business; you are speculating about something where the outcome is unsure. "Have-mode" according to Fromm, as in Auction, Loot, Attaché Case, Shares; usually refers to your finances.

YOU'RE WELCOME FOR THE TIP

You might dream you are on the floor of the New York Stock Exchange—which is where the bastards threw you after they chewed you up and spit you out.

STOCKING: Being grounded. In rare instances, may also have a sexual meaning (particularly putting on a stocking).

STOMACH/STOMACH ILLNESS: First, make sure that there are no real physical symptoms. If not, this symbol may be pointing to the ability to digest and to metabolize, to be receptive, and to deal with intellectual and emotional "food."

A full stomach points to overstimulation and too much consumption. An empty stomach is an indication of hunger; you feel shortchanged.

QUICK FIX

A not quite full enough stomach is an indication of having eaten Chinese food an hour ago.

STONE: Merciless, tough ("a heart of stone"); durability.

STONE/CLAY (FLOOR): Points to the necessity of becoming more grounded, but at the same time it is what separates us from the "naked" earth.

According to Jung, it expresses darkness, as in Forest.

STOOL: Elevation, as in podium, but also unsafe seat. You need more security, support, and grounding.

COMMUNICATION

To step on a stool is to step in a place of icky.

STORAGE ROOM: See also Food (Stored) and Closet. Here your energy reserves, your potential and unused abilities are being addressed. Pay attention to what is stored and what the individual items might symbolize.

STORK: Emotional strength, desire for family. Legend has it that it is the stork who "delivers" babies. It is also said that the stork never leaves its nest. According to Christian symbolism, the stork is the one who foretells the return of the Lord.

SECRET TIP

Comforting to know that the stork foretells the return of the Lord. We thought it was that guy on TV with the bad rug that's always asking people for money.

STORM: See also Hurricane, Wind. An obstacle dream or possibly a symbol of breaking out, being liberated from or through intellectual efforts. Storm of emotions. Try to be either more or less emotional.

STRANGER: Something new is announced. The image can also point to the shadow (the stranger within), rejected or unknown characteristics in yourself that you don't want to see.

STRANGULATION: Something is denying you the room to breathe; something has got you by the throat. "Spit out whatever is sticking in your throat," which means look at what is bothering you and get rid of it. Don't panic about this dream. The dream is giving you a chance to see what is holding you back!

SNAP OF THE FINGER

You might even be strangling yourself, a signal that it is you who is denying yourself the room to breathe. Thank you, that'll be $125, please.

STRAW: Troublesome work or difficulties. Also refers to bed and camp/cot (in the past consisting of fresh straw or mattresses stuffed with straw).

STRAWBERRY: Sexual symbol (like nipple). Marriage, becoming a mother, summer fun.

STREET/SIDEWALK/PATH: Life's path. What is happening on the street is normal and available to everybody. Important is the condition of the street and possibly the direction in which you are walking. Who or what are you meeting on the street? What is your destination? Intersections symbolize decisions, street signs are an aid in finding direction.

According to Freud, sexual organs. According to Jung, the collective world of awareness.

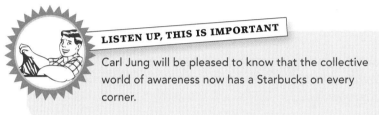

LISTEN UP, THIS IS IMPORTANT

Carl Jung will be pleased to know that the collective world of awareness now has a Starbucks on every corner.

STREET CAR/TROLLEY: As in Train. A symbol of collective forward movement. Do you need a trolley right now in order to get ahead?

STRETCHER: Symbol for resting, particularly during times of stress. Support and help, but also fear of an accident or death.

STRING: See Ribbon.

STRIPPING (CLOTHES): Being open and refraining from pretense, as in Bareness, Naked. Enjoying fully the sensuous beauty of yourself or somebody else. Do you want, no matter what the subject actually is, to bare yourself? A warning against lack of boundaries and being insolent. Shedding clothes, according to Jung, is always the shedding of parts of ourselves. See also Amputation.

STUMBLING: Something is out of order—a dream of obstacles or the opposite: you have found a new order, meaning that you have lost your customary rhythm.

SUBMARINE: Wanting to hide and look at the world from the emotional side (Water). It suggests regression and a weak ego, or being submerged in oceanic feelings and being powerless over them. Even in the presence of great emotional turmoil, maneuverability is still intact. See Diving.

SUBURBS: Not being quite inside and not quite outside. Boredom.

SUCCESS: Do you want to be successful?

SUFFERING: Fear of suffering and illness. Such dreams usually offer constructive advice on how to transcend the suffering in your life.

SUFFOCATING: First determine if you had a real breathing problem while you slept—a cold, for example. Were you feeling emotionally constricted? Were you bothered by unspoken and ambiguous thoughts that took your breath away and which you denied, creating tension and stress? Here it is not a question of your being in danger of your life, but rather a desire to get more Air, as a symbolic expression for more intellect and greater mental clarity.

SUGAR: Though sugar in a dream usually is not sweet, still you would like to sweeten your life.

SECRET TIP

Not that this is much healthier than the high-fructose corn syrup dream.

SUIT: The rigid, conventional side. Initiation into manhood. Wanting to amount to something in life. The persona in the Jungian sense (that which is presented to the outside) in contrast to Naked.

COMMUNICATION

Initiation into manhood, perhaps. Although if that suit you wore to your confirmation or bar mitzvah is any indication, more like an initiation into dorkhood.

SUITCASE: Container, Luggage. Burden and problems that you carry around with you; but also a reservoir of abilities and talents. Very important here is the weight of the suitcase. A heavy suitcase usually symbolizes unsolved tasks, unused talents, and similar burdens. A light suitcase is a symbol of talents and abilities that are being used.

According to Freud, it refers to the female body, as in Oven.

SUMMER: See also Sun. Energy, vitality, and success.

SUMMIT: The achievement of higher consciousness, spirituality or a case of arrogance, career ambition, and lack of humility. What do you believe is your calling? What is the price you are willing to pay for achievements? In addition, it is also a connection to your inner center (and to God). Are you taking time for yourself? It represents the growth and maturity you have set as a life goal. Also, fear of depth and confrontation.

SNAP OF THE FINGER

Try to preserve the memory of your ascent to the summit in your dream by finding some gullible tourist to take your picture.

SUN: See also Summer. Creative energy. If the sun is shining in your dream, it always refers to consciousness. If the sun does not shine, you are approaching either the unconscious or a loss of energy. The sun equals the father, midlife, the danger of being dazzled.

SUNDAY: Rest.

SUPERIOR: The mirror or image of the dreamer's own tension over what life is presenting, tasks that are assigned. See also Chief.

SUPERMAN: Comic book characters and those from science fiction and Westerns are modern symbols for the Hero. They often, however, also express immature masculinity, delusions of grandeur, and being all-powerful in situations where they are surely powerless. This dream image is about the antiquated ideals and unfulfilled goals of the dreamer.

SECRET TIP

Recent studies provide a simpler explanation. A Superman dream is merely an expression of your repressed desire to wear your underwear on the outside.

SUPERVISOR: Order and discipline, as in Office. Restriction, male authority; can also mean negative masculinity. Pressure at work, but also having a good perspective/overview.

SURF: Accumulated urges, as in Fire, but with a more intense emotional depth (Water). Waves of emotion, but also vacation and experiencing nature. In most cases, the surf is a surging soul that is expressed through the force of nature, but it can also address oceanic feelings that you are afraid of or longing for.

SURFING/RIDING THE WAVES: Being carried away by emotions (Water), being transported by and giving in to the existing Rhythm. Here the power of the Winds, as well as the intellect, is used for moving forward. This is an expression of fear about going under, in the sense that the Head would be submerged under Water (similar to fear of emotional chaos, as in Swamp). This is also a sexual and virility symbol ("Surfers do it standing up"). See also Captain, Admiral, Sailboat.

STRETCHING THE TRUTH

Most surfer dream subjects report a totally tubular experience with some awesome ten-foot breakers, only to awaken with a start and find that their mellow has been completely harshed.

SURGEON: By cutting off (forgetting) something, something needs to be healed. Being saved in times of distress.

Authority, often the male hero; or appearing in a dream of a contemporary woman, the limitations of the hero.

SWALLOW: Domestic bliss and Spring, announcing the end of winter. Great speed and mobility. According to *Physiologus*, the most widely read book of the Middle Ages, the swallow reproduces only once and possesses great knowledge about herbs.

SWAMP: See also Moor. Being stuck, afraid of being trapped in the unconscious. Fear of emotions, of being "devoured back into the feminine." This means that the masculine side in the man and the woman (animus) fears that consciousness—fought hard for—will be sucked up by the vortex of emotions. Expressed here is the desire for and fear of emotional chaos.

SWAN: Swans are a symbol for family. They mate for life and raise their young together. Intellectual interests, idealism. A symbol of beauty.

According to Celtic tradition, swans and geese were considered messengers from another world and for that reason were not used as food.

The black swan is a messenger of bad luck or death.

YOU'RE WELCOME FOR THE TIP

Remember, too, the ugly duckling, who did not know what a beautiful swan he really was. Nice story, but hardly applicable to the harsh realities of daily life. Your precious ugly duckling would be broken on the wheel of low self-esteem before you could say "propaganda."

SWEAT: Trouble and work, but also success.

SWEETS: Sensual pleasures, according to Freud. Often sexual pleasures; at least, desire for love. See Paradise.

SWIMMING: See also Water. Relaxation, the world of feelings. It is often connected to liberation. Where does the swimming taking place; what is the condition of the water? According to Freud; urine and the life of the unborn. Also, a symbol of pollution.

COMMUNICATION

Freud must have spent an awful lot of time in public swimming pools.

SWING: Mood swings; the ups and downs of life—either we give in to them too much or we repress them too much. The symbol of the rhythm of life. Are you being "taken for a ride"?

It may also be connected to memories from your childhood. Playfulness. A sexual symbol.

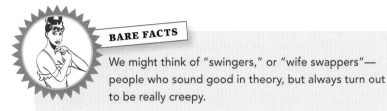

BARE FACTS

We might think of "swingers," or "wife swappers"—people who sound good in theory, but always turn out to be really creepy.

SWITCH: Is the switch turned on or off? That would point to your vitality. It is in your power to regulate and switch things and modes.

SWORD: Appears rarely in dreams. It is a symbol of power and intellect. See Knight. Seeking power, as in Monument and aggression. Frequent symbol for intellectual work since the sword separates and, therefore, leads us to make decisions. We use the sword to fend off somebody and it is, in that sense, a sign of distancing and individualism.

According to Freud, a phallic symbol, as is Knife. In psychoanalysis, separation or fear of separation, as in Good-bye, Abortion, Corpse, Death, Divorce, and Funeral.

SYRINGE: The male sex organ. Fear of a syringe points to sexual inhibitions. At present, the syringe is also a symbol of fear of AIDS, and fear of something intruding on you. Often a hint that you should be more open. If a diabetic dreams of syringes, it could be a message from the inner healer to think about the right dose.

SYRUP: A symbol of everything that is sweet, or everything that is sticky.

COMMUNICATION

Bad dramatic movies are said to be "syrupy" or "sickeningly sweet." We prefer the term "piece of crap."

TABLE: The desire for unencumbered connections to others, or a hint that whatever the connections presently are, you'd do better to accept them. Sticking together and belonging. Also refers to a noble attitude that either is to be adopted or has already been incorporated (Knights of the Round Table). See also Feast, Communion, Restaurant.

TABLE/DESK: See also Furniture. Vitality. The symbol of matter as well as Earth (world). Ancient Egyptian dream interpretation states that a table indicates the arrival of guests, and that they must be entertained lavishly.

According to Freud (as well as the Talmud), it is a symbol for the body of women.

YOU'RE WELCOME FOR THE TIP

Men! Score points with your wife or girlfriend tonight by telling her you had a wonderful romantic dream in which she had a body like a table!

TABLET/PILL: See Medication, Pill. Medicine.

TAIL: Always a sexual symbol, but also symbol of the Devil.

TAILOR: See also Dress, Needle, Thread. The traditional meaning is cunning and being a coward. Vanity, as in Jewelry.

TAKING AN OATH: Suggests you ought to make a decision in a particular situation, or that important responsibilities to yourself are being neglected.

TAKING APART: Excavation. Looking inward, understanding, and analyzing. Often appears as a dream image when living without much thought. Pay attention to what is being taken apart. What do the individual parts look like? See also Puzzle.

TANK: Energy reserve.

TANK/SHELL: An object of war as well as a protective shell, as in the turtle or lobster, for instance. Fear of war, or do you want to get your own way regardless of the consequences? Are you feeling overwhelmed? These are symbols of toughness, of protection of your emotional qualities.

STRETCHING THE TRUTH

Researchers have named the protection of your emotional qualities with an outward shell your "Inner Sherman," after the tank of the same name. We all have an Inner Sherman. Embrace it, love it, give it a hug.

TAPE RECORDER: A suggestion that something has to be recorded (documented) very precisely. See also Ear, Radio.

TAR: This image refers to dependency (it clings) and the dark. See also Black.

TARGET: Focus, the ability to assert yourself.

SECRET TIP

Recent Target dreams involve walking around a fantastical landscape of super low prices and people in red vests called Team Members who roam the aisles with no other purpose than to help you get what you need.

TASTE: The kind of taste determines the symbolic meaning. Taste is what is on the tip of your tongue, what is felt and should be expressed.

TATTOOING/TATTOO: Courage, boldness, and masculinity. To display an eccentric and sensual Self in the skin.

SECRETS TO MAKE YOU LOOK GOOD

The tattoo, once a symbol of boldness and eccentricity, has been demoted as a dream symbol recently. This occurred after the number of high school girls who got a tattoo of a butterfly on their ankle reached 11,212,008. Sorry, now it's 9. Wait, 10. We better go.

TAXI: You are not in charge of your life journey, even though you have chosen the goal.

DON'T BE A JERK

Not in charge of your life journey? In a taxi, you're not even in charge of your *life*.

TEA: Stimulation. Practice patience.

TEACHER: Functioning as an emotional aid. Points to the times when you were in school. The teacher is an archetypal figure of authority. Bad conscience, often connected to sensuality. Teachers are almost always the leaders that guide us into adulthood. This may also be an initiation dream. The inner guide teaching about maturity and self-discipline. On the other hand, there may be the tendency to preach to oneself and to others.

COMMUNICATION

If this dream indicates a tendency to preach to oneself and others, it is usually followed by a dream in which you stay after school and write "I will not preach to myself or others" a hundred times on the blackboard.

TEARS: Similar to Drink. The Water of life is able to flow. It is a sign of solution and resolution. See also Crying.

TEDDY BEAR: Usually an expression of a desire for security and simplicity. A teddy bear may also indicate the desire for children.

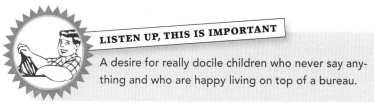

LISTEN UP, THIS IS IMPORTANT

A desire for really docile children who never say anything and who are happy living on top of a bureau.

TEETH/LOSS OF TEETH: Vitality, relatives, friends, and lovers; but this image also has a predatory and destructive side. See also Vampire.

As far back as Greek mythology, teeth were said to refer to children. The reason probably was that, during pregnancy, mothers experienced the rapid loss of their teeth ("Each child will cost you a tooth").

In mythology teeth are considered similar to seed corn, comparable to dragon's blood. In addition, teeth symbolize the oral qualities of the dreamer. The possible reason for this might be an eating and biting urge, or the repression of it. And, last but not least, teeth, like Mouth, are used to take in food. See Beauty, Face, Bones, Bite.

According to Jung and Freud, teeth are often a phallic symbol; according to Freud, dreams about toothaches are considered masturbation dreams.

According to the newest dream research, women often dream about teeth during menopause.

STRETCHING THE TRUTH

What is not addressed above are dreams about flossing. Flossing dreams indicate that even in your damn dream you are stuck doing the most tedious activity on the face of the planet.

TELEGRAM: See also Letter. Something important and urgent.

TELEPHONE: Frequent dream for men, suggesting good connections. It also symbolizes contact with the other side of the self. Important is whether you have reached your party or not. Not reaching the other party could be a sign of difficulty in making/maintaining contact. Once the "busy signal" is removed, the dreamer can improve communication with the outside world. Pay attention to the style of communication, especially in relationships.

COMMUNICATION

The cell phone has introduced an entire new dream lexicon. "Can you hear me now?" indicates that your loved one seeks more communication from you. "Unlimited nights and weekends" reveals the desire for sexual liaison. And "You're breaking up," well, we think you know what that means.

TELESCOPE: Should you take a closer look at something? Or, do you need more distance?

TELEVISION: Openness, enjoying contact, or lack of contact; mindlessness, superficiality, and diversion. Possibly a mirror of the dream.

Searching for orientation. Are you appearing on TV yourself? Or what are you watching? It is important to know what kind of program is running—the program mirrors your mood.

TEMPLE: One of the luckiest symbols, meaning completeness, zest for life, getting ahead, and always finding your way to the center of things. Also a symbol for Mother, and in that case is usually an idealization of mother. See also Priest.

TEN: A new beginning, after having reached the goal. In the Egyptian tarot, the Wheel of Fortune. And a "10" is, of course, the perfect woman.

TENT: Adventure, something momentary and temporary. Wanderlust, wanting a vacation, longing for a more natural life. See also Snake, Home, Roof, Skin.

TERMINATION: 1. In the sense of ending—ending something, or longing to end a relationship or a situation.

2. In the sense of demolition (such as demolishing a house), it points to the need to be aggressive; or fear of aggression. It is usually based on feeling either destructive, disappointed, or both.

Confrontation with Death, if a house is being demolished, similar to Funeral, and Grave. Often it indicates underlying desires that are being repressed, as in Attack, Fire (Surf), and Violence.

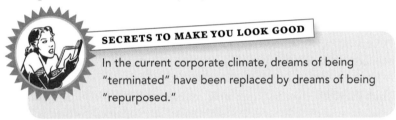

SECRETS TO MAKE YOU LOOK GOOD

In the current corporate climate, dreams of being "terminated" have been replaced by dreams of being "repurposed."

TERRACE/PATIO: Tentatively moving into a new, usually public area, and presenting the Self to the outside world. Relaxation and free time.

TERRORIST: Breaking out of rigidity, necessitating change. See Adventure and Hero, who is dissatisfied with the social situation or who is a social outcast. When images of rebellion and protest appear repeatedly, ask yourself what your goals are. Often in such dreams we are looking for the Leader in us or for a sustaining principle.

THEATER: Take life a little easier and don't be so dramatic. Vanity, and the need for acceptance, but also a symbol of personal dreams and ideals. The theater/stage is in some ways the model world for the dreamer. See also Actor.

SNAP OF THE FINGER

Are you acknowledging your own importance? Are you taking "center stage" in your life? That's fine—unless you have kids, in which case you are in a constant state of realizing you are no longer important and you might as well just sit back and wait for death.

THERMOMETER: This image is always a barometer of the dreamer's moods.

THIEF/STEALING: Fear of loss, particularly in personal relationships, or you want to "steal away" from a relationship. Is something being stolen from you or are you the thief? What is being stolen?

THIRST: Often you actually are thirsty. Restlessness, dream of obstacles. It is important what you are thirsting for; often a sign of emotional longing.

THISTLE: Work, troubles, and fighting. According to second-century dream interpreter Artemidorus: problems and difficulties with a man.

THORNS: See also Spine, Thistle. According to dream interpreter Artemidorus, obstacles and difficulty with a woman.

THREAD: Fleeting ideas, spontaneous thoughts, or making meaningful connections. The red thread of Ariadne (in the Labyrinth) symbolizes life's journey and life itself.

THRESHOLD: Crossing over to something new. Separation. The connection between two or more worlds. See also Step, Buckle, Bridge.

THROAT: Inexhaustible and unquenchable.

THRONE: Desire to rule. Have you elevated yourself to the throne? Are you the heir to the throne or have you been asked to abdicate? Are you the power that stands behind the throne? See also Chair, King/Queen.

THRUSH: As with all Birds, connection between heaven and earth, between the gods and humans. Perspective and overview. According to a medieval interpretation, the thrush in a dream means new acquaintances for women; for men, unexpected affection.

LISTEN UP, THIS IS IMPORTANT

And, for both men and women, thrush droppings making their symbolic way from heaven to earth (more specifically, your shoulder).

THUMB: Indicates male and female productivity (also seen as a symbol of male and female genitals). Symbolic expression of creativity. Often points to the dreamer feeling small. The position of the thumb can mean life or death, as in the fights of gladiators in ancient Rome. According to Freud, sexual urges.

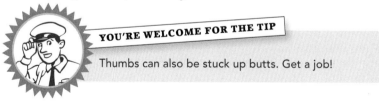

YOU'RE WELCOME FOR THE TIP

Thumbs can also be stuck up butts. Get a job!

THUMB SUCKING: Flight back into childhood. In psychoanalysis, a well-known symbol for masturbation.

THUNDER: See also Lightning. Be more assertive and don't put up with everything. "Let it roar!" The task here is to shape your own personal world. According to the *I Ching*, thunder indicates excitement and, by implication, the firstborn son. According to ancient Egyptian dream interpretation bad news, anger, rage, aggressive emotions. According to Homer, Zeus, the jovial "thunderer."

That which destroys and cleanses. Thunder gives your aggression a voice.

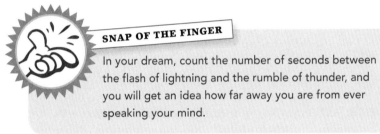

SNAP OF THE FINGER

In your dream, count the number of seconds between the flash of lightning and the rumble of thunder, and you will get an idea how far away you are from ever speaking your mind.

THUNDERSTORM: See Thunder, Storm, Hurricane, Wind.

TICKET: Pleasure of traveling, new plans for your life; changes.

TIE: An emphasis on masculinity. A hint either that you are conceited, or that the Knot on your Neck refers to self-control. Often also a phallic symbol.

TIGER: See also Leopard. An image frequently dreamed by women. Longing for powerful love while, at the same time, also being afraid of the experience. The tiger and the Lion are both symbols of vitality and passion. The tiger is more a symbol of female sexual energy, while the lion is more a symbol of masculine sexual energy. The tiger possesses great energy, and one of its main strengths when it attacks is the surprise factor. It is also the symbol of severe loss. In the Shinto (of ancient Japan), the tiger was considered a holy but people-devouring predator, the personification of horror and fear who stops at nothing. According to Jung, it is also the symbol for female compulsion, as in Cat, Bear, Snake.

COMMUNICATION

People who are aggressive are said to be "tigers." Well, put these cocky bastards into the ring with an actual tiger and see who ends up without a spleen first.

TIME: How you use your time is a hint of your stage of development and your personality. It symbolizes how you organize and plan your life. It is meaningful to know what time period your dream represents—noon or night? Summer or winter? Also the century could be important.

As happens in many dreams, time sometimes seems to stand still (stagnation) or is passing quickly (stress). If time is standing still, it could mean it's time to slow down, to look at something more closely. Time speeding up—as in a time-lapse photo—often symbolizes expanded awareness.

TIN: Nonsense; malleability, of little worth.

TOBACCO: Pleasures (sometimes with regrets), restfulness but also addiction. See also Sweets, Smoke, Fog.

TOES (TIPTOE): Suggests that you become more careful in your present situation. Do you want to perform at the highest level? However, it could also mean that you are not resolute enough and lack wholeness. See also Dance, Thumb, Finger.

TOILET: The zone of the root chakra, where the Kundalini resides. This image may point to the need for relief from bodily urges or from the problems of your life. The suggestion here is to "let go."

From time immemorial, the toilet has been seen as a dark and scary place—in dreams, all places connected to natural functions are demonized. It is the place of forbidden sexuality—self-gratification and homosexuality—a place full of danger and frightening activities. It is a place where ghosts and devils do their bad deeds, and the reason why toilets in the past were always outside. It is a place of taboos, of secrets and forbidden things, a place where budding sexuality and puberty fantasies run amuck.

This dream image also expresses the finality of nature. On one hand, it addresses everything that is transitory and points out that everything material will pass on and has no value. On the other hand, it addresses the meaning of accomplishment, completion. It is, again, an example of the alchemistic idea that gold can be made out of feces. In one sense, the toilet is the place where products are transformed. Such dream images almost always point to a necessary change: you must let go of something, while, at the same time, you must produce something positive. In Norse fables, King Olaf warns his guests not to go to the toilet alone during the night, because they might end up in a dangerous adventure with the Devil. The toilet has also been considered the place of ghosts.

According to Jung, it is the place of the highest creativity.

STRETCHING THE TRUTH

In ancient times, a common refrain from the man of the house was "If you want me, I'll be in the root chakra catching up on my Kundalini." Also, you can still visit King Olaf's royal toilet, on the wall of which is a poem which begins "Here I sit, brokenhearted . . ."

TOMATO: See also Red. The tomato is a symbol of fertility. As a nightshade plant, something is scary about it. According to Rudolf Steiner, the tomato is the expression of eroticism and passion.

TONGUE: Language, intellectual creativity, communication. The tongue always refers to the throat chakra and thereby to the honesty of your communication, or the lack of it. See also Speech (Giving A) and Lecture.

TOOLS: Used for and aiding work. According to Freud, all tools are symbols of the male organ.

BARE FACTS

So God knows what's going on out in that garage workshop.

TOOTHACHE: You are lovesick.

TOP HAT: In a man's dream, a desire for greater virility. In a woman's dream, often a wish for marriage. A top hat was worn only to very formal events, such as a Wedding or a Funeral. Pay attention to the symbolic meaning of the event to which the top hat is worn.

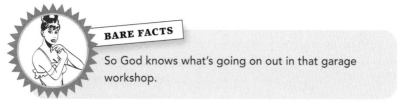

YOU'RE WELCOME FOR THE TIP

For example, if you are wearing a top hat to a Monster Truck Challenge, you may have a subconscious desire to get pummeled.

TORCH: Once a symbol for marriage, because the fire in the hearth was lit in a ritual ceremony with a torch. Then it became a symbol of passing on psychic energies and ideas (Olympic torch); the light of reason and freedom (Statue of Liberty). Today, however, it is more a symbol of light and consciousness that penetrates the dark (that which is not understood). Also, a symbol of honoring somebody (torchlight procession).

TOWEL: You want to wipe something away, as if it never happened. Or, when you throw in the towel, you are giving up (usually on yourself). A wet towel is a sign of something unsuitable and dysfunctional.

SECRETS TO MAKE YOU LOOK GOOD

A wet towel left on the floor is a sign that your girlfriend is ready to murder you, which is about as unsuitable and dysfunctional as it gets.

TOWER: A frequent phallic symbol, particularly in women's dreams. More perspective is needed (watchtower). A symbol of power (compare the similarity of the words "tower" and "power." Being locked up in a tower points to sexual inhibitions in women (Rapunzel), and also is an indication of an unusual and highly developed sexuality that has no outlet.

TOWN HALL: Office and honor. Points to an inner, psychic organization of your personality.

LISTEN UP, THIS IS IMPORTANT

Although, as in life, in a town hall dream, it usually takes all freaking day to get seen.

TOYS: Childlike, childish, immature.

TRACK/TRACE/SIGN: You are beginning to understand your problems; you have discovered the signs and are on the right track.

TRACKS/TRAIN TRACKS: The path of life is foreordained. Or it can reflect security and rigidity (everything running on track).

TRAFFIC LIGHTS: Traffic, stress, order, an indication of needing to understand the signs of the times, or to establish these signs. Green light: idea, insight, understanding. Red light: Repressive dream.

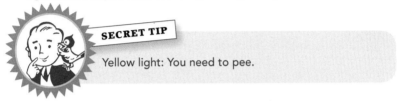

SECRET TIP

Yellow light: You need to pee.

TRAFFIC SIGN: Often a symbol for sexual behavior. What the traffic sign announces is important.

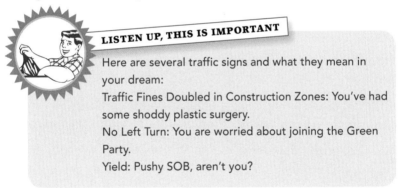

LISTEN UP, THIS IS IMPORTANT

Here are several traffic signs and what they mean in your dream:
Traffic Fines Doubled in Construction Zones: You've had some shoddy plastic surgery.
No Left Turn: You are worried about joining the Green Party.
Yield: Pushy SOB, aren't you?

TRAIL: You are on to something, or you are on to yourself. You are looking for something.

TRAIN: See also Railway Station. Vacation or business trip? Fear of "missing" the train; or it is high time (if you want to catch the train). See Haste. Developing one's personality, striving for success and being sociable. Fleeing from the present situation.

Are you observing the train or are you traveling on the train (you are either wanting to move or part of the movement). What is happening on the train and how would you characterize the action?

According to Freud, leaving on a train and traveling on a train means death. However, Freud suffered from a phobia about trains.

QUICK FIX

Finally, we find Freud's weak spot. Too bad he's dead, or what fun we could have had exploiting it.

TRAIN/CONDUCTOR: Enjoying contact and communication, travel. The conductor may represent the guide of the soul (travel guide and signpost). You know where your travel will take you.

TRAIN (GOWN)/VEIL: Something is dragging behind you. To take somebody in tow. But also dignity, splendor, and worship. Often this image refers to Bride. Sometimes it may suggest time is "dragging," addressing the subject of patience.

TRAP: Difficult situation, being imprisoned; more prudence and caution is in order. Feeling restricted, as in Siege, Amber, Village, Cage, and Elevator. See also Falling.

TRAPDOOR: In contrast to Parachute, this is unpleasant Falling, as in Abyss, and particularly as in Shooting. See Hiding Place, but this image also accesses layers of your character.

TRASH CAN: See also Toilet. Symbol for repression and cleansing.

TRAVEL: The life's path of the dreamer. Rejuvenation of the psyche. You are moving, searching. What is important is the kind of trip and how it is proceeding.

According to Freud, traveling is usually the symbol of death.

SNAP OF THE FINGER

You can save time and money by booking your travel dream online.

TREASURE: Something of value. You need to activate old and forgotten skills. Treasure symbolizes the goal of the search and represents either the beginning of or the reason for personal efforts and endeavors. See also Wealth. According to Freud, treasure stands for the person we love.

TREE: Protection; archetypal symbol for life (tree of life, tree of the world, family tree) and for being human, rooted in the earth. The crown of the tree, like the head of a human being, reaches for the sky. Part of two worlds—reality and obligation (earth) and spirit and freedom (heaven). Personal development and growth of the dreamer. Family situation across several generations. Connected to nature, as in Field, Ear (of corn), Farmer, Farm. Concern for the environment as well as personal growth.

Does the tree grow Fruit? In what season did the image appear?

What is the condition of the root system (base of the root as a symbol for soul), the Trunk, and the Crown? Where is the tree and how does it stand—alone, in a small group, in the forest, in a park?

According to Freud, the tree trunk is a phallic symbol.

STRETCHING THE TRUTH

One would think that the tree *branches* would be the more obvious choice for a phallic symbol, but apparently the tree vetoed it. Said he didn't want people getting the wrong idea and that he had plenty to offer in that department, thank you very much.

TREE (BLOSSOMS ON): Luck, fullness. A frequent dream symbol that appears during nocturnal ejaculation.

TREE-OF-LIFE: See also Tree. Growth. Connection between heaven and earth.

TREE TRUNK/TRUNK: Tree. Security, stability and productivity, similar to Family, Notice-of-Intention-to-Marry. It often has a negative connotation when the trunk is either split or cut off. However, the chopping of the wood may also point to warmth (food for the inner fire) and (allocation of) one's inner energies. Is the trunk straight and strong?

TRIAL: If you are the accused, pay close attention to what you have been accused of doing. If you are the accuser, take a look at what injustice has been done. You need to be objective, focused, and fair in your everyday life. See also Attorney.

TRIANGLE: Spiritualization. It is a female sexual symbol if the tip points down; male, if the tip points up.

TRIP (OUTING/EXCURSION): Recuperation, fun, change of scene. Well-known dream symbol when overworking. Where are you going on your trip?

TROPHY: You want to be recognized.

TROUT: Fish. Enjoyment of life; you are able to move freely in the waters of your emotions.

TRUCK: You are carrying a heavy burden. Or are you the authority that is steering the truck? Important is the symbolic meaning of the products that the truck is transporting.

TRUMPET: Attention getting and trying to awaken energies that are asleep. The expression of powerful energies.

TRUNK: See Tree Trunk.

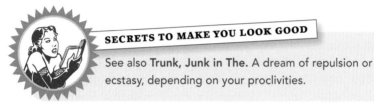

SECRETS TO MAKE YOU LOOK GOOD

See also **Trunk, Junk in The.** A dream of repulsion or ecstasy, depending on your proclivities.

TUB: Cleansing, as in Shower, Bath, Sauna.

TUBER: Concentrated energies that now need to be used for further development, similar to Bud. According to Freud, a phallic symbol. See also Potato.

TULIP: A dream of women, rarely men. Being connected to nature. As is the case with all flower symbols in dreams, the image of the tulip also has sexual meaning.

TUNNEL: In most cases, this is a dream about birth—looking back to the starting point. A dream of rebirth. In a tunnel we often meet the unconscious.

According to Freud, a reference to intercourse, especially when Trains drive in or out of the tunnel.

TUNNEL (AS IN A MINE): That which is unconscious and from which inner treasures need to be brought to light.

According to Freud, symbol of the vagina.

TURTLE/TORTOISE: Hiding behind a character trait (according to Wilhelm Reich). Patience, wisdom; or hiding something essential.

TWELVE: The number we use to keep time (hour, months), it represents completion, an end and/or a new beginning. Twelve apostles, twelve astrological signs, and so on.

TWIG: See also Branch, Tree. Growing and thriving. It is a symbol of your own foundation (don't cut off the branch that you are sitting on), your own growth and ability to branch out—to understand the outside world in its many different aspects. See Y-Shape. According to Freud, a twig with blossoms is clearly a sexual symbol.

TWILIGHT: Romance, a transitional period. One is standing between two worlds and is not quite sure. Twilight indicates a moment of transition, in which everything seems undefined and undecided. Dusk is connected to fears, but in part it is also a symbol for new beginnings, curiosity (what does the new day have in store?) and openness. Morning sunrise and evening sunset are times of pleasure. See also Red.

LISTEN UP, THIS IS IMPORTANT

See also **Twilight Zone**, a place where these guys think they landed on some weird other planet, only in the end you realize they were, like, on Earth the entire time. (See also **The One Where the Guy Realizes He Was Dead the Entire Time.**)

TWINS: See also Two. Talking to both sides within the Self, or one specific side—the side represented by the image of the twins. "The better half" and "the other self" (alter ego).

TWO: The opposites and contradictions that are in need of differentiation and balance. Your ambivalence is becoming known, which is a positive development.

According to Jung, two identical symbols refer to the unconscious, because they cannot be distinguished from one another. Messengers from the underworld, for that reason, usually appear in twos.

STRETCHING THE TRUTH

Messengers from the underworld usually appear in twos? That would explain your manager and the assistant manager.

UMBRELLA: You are rejecting insight and ideas; have no direct contact with reality; no contact with the water of the emotion. Or, the umbrella could mean flexibility —a Roof over your head.

YOU'RE WELCOME FOR THE TIP

Hey, you may have no direct contact with reality, but at least you're dry.

UNCLE: "Elder people" and authority.

UNDERGROUND: One of the most frequent symbols for the unconscious. The task is to discover the unconscious and that which has been unconscious, and to become familiar with it.

UNDERGROUND GARAGE: The place of the unconscious and everything frozen and rigid. See also Forest, Basement.

UNDERWORLD: See also Underground. Mythological symbol of the unconscious—the dark or shadowy gods of the deep.

UNDRESSING: Openness, exposing oneself. What is underneath the surface (the clothing)?

UNIFORM: Authority, self-affirmation, ambition, and seeking power; but also a lack of self-awareness and/or a weak ego. It may also signify lack of order or too rigidly adhering to order. In the case of women, longing for or fearing a strong man. Uniforms also point to a lack of individuality, repetitiveness.

According to Freud, nakedness that one is trying to hide.

UNIVERSE: The spiritual environment of the dreamer.

UNIVERSITY: See also School. Mother symbol (alma mater), but also a symbol of masculinity. It represents the intellectual side of life.

UPHILL: The effort of Ascension. Succeeding in a task.

URINE: Magical liquid, like all body liquids. Points to sexual or domestic problems.

URN (CONTAINER FOR ASHES): See also Death and impermanence.

UTERUS: Fertility and inner wealth. With this image, are you remembering your own heritage, or a "past life"?

VACUUM CLEANER: Symbol of cleanliness and an orderly house.

VAGABOND: Freedom, breaking with rigid convention. This dream usually appears in times of social pressure.

VALLEY: Low point, crisis, and turning point. Going down into the valley means either getting to the bottom of something, or descending into the unconscious. Pay attention to the kind of valley (its shape and what is growing there). If the valley is already in the shadows, it symbolizes dark areas. A valley that is shaped like a canyon symbolizes either female sexuality or sexual anxieties.

VAMP: Are you posing as a cunning female? Should you become sexually more provocative? In a man's dream, a desire to be more clever in sexual matters.

VAMPIRE: See also Monster/Mythical Creature, Bat. Guilt feelings, and the sense of being sucked dry. These dreams often appear during depression. The vampire image points to insufficient boundaries toward the world of shadows.

LISTEN UP, THIS IS IMPORTANT

Remember, too, that vampires are known as the "undead." Are you dreaming about an insurance salesman? (Or maybe that one waitress down at the diner?)

VASE: See also Container. You are depending too much on external things. Also a suggestion that you are guided by sexual moods and feelings that are confusing. In women's dreams the demanding side of your sexuality needs to be lived out more fully, or in a way that causes conflict in a male-dominated society.

According to Freud, a symbol of the female.

SECRETS TO MAKE YOU LOOK GOOD

In men's dreams, the demanding side of your sexuality needs to be clubbed on the head *with* a vase.

VAULT: As in Cave, a symbol for mother and security.

VEGETABLE: Stands for young people and children. See also Food.
According to Jung, usually a reference to eroticism.

VEHICLE: Driving. Freedom of movement. You want to get away. You want to keep moving. You would like to arrive. The type of vehicle indicates whether you are pursuing your own path and what progress you are making. Also, symbol for emotional independence and momentum.

VEIL: A symbol for secret. Something is being hidden—something is being portrayed falsely. See also Virgin. Tearing down a veil symbolizes Defloration. But it also refers to protection in the sense of having essential emotional boundaries. Warning of, and emphasis on, emotional immunity.

DON'T BE A JERK

A black veil is a traditional symbol of mourning. What deep and significant loss is your dream helping you to mourn? And no, the cable going out during the game does not count.

VELVET: Luxury and sensuality. The symbolic meaning of the color is important.
According to Freud, pubic hair, as in Fur, and sexuality.

VENGEANCE: Should you be more aggressive?

VICTIM: Some emotions, characteristics, and behaviors need to be given up. If you are making a sacrifice in the dream, or giving something away, ask how easy it is for you to let go in real life. What you may have to let go of is symbolized by what you give away or sacrifice in the dream. On the other hand, giving something away shows how compassionate you are, and how much empathy you are capable of. If you are a victim, pay close attention to the perpetrator and figure out how you came to be cast in the role of victim and what kind of fearful or enjoyable emotions are connected with that role.

COMMUNICATION

We spent a long time analyzing this victim stuff, and all we know is the world is against us. And it's all your fault.

VICTORY: Desire for success and for the ability to achieve. Since our most significant arguments take place internally, this dream image refers to conscious development. You are now able to win over your own problems and blocks.

VILLA: A symbol of wealth that one would love to possess. It is a wish dream, representing the popular belief that emotional emptiness can be filled with possessions.

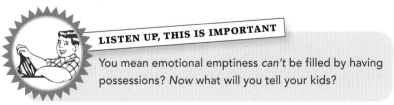

LISTEN UP, THIS IS IMPORTANT

You mean emotional emptiness *can't* be filled by having possessions? *Now* what will you tell your kids?

VILLAGE: Symbolizes the personality of the dreamer: unsophisticated but well-balanced (at least as an ideal). But can also mean restriction, as in Siege, Amber, Trap, as well as a phony idealist. According to ancient Egyptian dream interpretation, peaceful existence, family, protection, belonging.

VINEGAR: Insult, disappointment; you are sour. Something is getting ruined (turning sour).

SECRET TIP

Also the balsamic vinegar dream, had mostly by waiters.

VIOLENCE: Discipline is necessary. Or let go of too much discipline. Similar to Obedience. Repressed urges.

VIOLET (FLOWER): Modesty, a pure woman or girl ("shrinking violet"). On one hand, the color violet points to emancipation. The emancipated woman is one who walks new frontiers. Violet, from a language point of view, is connected to the Latin word *violatio*, which means force and rape.

VIOLIN: An idealization of the female body. Or wanting to "play the first violin." As with all musical instruments, harmony is addressed; and as with all string instruments, the image symbolizes the "string of nerves," as well as the mood and tension of a person. The resonating power of a violin also points to how our inner world resonates. It could be interpreted as the "echo of the soul."

If a string breaks, it means quarrels.

VIRGIN: As with all strange women who appear in a man's dream, this image represents his own feminine side, which in case of a mother complex he is unable to integrate.

In a woman's dream, it represents her own unknown, often disowned, feminine side. It also reflects a strong connection to the father, egocentricity in love, and possible frigidity. See also Defloration.

Something new should be undertaken. Also a warning about an action that cannot be undone. The action of the virgin in the dream points to unknown characteristics and behaviors of the dreamer.

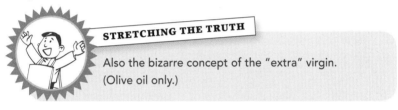

STRETCHING THE TRUTH

Also the bizarre concept of the "extra" virgin.
(Olive oil only.)

VISIT: Change, period of development and transition, loneliness. A longing for social contact, or too much of it, as in Friend.

VISTA: A well-known symbol for perspectives and consciousness, almost always pointing to the future. The vista often appears in the dream as a mirror of the eyes and what the dreamer is seeing, meaning it is a symbol of the personal identity of the dreamer. What are you looking forward to? Are the choices good or bad? What do you see?

VITAMIN: What is nutritious and good. Do you have to take more?

VOICE: You need to make people to listen to you. Raise your voice.

VOLCANO: Drives repressed and drives released, stress or stress reduction. This implies a "test by fire." What is innermost comes to the surface. It might express a fantasy of merging in a relationship, or fusion of different parts of the Self in a developing personality. Also, what was hard is made to flow again.

VOMITING: Undigested concepts and emotions are being expelled, cleansed—similar to Sewer, Toilet. Letting go of unwanted emotions.

SNAP OF THE FINGER

Though it may be unsettling, it is important to inspect your dream vomit for exactly what undigested concepts and emotions have been expelled. (E.g., "Look at that chunk of unprocessed resentment toward my stepfather . . . No wonder I got sick!")

VULTURE: Exploitation has become a way of life It may serve as an explanation of why you have difficulty with the world around you.

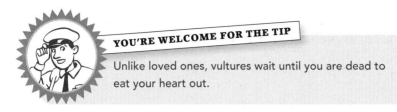

YOU'RE WELCOME FOR THE TIP

Unlike loved ones, vultures wait until you are dead to eat your heart out.

WAFFLE: Old and well-known symbol for female sexuality, domesticity, and enjoyment.

YOU'RE WELCOME FOR THE TIP

All three of which are better with syrup.

WAGES: How are you handling your emotional energies? Are you getting what you want?

WAGON: A wagon symbolizes an important transitional stage in life. It also indicates the dreamer's courage in steering his own course and making his own discoveries. According to Jung, although the wagon is a means of transportation made by man, its wheels are a symbol of the wheel of the sun that symbolizes Mandala. It is a frequent dream symbol when making changes.

WAGON/WHEELBARROW: On one hand, this symbol points to difficulties ("pulling the wagon out of the ditch," for example); on the other hand, it is also a symbol of mobility. A wheelbarrow in a dream often points to the dreamer's body, as does the Carriage. In addition to checking the condition of the wagon, also pay attention to the condition of the road.

WAIST: Those who want to lose weight probably dream about the waist more often than those who don't. See also Stomach.

WAITER: Friendliness, help. Should you be more humble and think more about service? Similar to Chauffeur.

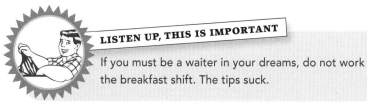
WALK: Often a dream of birth. A dark walkway may point to helplessness.

WALKING: Making progress in life under your own power, slow but steady. Independence. How you walk is a clear indication of your present situation.

COMMUNICATION

If your present situation was your annual checkup, you might be walking a little funny.

WALKING STICK: Support. Symbol of a person that you can trust. Phallic symbol.

WALL: An obstacle dream, or support, protection. You should either be more open or have better boundaries.

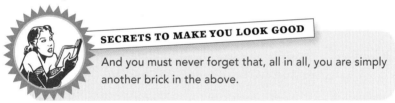

SECRETS TO MAKE YOU LOOK GOOD

And you must never forget that, all in all, you are simply another brick in the above.

WALTZ: Symbol of love as well as Rose, Circle, Dance.

WAR: Real fear of war. In addition, confrontation between different parts of the personality of the dreamer: inner conflict. This dream image points to current confrontations with your own aggressiveness. Check to see if you are too aggressive, or if you should express your aggression more directly.

WAREHOUSE OR DEPARTMENT STORE: Symbol of commerce or greed, but also may refer to an independent life and taking care of the Self. What is offered in the warehouse or department store refers to talents that are available.

YOU'RE WELCOME FOR THE TIP

That means your unavailable talents come in huge, honking blister packs of thirty.

WARMTH: A frequent dream symbol when the dreamer is actually cold while sleeping. Warmth and devotion, but also demanding and feeling restricted. If the temperature is falling, feelings are cooling off.

WARNING: A warning—though it is only in a dream—ought to be taken seriously.

SNAP OF THE FINGER

Especially if that warning is "Look out for that safe."

WARTS: Symbol of witches. See also Witch.

WASHBASIN: As in Washing, Tub, Shower, Bath, Sauna. A symbol of cleanliness and purity.

WASHING: A symbol for cleansing as in Tub, Shower, Bath, Sauna. In alchemy, being blackened is followed by washing; chaotic situations are followed by cleansing (from guilt feelings). Washing of the hands is a sign of innocence.

WASP: Aggression and egocentricity.

STRETCHING THE TRUTH

See also **WASP.** Loafers and sweaters wrapped around the neck.

WATER: See also River, Sea, Ocean. This dream symbol can be interpreted on five different levels:

1. on the sexual level
2. on an emotional level where your own emotions are perceived as undifferentiated and flowing
3. as a fear of flooding, being drowned by the unconscious
4. as a feeling of going with the flow
5. as a feeling that life is chaotic

This symbol is also the desire for a totally new orientation.

In alchemy, water is connected to feelings; it represents the wild nature of the soul in need of being conquered. Water is the place where the souls of the dead meet the spirits of the water; it is a place of repression, of secrets with unknown depths and an element of rapture. It can tear us away and sweep us off, and it can be very frightening. Water is the symbol of what is changeable. Diving into the water means to seek wisdom. Whoever looks into the water always sees the Self.

Water symbolizes women, the process of birth and pregnancy.

Running water means experiencing sexuality in a positive sense. Standing water means losing vitality and your very center. Or it might mean, as in Pond and the fountain of youth, that water is the carrier of life's energies and rejuvenation. Out of this understanding might have come the ritual of baptism.

Falling into the water means being swept away by emotion; but this may also be a warning dream, pointing also to Diving and Drowning.

According to the Chinese understanding of nature, water is a symbol of the elemental, female force of yin. For the Taoist, water is the essence of life, its movement an example for a life lived in harmony with nature. The holy water in the Catholic Church and the water used for baptism represent the healing powers of water.

According to Freud, a water dream is often the memory of our life in our mother's womb. And again, according to Freud, to come out of water represents the image of birth. Water for him was always connected to birth. See also Swimming, Bath, Diving, Tears, Drink, Birth.

LISTEN UP, THIS IS IMPORTANT

We start with a natural spring in a Taoist mountain range. Then we triple filter the sexual, emotional, and fear-based elements, careful not to lose the valuable minerals of baptism and the memory of birth. Finally, we bottle it at our plant, where the souls of the dead meet the spirits, and deliver it to you, the dreamer. Knock yourself out.

WATERFALL: See also Water. A symbol for letting go.

WATERING CAN: Abundance, wealth. Or economical distribution of your energies, as in Faucet. According to Freud, this is a phallic symbol, because what flows out of the "spout" brings about fertilization.

WATER LILY: The world of the emotions and a symbol for wholeness and completeness.

WAVE: See Water. An image of emotional excitement—tenderness, caressing, and sexuality. See also Surfing, Ship.

SECRET TIP

May also be a memory of "the wave," the dorky communal event which occurs in sports arenas. If so, then tenderness, caressing, and sexuality go right out the window.

WAX: Adaptability, steadfastness or the lack of it, and the power to shape. Symbol of temptation.

WEALTH: The expression of a desire for a full and spirited inner life. In dreams, wealth and money always are connected with psychic energies. This is a warning not to be too modest, or to allow yourself to have false expectations. Your existence and your personal qualities are your greatest wealth. How you are dealing with the world—protecting what is uniquely yours and developing it—makes a decided difference. See also Price, Treasure.

WEAPON: Particularly in women's dreams, fear of sexuality. In the
case of men, it is partly an expression of fear of the weapons of women.
Fear of war. A weapon in a dream also symbolizes internal poison or
corrosion. According to Freud and most of depth psychology, it is a
symbol of masculine sexuality, since bullets penetrate the body. Today,
this dream image is less relevant, because weapons so often totally
destroy the body. This expands on Freud's interpretation, which sees
it as an interesting tension between creating a body (sexuality) and
destroying a body (modern weaponry).

WEASEL: Symbol for speed.

WEDDING: Marriage. Important and frequent dreams during times
of marital and relationship conflicts. It is important how the wedding is
celebrated. Also, gains, in a spiritual as well as economic sense.

Longing for a permanent relationship, security, and home.
Today the image is often a symbol of being at the peak of your life,
expressing the idea that peak experiences should be present more
in your life.

In ancient Indian tradition, dreaming about a wedding points to impending death or pain.

According to Freud, a dream of desire. According to Jung, it always addresses the union of anima and animus—as in Bride or Bridegroom.

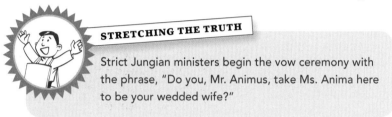

STRETCHING THE TRUTH

Strict Jungian ministers begin the vow ceremony with the phrase, "Do you, Mr. Animus, take Ms. Anima here to be your wedded wife?"

WEEDS: Unorganized and unknown instincts and impulses that may be destructive or helpful.

WEIGHT: Depression, burdened, as in Luggage. Or it may be an admonition not to take things so seriously. May also refer to your ability to "weigh" the facts.

WELL/FOUNTAIN: Strong bonding to the mother, regression, food, symbol of the female. If the dreamer is a man: passion, patience, true friendship. Rest and healing, as in Breast. Often the task is to become a "good mother" to oneself and to see oneself as "one's own child."

According to Freud, early childhood sexual symbol.

WET NURSE: Food, comfort, closeness; in the case of women, often the desire for conception, pregnancy, and children. In the case of men, often the fear of the female and, specifically, motherliness (a nursing woman, because of the fear of her fertility, was once called a "milk-cow").

DON'T BE A JERK

Uh-huh. Call a nursing woman a "milk-cow."
I dare you.

WHALE: The feeling of being swallowed up by a task that needs to be completed, like Jonah in the Bible, who was swallowed up by the whale. Also a symbol of the endangered species in the world.

COMMUNICATION

Dreams of whales may also indicate a desire to communicate with a beautiful and complex series of clicking sounds—which is more than what you've been able to achieve with your boyfriend.

WHEAT: See Grain.

WHEAT FIELD: Life's tasks, productivity, and success. See also Grain, Field, Seed, Harvest. Compare this also with the allegory about the wheat kernel that must die in order to bear fruit many times over.

WHEEL: See Mandala.

WHEELBARROW: See Wagon.

WHEELCHAIR: On one hand, restriction, suffering, and the inability to escape from problems. On the other hand, in spite of a psychological handicap, moving forward. Often such dreams are a challenge, in a sense, to learn how to walk again.

WHIP: Subjugation; the power of aggression. Masochistic tendencies that are lived out. Or, you are doing damage to yourself, and the dream is pointing that out. You need to find your Self.

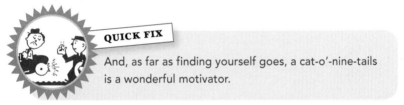

QUICK FIX

And, as far as finding yourself goes, a cat-o'-nine-tails is a wonderful motivator.

WHIRLPOOL: Sinking into emotions, into the unconscious. See also Diving.

WHISTLING: A rare dream symbol. You want to be noticed. As in Scream, a primeval outburst of psychic energy.

WHITE HORSE: Positive image of nature, energy, vitality, and purity.

STRETCHING THE TRUTH

It is often said that women desire a shining knight to come riding up on a white horse, and such a dream may indicate this. However, 85 percent of test subjects report that they stuck with the horse and were just as happy, if not more so.

WHITE THORN: White thorn is the bush Viviane hides behind to put a spell on Merlin. The wood of the white thorn also is used to make magical wands. Considered a holy plant in Christianity, the white thorn grows in Glastonbury in southern England and is said to have been brought there by Joseph of Arimathea. It blooms twice every year.

WIDOW: Loss of masculinity.

WIDOWER: Loss of femininity, loneliness, brooding, grief. See also Death, Divorce.

WILD/PRIMITIVE MAN: Romanticizing the simple life. A suggestion to live more on the wild side and to dismiss prejudice and reservations. This means trusting the Self more, having the "courage to not be perfect." See also Fool, Tiger.

WILDERNESS: The wilderness in dreams refers to the place where wild emotions and uncontrolled urges and drives reign, and suggests coming to terms with them. The wilderness, in addition to the so-called jungle characteristics, may also indicate a desert, meaning unproductive or unused talents within the Self.

BARE FACTS

Television was once referred to as a "vast wilderness." Thankfully, we now have hundreds of different channels to choose from, all of which offer deeply intellectual fare.

WILL: An attempt to bring order into one's affairs, gaining perspective about life already lived. Fear of death. Hoping for wealth without working for it. Coming to terms with a legacy, often in the sense of the dreamer's own past, talents, and abilities. The search for meaning. A desire for productivity and fulfillment, particularly after one period in life has come to an end.

YOU'RE WELCOME FOR THE TIP

In dreams as in life, a will is a wonderful opportunity to give the shaft to that one kid you never could stand.

WILLOW TREE: Flexibility, smoothness, but also sadness (weeping willow). It is a light in the darkness.

WIND: See also Storm, Hurricane, Air, Breath. Here the spirits of the air are being addressed. They personify intellect or spirit. The wind can also mean an idea or a new understanding. If it conveys a sense of fresh air, something new is going to happen.

WINDMILL: Intellectual powers. Intellectual or spiritual work. Battling with imagination, as in Cervantes's Don Quixote.

WINDOW: House. Here, almost always, internal and external references are being addressed. With this dream symbol, it is important to note what you see when you look through the window. In what direction are you looking? Is the window clean and clear or opaque? All this is of great symbolic meaning.

According to Freud, this image points to the body's openings (the house is the body, the windows are the eyes).

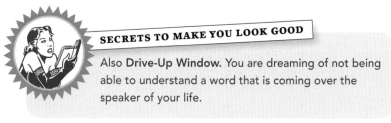

SECRETS TO MAKE YOU LOOK GOOD

Also **Drive-Up Window.** You are dreaming of not being able to understand a word that is coming over the speaker of your life.

WINDOWSILL: According to Freud, projections from the human body—for instance, the breast.

WINE/GRAPE WINE/VINEYARD: Intoxication and hard work; the juice of life and sensual enjoyment. *In vino veritas*—do you need to tell somebody the truth?

WINGS (FOR FLYING): You need to live an easier life, be more open to playful energies, be more spiritual (soar). This is a direct challenge to think big and to have courage to do great things. This image fits the observation in the *I Ching*: "It furthers one to cross the great water."

According to Homer, wings symbolize thought.

STRETCHING THE TRUTH

Flying is the ultimate symbol of freedom. And up to now you thought the ultimate symbol of freedom was those maxipads with wings.

WINNING: In every instance, a symbol of success.

WINTER: See Ice, Cold.

WIRE (HIGH-TENSION): Connection to somebody, to another place; or being informed and clever. It is a frequent symbol for nerves and intellectual connection. An electrical wire usually indicates the tension the dreamer is under.

WIRE (HIGH-VOLTAGE): Drives and urges must be guided sensibly. This image points to severe nervous tension—or exceptional strength.

We speak, as well, of someone who is "wired," or full of nervous energy. Encountering such a person in your dream is a warning to stop drinking caffeine. If the wired person in the dream is yourself, it is a warning to stop *injecting* the caffeine.

WISE MAN: An archetype of the wise old man as a guide for life's journey. Particularly in women's dreams, it is the expression of a longing for positive masculinity and "the better" father.

WITCH: Hedge. A negative symbol for Mother, the overpowering, malevolent woman who is feared. Often points to a mother who does not care properly for her children (particularly in children's dreams). Less often, the image of a witch points to the wise woman (particularly in women's dreams) who exudes great magnetism. The witch is almost always a symbol of the power of the unconscious—Magic. In fairy tales as well as in dreams, the witch plays an important, archetypal role, because she separates the hero or dream-self from his (usually royal) origin, which can then only be recaptured after he passes a certain test.

WITNESS: What we have witnessed in a dream—what we have seen—should be taken very seriously and remembered as accurately as possible. You are feeling included and part of the event. Being a witness means being productive and possibly an originator.

WOMAN: If a woman dreams about women, it is almost always about her shadow and seldom about herself. If a man dreams about a woman, he is dreaming about his emotional side, which, in the end, is about his connection to his mother. In the case of a man, the behavior of the woman in the dream often gives insight into his unconscious life, his unknown characteristics, physical urges, and behavior.

According to ancient Egyptian dream interpretation, the image of a beautiful woman is always a warning that a task is too large.

According to Jung, a strange woman in the dream of a man is always the feminine side of the dreamer, his anima. Jung also thinks that a woman in a man's dream always represents his emotional "teacher."

Women also appear in many dreams as old and wise (woman or hag), lecherous (threatening or liberated), imprisoned (like Rapunzel's trapped physical drive), ugly (as a witch), young (as a temptress), powerful (as the mother), and beautiful (the lover, the ideal).

WONDERS: In dreams, wonders and miracles are "normal." They suggest forsaking limitations. The dreamer is living life too rigidly.

WOOD INSTRUMENT: Music, relaxation, enjoying art, but also screaming silently. In most cases, it is an expression of great vitality.

According to classical depth psychology, a phallic symbol.

WORK: Problems and burdens of the day are being carried over into sleep. Image of emotional work done in a dream.

WORKER: Something is being accomplished; one must do something, be active. Social decline or social romanticism.

WORM: The Snake is often called a worm, a symbol of the lowest stage of the animal kingdom, often indicating bad conscience or troubles, usually with a sexual connotation.

According to Jung, worms represent the first movement of an unevolved soul, without "color," emotions, and reason—representing blind instincts.

SECRETS TO MAKE YOU LOOK GOOD

In a sense, we are all worms, unevolved souls—especially people who drive alone in the carpool lane.

WORSHIP: Prayer, peace, meditation; centering is necessary. This is a frequent dream image when life is oriented too much to materialism.

WOUND: See Injury. Painful emotional experience.

WREATH: Disappointment. A female sexual symbol, it may indicate the end of a relationship. In the form of a victory or funeral wreath, it expresses maturity and the completion of a task. Here you should check on your life goals.

WRECK: Fear of going under.

WRESTLING MATCH: You are fighting with yourself about something. It is important who the opponent is. Are you courageous, or do you feel like a coward? Meaning: Are you facing your problems or denying them?

LISTEN UP, THIS IS IMPORTANT

And can your denial face five minutes in the ring with The Crusher?

WRINKLES: Experience and age.

WRISTBAND: Bond/relationship; a feeling of one's activity being restricted, similar to the symbol of Chain or Cage. Also, an emphasis on independence. In the form of Jewelry, it implies vanity, but jewelry can also be an expression of pleasure in one's own beauty.

WRISTWATCH: Order in everyday life, rushing, stress, and time pressures. See also Clock, Time. In addition, take a look at your own life span. How are you using time? The image of "time" in this context is closely connected to your personality. What have you achieved? Are you satisfied?

YOU'RE WELCOME FOR THE TIP

Luckily, if you're one of those people without a wristwatch who simply checks the time on a Blackberry, then you are not caught up in rushing, stress, or time pressures at all!

WRITING: Thinking, planning, and organizing. To account for something to yourself. But it may also mean an important message or tip. You need to turn to a particular person and discuss something important with him or her. Or, if you have an important question, this person may have an answer.

YACHT: Symbolizes spoiled and expensive women, and a longing for more femininity. If the sea is calm, luck is indicated; your ambitions are being fulfilled. A wild sea represents danger.

BARE FACTS

There is nothing wrong with dreaming about a yacht—if you're a soulless, materialistic, and basically nasty person.

YARD: Points either to something hidden, as in Backyard, or to the open side of the dreamer's personality.

According to Freud, the yard symbolizes the vagina, but today this meaning is only thought relevant if sexual drives are repressed. However, these interpretations remain in the imagination, because once a meaning has been culturally established, the human soul does not ever forget.

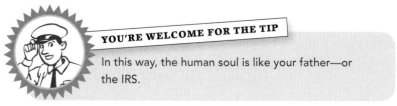

YOU'RE WELCOME FOR THE TIP

In this way, the human soul is like your father—or the IRS.

YARN: See also Thread. A relationship that should be kept intact. Red yarn is the red thread that Ariadne gives Theseus to help him to find his way out of the Maze.

YARN (STORY): Untruthfulness, "spinning a yarn," or thoughts and feelings that are taking shape very slowly. See also Thread.

YEAST: What drives us; the important, small things in life.

QUICK FIX

We simply couldn't have come this far and not mentioned a yeast infection. You know you would have wondered why we let it slide.

YELLOW: Refers to intuition and intellect (also in the sense of awareness). Symbol for the color of the sun. Yellow also stands for irritable feelings. It may also be a sign of mental illness that may be expressed, for instance, in the choice of yellow as a dominating color in paintings, such as those of van Gogh. The term "Yellow Peril" warns of mental and physical illness. This is a classic example of how a political term with an archetypal meaning has over time led to new associations, regardless of whether others share the same political opinion. Advertising works in a similar way.

If the yellow seems to have a golden tint to it—abundant harvest, intellectual activities. Dark or muddy/dirty yellow, on the other hand, means envy, greed, jealousy, and betrayal.

In Hinduism, yellow symbolizes the light of life; in Buddhism, humility and freedom.

Goethe wrote "[Yellow] is a happy, alive, gentle color, but it can easily become uncomfortable and with the addition of even the slightest amount of another color, it becomes devalued, ugly, and dirty."

YOGA: Body control and meditation. As a dream symbol, yoga usually suggests a more conscious way of dealing with the body.

YOGI: This dream symbol addresses the magical belief of the yogi. Expression of hope that one can overcome natural law.

YOUNG BOY: One whose life is in front of him. Start something new. It also points to weak masculinity and a poorly developed masculine side of the woman, as well as poor gender identity in a man. This is often connected to the aging process in a man. In the Koran, it means one whose wealth is increasing.

According to Freud, the male genitalia, often in connection with masturbation fantasies.

YOUTH: Primarily a symbol that appears in the second half of life. In the dream your life is seen in perspective, pointing to behavior that might have lead to problems (neurosis).

If such a dream happens to appear in the first half of your life, it usually points to undeveloped characteristics of the dreamer.

Y-SHAPE: The letter "Y" unites the masculine and the feminine. It also represents the dowsing rod that is used to find something hidden. The "Y" also represents a magical formula where one becomes two and two become one.

ZEBRA: Contradictions in life need to be better integrated or more clearly defined.

ZEPPELIN: See also Airplane. Phallic symbol.

ZERO: A sexual image, nothingness, triviality; less often death, quiet, and completion. See also Mandala, which, according to Jung, represent the Self as the center of a person. See also Fool.

ZINC: See Metal.

ZIPPER: This symbol is connected with Naked and Clothing. It might also have to do with the joining of Left and Right.

ZOO: Are you looking at your own animal side? This image refers to the animus anima (and your masculine and feminine sides).

LISTEN UP, THIS IS IMPORTANT

Do you feel like an animal in a zoo sometimes? Is your lunch slid in through a slot in the concrete? Is the floor covered in the droppings of your neighbors? Is there a sign nearby letting visitors know what the hell species you are? Welcome to our world, human!*

*Our final entry here submitted by guest contributors A. Rhino, A. Cougar, and A.N. Orangutan, representing AFCZE (the Allied Federation of Concerned Zoo Exhibits).

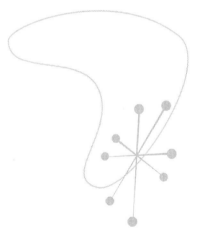

Dealing with Your Dreams

Practical Advice

DREAM DIARY

If you have decided to work systematically with your dreams, it is essential that you begin to keep a dream diary. Just the act of using one will allow you to remember your dreams much more often and more clearly.

What you should keep in mind if you start a dream diary:

1. Make a note about the date of the dream (use the date of the morning following the dream).
2. Start out by describing the events in the dream without any kind of interpretation and in the sequence you remember them.
3. Write whether the dream you remembered is complete or only a fragment.
4. Write how you felt before and after the dream.
5. Give each dream a title at the conclusion, one that best characterizes the content of the dream.

For interpretation, remember the following:

1. The attitude you adopted toward the dream. Were you a passive observer or actively involved in the event?
2. Which persons appeared in the dream and what your attitude is toward them, emotionally and behaviorally.
3. The mood of each individual scene and of the dream in general.

YOUR PERSONAL DREAM SYMBOLS

An alphabetically arranged address book lends itself well to keeping track of the most important symbols in your dreams. First, make a note of the personal meaning and then the general meaning of each symbol. Choose those images that you consider most important, especially the symbols that continually recur. For each symbol, make note of the title and the date of the dream in which it appeared. A general interpretation of a symbol listed in this handbook should only be noted if it expands or changes your understanding of your personal dream symbols.

HOW TO BEGIN

Most people who do dream work have found it helpful to establish a system that allows them to jot down the initial interpretation of the dream quickly. Such a system makes it easy to refer back to their dreams. The system should include the following:

1. Which persons in the dream could represent the animus (the masculine side—primarily in women but also in men) and/or the anima (the female side, primarily in men but also in women)?
2. Are there people in the dream whom you reject, whom you fight against or hate? Particularly when they are of the same gender, they are likely to represent your own dark and rejected side, the shadow.
3. What is the main symbol, and what is your attitude toward it? It is possible that there is more than one "main" symbol. Access to a clear understanding of the symbol is possible when you characterize it in one sentence.

4. Which objects are important in the dream? What is their objective function in your daily life? What is their subjective function?

5. Try to determine what, in yourself, each symbol refers to.

6. Go over the sequence of actions or situations in your dream once more and ask yourself: Where in my everyday life have such behaviors or situations occurred?

Only after going through these steps, should you attempt to interpret your dream in its entirety. Summarize each interpretation in two or three clear-cut sentences.

This type of system is for those who have very little time in the morning for any extensive and detailed dream work. It could well be called a system for the stressed-out city dweller, which however doesn't mean that it cannot be an effective and precise way for dealing with your dreams.

For those with more time, here are a few additional suggestions:

1. Before each interpretation, ask yourself: Where have I come from and where am I going? Examine your dream in that connection.

2. Look closely at each detail of your dream. The small things give important suggestions that are easily overlooked.

3. Look very closely to see if there are objects that appear in an unusual combination. Look for magical and fairy-tale elements: for instance, transformations, breaks in time, or other unusual incidents. This is often the case in short dreams that sometimes seem composed like a still life and where natural objects combine unnaturally to create a certain atmosphere. Arbitrary combinations of familiar things always create unusual images or special atmosphere, and that is significant here. Begin your interpretation with this atmosphere.

4. At the end of each interpretation, ask yourself: Can I transfer what I have learned in the dream to my everyday life? It is best to have a plan on how to immediately integrate these "lessons" into your life.

THE ATTITUDE OF THE DREAMER

Never interpret your dreams intellectually! Reasoning creates distance. Such distance often leads us to misunderstand symbols and whole dreams. Symbols are dealt with by the heart and not by the intellect, because their effect lies in moving something emotionally. Dreams therefore must always be approached on an emotional level. We can often recognize intuitively—and very quickly—what a dream is trying to tell us. Bring a little bit of your heart to every dream analysis and you will gain a lot.

YOU'RE WELCOME FOR THE TIP

Of course, the heart can be an organ of suffering, so bring a little humor and a bad ass attitude to your analysis, too (i.e. Denial).

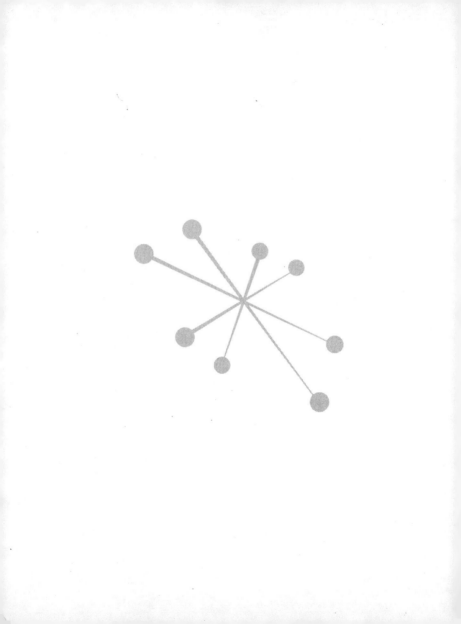